T0331917

CAUSALITY, PROBABILITY, AND TIME

Causality is a key part of many fields and facets of life, from finding the relationship between diet and disease to discovering the reason for a particular stock market crash. Despite centuries of work in philosophy and decades of computational research, automated inference and explanation remain an open problem. In particular, the timing and complexity of relationships have been largely ignored even though this information is critically important for prediction, explanation, and intervention. However, given the growing availability of large observational datasets, including those from electronic health records and social networks, it is a practical necessity. This book presents a new approach to inference (finding relationships from a set of data) and explanation (assessing why a particular event occurred), addressing both the timing and complexity of relationships. The practical use of the method developed is illustrated through theoretical and experimental case studies, demonstrating its feasibility and success.

Samantha Kleinberg is Assistant Professor of Computer Science at Stevens Institute of Technology. She received a PhD in Computer Science and a BA in Computer Science and Physics from New York University.

CAUSALITY, PROBABILITY, AND TIME

SAMANTHA KLEINBERG

Stevens Institute of Technology, Hoboken, New Jersey

CAMBRIDGE
UNIVERSITY PRESS

University Printing House, Cambridge CB2 8BS, United Kingdom

One Liberty Plaza, 20th Floor, New York, NY 10006, USA

477 Williamstown Road, Port Melbourne, VIC 3207, Australia

314-321, 3rd Floor, Plot 3, Splendor Forum, Jasola District Centre, New Delhi-110025, India

79 Anson Road, #06-04/06, Singapore 079906

Cambridge University Press is part of the University of Cambridge.

It furthers the University's mission by disseminating knowledge in the pursuit of education, learning and research at the highest international levels of excellence.

www.cambridge.org
Information on this title: www.cambridge.org/9781107026483

© Samantha Kleinberg 2013

This publication is in copyright. Subject to statutory exception and to the provisions of relevant collective licensing agreements, no reproduction of any part may take place without the written permission of Cambridge University Press.

First published 2013

A catalogue record for this publication is available from the British Library

Library of Congress Cataloging in Publication data
Kleinberg, Samantha, 1983– author.
Causality, probability, and time / Samantha Kleinberg, Stevens Institute of Technology, Hoboken, New Jersey.
pages cm.
Includes bibliographical references and index.
ISBN 978-1-107-02648-3 (hardback)
1. Computational complexity.   I. Title.
QA267.7.K54   2012
511.3′52–dc23   2012021047

ISBN 978-1-107-02648-3 Hardback
ISBN 978-1-107-68601-4 Paperback

Cambridge University Press has no responsibility for the persistence or accuracy of URLs for external or third-party internet websites referred to in this publication, and does not guarantee that any content on such websites is, or will remain, accurate or appropriate.

Contents

Acknowledgments

From the beginning, this work has been profoundly interdisciplinary. I am deeply grateful to the collaborators and colleagues who have enabled me to explore new fields and who have enthusiastically shared their expertise with me. Immersing myself in philosophy, bioinformatics, finance, and neurology among other areas has been challenging, exciting, and necessary to this work. I also thank the audiences and anonymous referees from the conferences, workshops, and seminars where I have presented earlier versions of this work for their feedback.

This book began when I was a graduate student at NYU and was completed during my post-doc at Columbia. The support of my colleagues and their generosity with their time and data have significantly shaped and improved the work, bringing it closer to practice. In particular, collaboration with medical doctors has given me a new appreciation for the importance of automating explanation and for the practical challenges this work faces.

This material is based on work supported by the NSF under Grant #1019343 to the Computing Research Association for the CIFellows project. That fellowship provided salary and research support for the last two years and was instrumental to the completion of this work. This work has also been funded in part with federal funds from the NLM, NIH, DHHS, under Contract No. HHSN276201000024C.

Prior versions of this work have appeared in conference proceedings and journals. In particular, material in Chapters 4 and 7 are partly based on work that appeared in Kleinberg and Mishra (2009); Chapter 6 is partly based on work that appeared in Kleinberg and Mishra (2010); and portions of Chapter 2 previously appeared in Kleinberg and Hripcsak (2011).

Finally I thank my editor, Lauren Cowles, at Cambridge University Press for her support and enthusiasm for this book.

1

Introduction

Whether we want to know the cause of a stock's price movements (in order to trade on this information), the key phrases that can alter public opinion of a candidate (in order to optimize a politician's speeches), or which genes work together to regulate a disease causing process (in order to intervene and disrupt it), many goals center on finding and using causes. Causes tell us not only that two phenomena are related, but how they are related. They allow us to make robust predictions about the future, explain the relationship between and occurrence of events, and develop effective policies for intervention.

While predictions are often made successfully on the basis of associations alone, these relationships can be unstable. If we do not know why the resulting models work, we cannot foresee when they will stop working. Lung cancer rates in an area may be correlated with match sales if many smokers use matches to light their cigarettes, but match sales may also be influenced by blackouts and seasonal trends (with many purchases around holidays or in winter). A spike in match sales due to a blackout will not result in the predicted spike in lung cancer rates, but without knowledge of the underlying causes we would not be able to anticipate that failure. Models based on associations can also lead to redundancies, since multiple effects of the true cause may be included as they are correlated with its occurrence. In applications to the biomedical domain, this can result in unnecessary diagnostic tests that may be invasive and expensive.

In addition to making forecasts, we want to gain new knowledge of how things work. Causes enable us to explain both the occurrence of events and the connection between types of events. We do not want to know only that a particular drug is associated with renal failure, but rather we want to distinguish between whether this association is due to an adverse drug reaction or the disease being treated causing both renal failure and prescription of the drug. Associations do not have this type of explanatory power, nor can they help us with a second type of explanation, that of why a particular event occurred. When attempting to explain why a patient developed a secondary brain injury after a stroke, the goal is to determine which factors are responsible so that these can be treated to potentially prevent further brain damage. Knowing only that a particular event is correlated with secondary injury is insufficient to determine which factors made a difference to its occurrence in a particular case.

Finally, knowledge of the underlying causes of a phenomenon is what allows us to intervene successfully to prevent or produce particular outcomes. Causal relationships (actual or hypothesized) prompt us to make decisions such as taking vitamin supplements to reduce our risk of disease or enacting policies decreasing sodium levels in food to prevent hypertension. If we did not at least believe that there is a causal connection between these factors, we would have no basis for these interventions. Intervening on a side effect of the underlying cause would be like banning the sale of matches to reduce lung cancer rates. This is clearly ineffective, since smokers can also use lighters, but banning smoking or reducing smoking rates does have the ability to lower lung cancer rates. In general, to bring about desired outcomes we must know that the factor being acted upon is capable of preventing or producing the effect of interest.

However, causality alone is not enough. To use causes to effectively predict, explain, or alter behavior, we must also know the time over which a relationship takes place, the probability with which it will occur, and how other factors interact to alter its efficacy.

When finding factors that affect stock prices, we need to know when the effect starts and how long it persists to be able to trade on this information. Individual phrases may positively influence voter perception of a politician, but candidates must combine these into coherent speeches, and two phrases that are positive individually may have a negative impact in combination. With multiple targets for drug development, the likelihood of each being effective must be weighed against its potential risks to determine which candidates to pursue.

Few relationships are deterministic, so even if we know the details of a cause that can produce the desired effect and how long it takes to do so, we cannot be certain that this outcome will occur in all instances. In many cases, this is due to the limits of our knowledge (as it is rare that all factors relevant to the success of the cause can be enumerated) while in others the relationship itself may be probabilistic. Knowing both the timing of relationships and their probabilities is important for making decisions and assessing risk, as there are often multiple effects of a cause and multiple causes of a particular effect. Thus, we can rarely influence a cause in isolation, and must also choose between potential candidates. For many medical conditions, doctors have a choice of treatments where some may be extremely effective, yet come with the potential for severe side effects, while other less effective drugs may be desirable because of their limited side effects. When choosing a target for interventions, one must evaluate the strength of the relationship (likelihood of the cause producing the effect, or the magnitude of influence) against potentially undesirable side effects. This has been partly addressed by artificial intelligence work on planning, which finds both direct and indirect effects (ramifications) of actions to determine whether a strategy will achieve a goal. These methods assume that we already have a model of how the system works, but in many cases the first step of research is finding this model or creating it with the input of domain experts. By starting with a set of causal facts (essentially, ways of changing the truth value of formulas), these methods free themselves from answering the most difficult question: what exactly is causality?

This question has plagued researchers in many areas, but it has been a fundamental practical problem in medicine where doctors must always act with incomplete information. Causality is at the center of every facet of medicine, including diagnosis of patients (Rizzi, 1994), identification of adverse drug events (Agbabiaka et al., 2008), comparative effectiveness research (Johnson et al., 2009), and epidemiological studies linking environmental factors and disease (Parascandola and Weed, 2001). Yet as central as causality is to biomedical research, work on understanding what it is and how to find it has primarily taken a pragmatic approach, disconnected from the philosophical literature in this area. As a result, randomized controlled trials (RCTs) have come to be treated as the gold standard for causal inference, even though these can answer only a subset of the many causal questions researchers and clinicians aim to answer and sidestep the question of what causality actually is. The basic idea of an RCT is that a subset of a population has been randomly assigned to a particular treatment while the control group does not receive the treatment. Both are measured the same way for the same time, and when there is a difference in outcomes between the groups it is said that the therapy is responsible for it (as it is meant to be the only difference between them). These methods have many well-known limitations, in particular that the ideal of randomization to eliminate confounding may not always occur in practice (Schulz et al., 1995), and that the internal validity of these studies (that they can answer the questions being asked) often comes at the expense of external validity (generalizability to other populations) (Dekkers et al., 2010; Rothwell, 2006). Similarly, due to the difficulty and expense of enrolling patients, these studies follow fairly small populations over fairly short time periods.

Instead, new large-scale observational datasets from electronic health records (EHRs) may address some of these limitations (by studying the same population being treated, following patients over a long timescale, and using a large population). Columbia University Medical Center, for example, has a database of 3 million patients over twenty years. In other systems with less in and out-migration, these records can capture a patient's health over nearly their entire lifespan. Further, while many RCTs involve homogeneous sets of patients with few comorbidities, EHRs contain a more realistic set of patients (though they exclude those who have not sought or do not have access to medical care). Despite the potential benefits of using EHRs for research, they have been underused, as these observational data are outside the traditional paradigm of RCTs (here we have no control over the data gathered and patients may have many gaps in their records) and have been difficult to analyze using prior computational methods for causal inference (as few of their assumptions hold in these types of real-world datasets).

To address the challenge of causal inference from observational data, though, we first need to understand what causality is in a domain-independent way. Attempts have been made to create guidelines for evaluating causality in specific scenarios, such as Hill's viewpoints on causality (Hill, 1965), but these are simply heuristics. Over time though they have come to be treated as checklists, leading to a conflation of what causality might be with the evidence needed to establish it and tools we can use to recognize it. While I aim to develop practical inference methods, we must be clear about what is being inferred and this requires us to engage with the philosophical literature.

There is no single accepted theory of what it means for something to be a cause, but understanding this distinction between the underlying fact of causality and how inference algorithms identify causes (and which causes they identify) is critical for successful inference and interpretation of results. As will become clear in the later chapters, causality is far from a solved problem, but philosophical theories have succeeded in capturing many more aspects of it than are addressed in the computational literature. There is a small set of cases on which all theories agree, with only partial overlaps in others. Since there are generally no corresponding algorithms that can be applied to test datasets, the primary method for evaluating and comparing philosophical theories of causality has been by posing counterexamples to each, following a battery of tests that have evolved over the years. As no one theory addresses all potential challenges, this provides some idea of which theories apply to which scenarios, but has also indicated that the search for a unified theory may be unlikely to succeed.

In this book, I will not attempt to provide a unifying theory of causality, but rather aim to make clear where there are areas of disagreement and controversy and where certain assumptions are generally accepted. The book begins with a review of philosophical approaches to causality, because these works give us a vocabulary for talking about it and they provide the foundation for the computational literature. In particular, philosophy is one of the few fields that has extensively studied both type-level causality (general relationships such as that between an environmental factor and a disease) and token causality (specific relationships instantiated at particular times and places, such as the cause of a particular patient's hypertension), as well as the link between these levels. While philosophical approaches have attempted to find one theory that accounts for all instances of causality (arguing against any approach that does not act as expected in at least one case), this has so far not succeeded but has yielded a rich set of competing theories. Given the lack of a unified solution after centuries of effort, some philosophers have recently argued for causal pluralism (with a plurality of things one might be plural about, including methodologies, causality itself, and so on). On the other hand, computational work has honed in on a few inference methods, primarily based on graphical models (where edges between nodes indicate causal dependence), but these may not be appropriate for all cases. Instead, we may once again take inspiration from the philosophical literature to guide development of a set of complementary methods for causal inference.

One of the most critical pieces of information about causality, though – the time it takes for the cause to produce its effect – has been largely ignored by both philosophical theories and computational methods. If we do not know when the effect will occur, we have little hope of being able to act successfully using the causal relationship. We need to know the timing of biological processes to disrupt them to prevent disease. We need to know how long it takes for conditions to trigger political instability if we want to react quickly to it. We need to know a patient's sequence of symptoms and medical history to determine her diagnosis. Further, personal and policy decisions may vary considerably with the length of time between cause and effect (and how this relates to the relationship's probability). The warning that "smoking causes lung cancer" tells us nothing about how long it will take for lung cancer to develop nor how likely this is to occur. We often see people who smoke and do not develop lung cancer, so we immediately know that either this must occur on such a long timescale that other causes of death occur first, or that the relationship must be probabilistic. Without these details though, an individual cannot adequately assess their risk to make a decision about whether or not to smoke. While a deterministic relationship that takes 80 years may not affect a person's behavior, a relationship with a significantly lower probability at a timescale of only 10–15 years might be significantly more alarming.

To successfully make and use causal inferences we need to understand not only what causality is, but how to represent and infer it in all of its complexity.

I argue that it is futile to insist on a single theory that can handle all possible counterexamples and applications, and instead focus on developing an approach that is best equipped for inferring complex causal relationships (and their timing) from temporal data. While this method builds on philosophical work, the goal is not to develop a theory of causality itself, but rather a method for causal inference and explanation that aims to be philosophically sound, computationally feasible, and statistically rigorous. Since the goal is to use these methods in many areas – such as biology, politics, and finance – the definitions must be domain independent and should be compatible with the types of data that are realistically encountered in practice. This method needs to capture the probabilistic nature of the relationships being inferred, and be able to reason about potentially complex relationships as well as the time between cause and effect. I will discuss why previous methods for causal inference (those that result in the creation of networks or graphs, and those allowing simple lags between cause and effect but not windows of time) do not achieve these goals. Instead, I present an alternative approach based on the idea of causal relationships as logical statements, building on philosophical theories of probabilistic causality and extending probabilistic temporal logics to meet the representation needs of the complex domains discussed.

In this approach, cause, effect, and the conditions for causality are described in terms of logical formulas. This allows the method to capture relationships such as: "smoking and asbestos exposure until a particular genetic mutation occurs causes lung cancer with probability 0.6 in between 1 and 3 years." While I focus on the case of temporal data, the working definitions developed allow us to correctly handle many of the difficult cases commonly posed to theories of causality. Further, the use of temporal logic, with clearly defined syntax and semantics, allows us to efficiently test any relationship that can be described in the logic. The approach is based on probabilistic theories of causality, but probability raising alone is insufficient for identifying causal relationships since many non-causes may precede and seem to raise the probability of other events. Instead, to determine which relationships are significant, I introduce a new measure for the significance of a cause for its effect that assesses the average impact a cause makes to an effect's probability. Using the properties of this measure we are also able to determine the timing of relationships with minimal prior knowledge. Similarly, the distribution of this measure allows standard statistical methods to be applied to find which causal significance values should be considered statistically significant. The inference methods here build on philosophical theories of probabilistic causality, but introduce new computationally feasible methods for representing and inferring relationships.

In addition to inferring general relationships such as that smothering someone causes their death, we also aim to find causes for specific events, such as that Othello smothering Desdemona caused her death. These singular, token-level, relationships need not correspond exactly to type-level relationships. For example, seatbelts may prevent death in the majority of accidents, but can cause it in others by preventing escape from vehicles submerged under water. However, methods that make use of type-level relationships without being constrained by them can enable us to automate this type of reasoning. Finding the causes of particular events is a significant practical problem in biomedicine, where clinicians aim to diagnose patients based on their symptoms and understand their individual disease etiology. Algorithms that can do this without human input can have a particularly large impact in critical care medicine, where doctors face an enormous volume of streaming data that is too complex for humans to analyze, yet knowing not only what is happening but why is essential to treatment. Since treatments can come with potential risks, doctors must be sure they are treating the underlying cause of a patient's illness and not simply symptoms that indicate their level of health. Timing is critical for automating this type of explanation, since it allows objective determination of whether an observed sequence can be considered an instance of the known general relationship and provides information on when a cause is capable of producing its effect. This must also be done with incomplete data (as we may not observe all variables and may have gaps in their recording), and must allow for deviations in timing (as we do not usually have continuous data streams at an arbitrarily fine level of granularity). There are many reasons inferred timings may differ from particular timings even though the particular events are still instances of the general relationship. Inferring, for instance, that a factor causes decreased potassium levels in 60–120 minutes does not necessarily mean that it is not possible for this to occur in 59 to 121 minutes. The need for this type of reasoning is not limited to biomedicine, but may also apply to finding causes of stock market crashes and software failures. In this book, I aim to close the loop from data to inference to explanation, developing methods for assessing potential token causes for an effect while allowing for incomplete and uncertain information.

1.1. Structure of the Book

This book is written primarily for computer scientists and philosophers of science, but it is intended to be accessible to biomedical scientists and researchers in finance among other areas. For that reason, the book is mostly self-contained, and assumes very minimal background in statistics, logic, or philosophy. Chapters 2 and 3 contain all needed background on causality, probability, and logic. Before discussing methods for inferring causes, one needs to understand what is being inferred. Thus, chapter 2 begins with a short introduction to philosophical theories of causality, beginning with historical foundations and then continuing with a critical discussion of probabilistic and counterfactual theories. This discussion covers the problem of defining and recognizing causal relationships, which is necessary before we can discuss how to find these in an automated way. The goal of this section is to make readers from all backgrounds familiar with potential problems in defining causality, providing a framework for evaluating other methods. Finally, I review recent approaches to inference, including graphical models and Granger causality. Chapter 3 is a gentle introduction to probability (covering what is needed for the later examples and algorithms) and temporal logic, concluding with a discussion of the probabilistic temporal logic that the approach builds on.

In the remaining chapters, we turn our attention to a new approach to causal inference. In chapter 4, I begin by defining the types of causes we will aim to identify. Rather than partitioning relationships into causal and non-causal, I focus on calculating the significance of relationships, introducing a new measure for this purpose that is computationally feasible, but based on the philosophical theories discussed in chapter 2. I relate the definitions to probabilistic temporal logic formulas and discuss how they deal with common counterexamples posed to theories of causality. By representing causal relationships as temporal logic formulas (and later extending this logic for use with data), this approach can address the previously ignored problem of representing and inferring complex, temporal, causal relationships. This will allow us to find relationships and their timing (how long it takes for a cause to produce its effect) while allowing this process to be automated in a computationally feasible way. Prior philosophical and computational work has left it to the end user to define variables in arbitrarily complex ways, but constructing these instead as logical formulas means that any relationship that can be represented in this manner can be efficiently tested. Further, this method will enable inference of relationships such as feedback loops that have previously eluded other approaches.

In chapter 5, I develop the algorithms needed for testing these causal relationships in data, discuss how to determine their causal and statistical significance, and finally develop algorithms for finding the timing of causal relationships without prior knowledge. First, I discuss how to check logical formulas in time series data (traces), and augment probabilistic computation tree logic (PCTL) to allow specification of formulas true within a window of time (rather than with only an upper bound on timing), developing a new trace-based semantics. I then discuss how the measure of causal significance developed in the previous chapter is calculated relative to data. This measure is the average difference a cause makes to the probability of its effect. We then need to determine which values of the measure are statistically significant. Since we are primarily interested in applications that involve a large number of relationships being tested simultaneously, we can relate the determination of a threshold for the level at which something is statistically significant to the problem of false discovery control, aiming to control how often a spurious cause is erroneously called genuine. Finally, *See* while we need to understand not only why things will happen but when they *appendix A* will occur, this is one of the largest remaining gaps in methods for causal *for an* inference. One can search exhaustively over a set of possible timings, but *introduction* this is computationally inefficient and dependent on the initial times pro- *to multiple* posed. Prior methods have been limited by their inability to suggest and *hypothesis* evaluate new relationships, refining rather than only accepting or rejecting *testing and* hypotheses. What is needed is a way to take user input as a starting point and *false* modify it during inference as new information is revealed. In this section, *discovery* we show that with a few assumptions (that the significant relationships are *control.* a small proportion of the overall set tested, and that a relationship will be significant in at least one window overlapping its true timing) the problem can be solved efficiently, allowing us to generate a set of hypotheses and candidate time windows, such as "*a* causes *b* in 1–2 weeks," and eventually infer "*a* causes *b* in 7–10 days."

In chapter 6, I discuss the problem of token causality in depth. The goal here is to take a sequence of observations (such as a patient's history) and a set of inferred type-level relationships and assess the relative significance of each type-level cause for a particular, actually occurring, event (such as a patient's seizure). This will allow for uncertainty in the timing of events by incorporating deviations from the known (type-level) timing into a measure of significance for a token-level explanation, ensuring that a case that differs slightly from a known relationship will not be immediately excluded while one that deviates significantly will be penalized (though can still be considered possible). I begin by discussing why we need a separate treatment of this type of causality and how, building on philosophical theories, we can use prior type-level inferences (made using the method developed in the previous chapters) as initial hypotheses, before developing a practical measure for token-level significance. I then examine several difficult cases found in the philosophical literature, showing that the approach can handle these in a manner consistent with intuition about the problems.

Finally, in chapter 7, the methods are applied to data from biological and financial applications. Here the approach is first validated on simulated neural spike train data, showing that it can recover both the underlying relationships and their timing. Through comparison to other methods (specifically graphical models and Granger causality), it is shown that the approach advanced here is able to make fewer false discoveries while retaining the power to make many correct discoveries. In fact, its error rates are an order of magnitude lower than for the competing methods. The approaches developed are then applied to a second domain, finance, using both simulated and actual market data. First, data is simulated using a factor model, with causality embedded in a series of randomly generated networks (some with randomly generated time lags between portfolios). Once again the method developed in this book outperforms Granger causality, a method commonly applied to financial time series. Finally, application to actual market data shows that over the long run, relationships may not persist while at a timescale of a year, causal relationships can be identified between stocks.

2

A Brief History of Causality

2.1. Philosophical Foundations of Causality

When discussing causality and causal inference we must first distinguish between the thing itself and how to recognize it. Most scientific work on causality involves developing methods for providing evidence for causal relationships, while work in philosophy addresses what it means for something to be a cause. This philosophical work is not immediately applicable to practical problems, but it provides a necessary starting point for work by computer scientists, epidemiologists, and economists. This section introduces readers not familiar with the philosophical literature to how philosophers have conceptualized causality and why this problem is still unsolved after centuries of work. I begin with a review of the primary ways philosophers have addressed causality leading up to more recent probabilistic methods. The review is not an unbiased survey of causality, but rather a discussion of its philosophical foundations through the lens of researchers aiming to build inference methods upon them. As a result, I omit large bodies of work such as process-based theories (Dowe, 2000; Salmon, 1994) and mechanistic models (Glennan, 1996; Machamer et al., 2000) because knowledge of these is not required to understand the later sections.[1] I also raise concerns (such as computational complexity) that differ from those of philosophers but are important when translating these methods to practice.

While Aristotle is often credited with the first formal theory of causality in his *Physics* and *Metaphysics*, the most influential modern discussion of causality comes from David Hume in the 18th century. Hume attempted to define both what a cause is and what is meant by the term; as well as how we can come to possess causal knowledge and what is needed to infer it from observations. The core of Hume's work is arguing that we come to

---

[1] We will pick up with process and mechanistic theories in the book's conclusion, discussing how these relate to the approach set forth here.

know of causal relationships by inferring them from observations, so they may also be subjective due to beliefs and perception. Before getting into the formal details, Hume broadly defined a causal relationship as being a regular connection, so that C causes E if every event of type C is followed by an event of type E. From experience, we learn these regularities and can use them to reason about what will happen, develop expectations based on our perceptions, and finally establish whether these beliefs are true or false through experimentation and observation. When hearing a noise outside in the morning, we may believe that a garbage truck is outside, since in the past we heard this noise and saw a garbage truck outside the window. We expect to go to the window and see the same thing this time. This belief may turn out to be false if today there is instead a street sweeper causing the noise. The key point here is that without empirical evidence we could not have made any predictions about the cause of the noise.

Addressing the concept of causality itself, Hume posited three essential relations: contiguity, temporal priority, and necessary connection (Hume, 1739). First, *contiguity* means that cause and effect must be nearby in time and space. While it may not seem that this condition always holds, since, for example, the impact of a tax policy on job growth will take some time, Hume believed that cases that seem distant are linked by a chain of contiguous causes.[2] The second quality, *temporal priority*, means that a cause must precede its effect in time. While Hume suggests that allowing cause and effect to be co-temporary leads right to the annihilation of time, it is true that if we allow this, we could not distinguish the cause from the effect and would only be able to find a correlation between the pair. Finally, *necessary connection* is the defining feature that allows one to distinguish between causal and noncausal relationships. Here it is stipulated that the cause always produces the effect, and the effect is not produced without the cause.

This view is violated by electron pairing (Skyrms, 1984).

In the empirical definition, necessary connection is replaced by *constant conjunction*, since we may observe two events as being conjoined, but this does not mean that they are necessarily so (and we do not have any basis for being able to make such a statement). Empirically, Hume defines a cause as follows:[3]

Definition 2.1.1. An object precedent and contiguous to another, and where all the objects resembling the former are placed in a like relation of priority and contiguity to those objects that resemble the latter.

---

[2] Hume 1739, 75.
[3] Hume 1739, 172.

One common counterexample to this approach is that "day causes night" satisfies all three criteria, although we would not call day a cause of night. Another example is that of umbrella vendors and rain. In Manhattan, umbrella vendors are quite efficient and I always have the opportunity to buy an umbrella when it is raining. In fact, the vendors, anticipating the need for umbrellas, are always around right before it starts raining. Using Hume's criteria, one may erroneously conclude that the presence of umbrella vendors causes rain. Cases can be made against each of the criteria: the absence of an event can lead to an effect, physics has found simultaneous causal influence, and when there are multiple causes of an effect each is no longer individually necessary. These criteria nevertheless represent the first step toward a theory of causality that can be verified through empirical data. Hume freed researchers from looking for some elusive special quality that makes something a cause, reducing the inference of these relationships to the identification of regularities.

2.2. Modern Philosophical Approaches to Causality

2.2.1. Regularity

Hume's proposal, that causality is essentially routine occurrence of an effect following a cause, is what is known as the regularity theory of causality. As described, there are many examples of noncausal regularities (the presence of umbrella vendors and rain) and causation without regularities (a drug causing the death of a single patient), but this provided the basis for developments such as Mill's methods (Mill, 1843) and work in epidemiology (Hill, 1965; Koch, 1932; Naranjo et al., 1981; Susser, 1973).

One of the major omissions from Hume's approach is that there is no method for separating which parts of a regular sequence of events are essential from those that are just correlated with the others. For example, I may always open the door to my office, turn on the light, and then begin writing papers or code on my computer. While the light being on is useful for writing, it is not essential (particularly if I have candles or a window in my office). Many effects have multiple causes that are comprised of interacting components, such as the impact of environmental factors and genetic mutations on health. An approach like Hume's does not easily allow for reasoning with these types of causal complexes.

John Leslie Mackie formalized the ideas of necessity and sufficiency for causes, updating Hume's theory to take into account multiple components of a cause and multiple causes of an effect. An event C is a *necessary*

Mackie's approach is strongly paralleled by Rothman's sufficient component cause model for the health sciences (Rothman, 1976).

condition of an event E if whenever an event of type E occurs, an event of type C also occurs, and C is a *sufficient condition* of E if whenever an event of type C occurs an event of type E also occurs. According to Mackie, a cause is an INUS condition, "an *insufficient* but *non-redundant* part of an *unnecessary* but *sufficient* condition"[4] (taking the name INUS from the first letters of each italicized component). There are sets of conditions that result in an effect and a cause is a necessary part of one of those sets, even though it alone may be insufficient for producing the effect and there may be other possible causes of the effect (making it unnecessary).

Definition 2.2.1. C is an *INUS condition* of E iff, for some X and some Y, $(C \wedge X) \vee Y$ is a necessary and sufficient condition of E, but C is not a sufficient condition of E and X is not a sufficient condition of E.[5]

Unpacking this, we have that:

1. $C \wedge X$ is sufficient for E.
2. $C \wedge X$ is not necessary since Y could also cause E.
3. C alone may be insufficient for E.
4. C is a non-redundant part of $C \wedge X$.

A lit match (C) may be a cause of house fires but there are many other situations when a match is lit and does not cause a fire ($\neg X$), and in which a fire occurs without a lit match (Y). For the match to cause the fire, some set of circumstances (X) is required, where each of its components is necessary and they together with C are sufficient for a fire to occur. This gives the minimum conditions for something to be a cause, so a cause may be more than an INUS condition as it may be necessary or sufficient.

This definition addresses types of events, but Mackie also gives a method for using INUS conditions to find the causes of individual, actually occurring, events. To do this, we need two more definitions.

Definition 2.2.2. $A \wedge B \wedge C$ is a *minimal sufficient condition* for P if no conjunct is redundant (i.e., no part, such as $A \wedge B$, is itself sufficient for P), and $A \wedge B \wedge C$ is sufficient for P.[6]

Definition 2.2.3. C is *at least an INUS condition* of E iff either C is an INUS condition for E, or C is a minimum sufficient condition for E, or C

---

[4] Mackie 1974, 62.
[5] Mackie 1965.
[6] Mackie 1974, 62.

is a necessary and sufficient condition for E, or C is part of some necessary and sufficient condition for E.[7]

Then, for C to be a cause of E on a particular occasion (what is referred to as token, or singular, causality), according to Mackie, the following must all be true:

1. C is at least an INUS condition of E.
2. C was present.
3. The components of X, if there are any, were present.
4. Every disjunct in Y not containing C as a conjunct was absent.

Token causality is the subject of chapter 6.

Using the house fire example, a lit match was the cause of a specific fire if it was present; oxygen, flammable material, and the other conditions needed for a lit match to cause a fire were also present; and there was no unattended cooking, faulty electrical wiring, or other factors that cause fires in the absence of lit matches. The third and fourth conditions in the previous list ensure that the other factors needed for C to cause E are present, while avoiding the problem of overdetermination. If instead there was a lit match and the house was simultaneously struck by lightning, the fourth condition would be violated and neither would be deemed the cause of the fire. Mackie's rationale for this is that if two separate INUS conditions were present, either could have caused the effect and there is no way to assess their individual contributions to it using only regularities. This is one of the biggest limitations of the theory, but there are other impediments to practical usage. This approach does not easily allow for anomalous events, such as a factor that normally prevents an effect bringing it about in some unusual scenarios – such as a drug that normally cures a disease but causes death in a small fraction of the people who take it.

2.2.2. Counterfactuals

One of the key problems faced by regularity theories is distinguishing between a relationship that regularly occurs and a factor that made a difference to the occurrence of an effect on a particular occasion. Counterfactual approaches to causality usually aim to address these types of questions, assessing whether a particular instance of an effect would have occurred in the absence of the cause on that particular occasion. This is known as token (or singular) causality. Although counterfactuals can also be applied

---

[7] Mackie 1965, 247.

to type-level cases, they are primarily used to analyze situations where the cause did actually happen and one wants to determine what difference it made to the effect. Interestingly, this work can also be traced back to Hume's foundations. When Hume defined causality, he wrote that a cause is "*an object, followed by another, and where all the objects similar to the first are followed by objects similar to the second. Or in other words where, if the first object had not been, the second never had existed.*"[8] Though these are supposed restatements of the same theory, the first part (known as the regularity definition) is quite different from the second part (the counterfactual definition). Using the first half, the presence of an umbrella vendor may still seem to cause rain due to the regular occurrence. However, if the umbrella vendors went on strike, rain would still occur so we can see that there is no counterfactual dependence.

David Lewis developed the primary counterfactual theory of causality, discussing how we can use these conditional statements (Edgington, 1995; Stalnaker, 1968) to analyze token causality between events (Lewis, 1973). Central to Lewis's work is being able to reason about what would have happened using possible worlds, and comparative similarity between possible worlds. A *possible world* may be thought of as a maximally consistent set of propositions true in that world, and a world is closer to actuality than another world is if it resembles the actual world more than any other world does. While there is no standard method for comparing possible worlds, we can still reason about their similarity. A possible world in which Al Gore became president of the United States in 2000 is closer to the actual world than one in which Hillary Rodham Clinton became president that year. This is because it takes less of a departure from reality to access a world in which Gore was president (since he ran and was the Democratic Party nominee) than one in which Clinton was president (since she was running for United States Senator from New York at that time). Lewis introduced two constraints on the similarity relation: (1) any two worlds may be compared, but it is a weak ordering so they may be equally similar to the actual world; (2) the actual world is closest to actuality since it is more similar to itself than any other world is.

Possible worlds are discussed further in section 3.2.1.

One can use these types of comparisons to define counterfactual dependence, and then causal dependence. The *counterfactual* of two propositions A and C (represented by $A \square \rightarrow C$) means that if A were true, C would be true. Where $A \square \rightarrow C$ is true in the actual world if and only if (1) there are

---

[8] Hume 1748, Section VII.

no possible worlds where A is true (vacuous case), or (2) a world where both A and C are true is closer to the actual world than any A-world where C does not hold. As Lewis says, "it takes less of a departure from actuality to make the consequent true along with the antecedent than it does to make the antecedent true without the consequent."[9] One can then express statements such as "had someone not thrown a rock at the window it would not have broken." These statements talk about what would have been if things were different, so it is natural to attempt to define causality in terms of this type of difference making.

Causal dependence is represented using two counterfactuals, stating that had c not occurred e would not have either ($\neg c \Box \to \neg e$), and that had c occurred, e would have too ($c \Box \to e$). While this causal dependence also implies causation, according to Lewis causality is transitive, so one may also have cases of causation without causal dependence. If there is a chain of causal dependence, such that e depends causally on d, and d depends causally on c, c is a cause of e even though e may not depend counterfactually on c. In Lewis's theory c is a cause of e if e is causally dependent on c or if there is a chain of causal dependence between c and e.

The main problems facing this approach are transitivity and overdetermination. In the first case, we can find situations such that some event a would generally prevent some event c from occurring but in the actual events, a causes another event b, which in turn causes c to occur. Thus, the counterfactual account can lead to events counterintuitively being labeled causal. McDermott (1995) gives one such counterexample. Suppose I give Jones a chest massage (C), without which he would have died. Then, he recovers and flies to New York (F), where he eventually has a violent death (D). Here, C was a cause of F, as without the massage he would not have been well enough to travel, and F is a cause of D, but C did not cause D. Whether or not C occurred, Jones still would have died, but there is a causal chain between C and D. It is counterintuitive to say that preventing death in one manner caused it in another simply because it allowed the person to live long enough to die differently. However, transitivity is needed in this method for reasoning about cases where there is causation without causal dependence.

Dependence here refers to token cases, and may differ from general properties.

The second problem for the counterfactual theory of causality is with redundant causation. Say there are two potential causes for an effect (both present) and the effect would have been the result of either, so that the effect

---

[9] Lewis 1973, 560.

depends causally on neither and the system is overdetermined. One common example is that of a firing squad: if one shot had not killed the prisoner, another would have. This redundant causation may be either symmetrical (each potential cause could equally well be called the cause of the effect, there is nothing to distinguish which was the actual cause) or asymmetrical (there was one cause that *preempted* the other). In the asymmetrical case, if we say c_1 was the preempting cause, c_2 the preempted and e the effect, then had c_1 not occurred, c_2 would still have caused e, and thus c_1 is not the cause of e despite its causing e. Imagine an alternate ending to *Thelma and Louise*, where the police have deemed them a danger. In this scenario, if the women had not driven off the cliff to their deaths, the police would have shot them instead. There is no causal dependence between their deaths and driving off the cliff, yet it is clearly the cause of their deaths as the police did not actually shoot (but would have).

Many events may occur even in the absence of a particular cause but the manner in which they occur may differ, whether this means for example their location or time or intensity. There may be cases, particularly in biology, where systems have backup mechanisms that ensure the result is produced and the manner of its occurrence may not differ substantially between the various possible causes. In the example of Jones's death, we took for granted that we were attempting to assess his death at that particular time, since had he not died violently he would have died of old age or disease or in some other manner. The inconsistencies in this theory led to a later revision, where causes affect how, when, and whether their effects occur (Lewis, 2000). This theory still has problems with incorrectly calling some factors causes, though, while failing to find others as causes. Any event that has a small influence on the timing or manner of the effect can be said to be a cause, as there is no discussion of the degree to which a cause influences an effect. Second, even though the idea is that altering the actual cause should alter the effect while altering a non-cause should not, there are cases where this fails (for example if the backup cause was instead earlier than the preempted one). According to Lewis, this happens if alterations are too distant from the actual events, but there is no method for measuring such a distance.

2.3. Probabilistic Causality

Both regularity approaches and Lewis's counterfactuals generally view causality as a deterministic relationship between events, where causes produce their effects without fail.[10] There is a key distinction here between theories that believe the relationship is, at its core, deterministic (so that if a cause is fully specified, it always produces its effect when it occurs), and probabilities are only introduced through lack of knowledge, and theories that hold that it is possible for a relationship itself to be probabilistic, such that the cause is not always sufficient for its effect. In the second case, even with complete knowledge of the world and all relevant information, we would still find that the cause does not always produce its effect. The other probability is due to our normally incomplete information about a system but has no bearing on what the underlying relationship is. Probabilistic theories of causality do not usually distinguish between these probabilities. When making inferences from data, note that we must also assume that the observations are representative. There may be cases such as a fair roulette wheel coming up red 20 times in a row or a fair coin flipped 20 times and coming up heads on each, where these observations are not indicative of the underlying probabilities. However, as the sequence of observations gets longer we will come closer to observing the true probabilities of the system.

Even if a relationship were deterministic, it is unlikely that one could ever infer this. First, the cause would need to be fully specified, such that every condition needed for it to produce the effect is accounted for (the conjunct X in Mackie's theory). However, we rarely have such detailed knowledge and should be able to reason instead about what happens in the majority of cases. Second, we could never observe enough events to pronounce with certainty that one thing causes another with probability one. For example, we may note that in all the years we have known each other, every time you call me, my phone has rung (let us assume I do not have call waiting, no one else has called, and I do not make calls on my own). We cannot be sure that my phone will always ring because you have called, that is, that your call is the cause of my phone ringing. What we can infer is that your calling makes it very likely that my phone will ring. We can predict with a high probability that when you call my phone will ring but cannot say this will always, without fail, be the case.

There have been a number of different probabilistic theories of causality (Eells, 1991; Good, 1961a,b; Reichenbach, 1956; Suppes, 1970), but these all share the core premise that (positive) causes raise the probabilities of their effects, so that once the cause has occurred there is a greater

---

[10] Lewis also formulated a probabilistic counterfactual theory (Lewis, 1986b), but it is not often discussed.

chance of the effect occurring. With cause C, effect E, and the conditional probability $P(E|C) = P(E \wedge C)/P(C)$, the basic probabilistic theory of causality is that C is a cause of E if:

Conditional probabilities are discussed in detail in section 3.1.1.

$$P(E|C) > P(E|\neg C). \tag{2.1}$$

However, probability raising alone is not sufficient for causality, so these theories then set about determining which of the probability raisers are most informative.

2.3.1. Screening off

One of the key problems for probabilistic theories of causality is that there can be cases of probability raising without causality (and causality without probability raising). If two events such as yellow stained fingers and lung cancer are the result of an earlier common cause, one would find that yellow stained fingers raise the probability of lung cancer even though neither one causes the other. With more information, we can find that smoking explains this seeming connection between its effects. This is called *screening off*, as when we hold fixed the common cause, the relationship between its effects disappears.

The idea of earlier screening off causes was introduced by Hans Reichenbach (1956), who attempted to characterize the direction of causal relationships without reference to time by making use of the asymmetry between cause and effect. The probability relations characterizing causal relationships are symmetric – a cause raises the probability of its effect and vice versa – yet we do not say that the effect produces the cause. Rather than relying on knowledge that the cause is earlier than the effect, Reichenbach uses the properties of probabilistic relationships to find the direction of time.

This is done using the *common cause principle*. The idea is roughly that if two events are correlated, one is a cause of the other or else they have a common cause (that occurs earlier than the two events). When there are correlated simultaneous events A and B, where $P(A \wedge B) > P(A)P(B)$, if there is an earlier common cause, C, of both, C screens off A and B from one another if and only if:

1. $P(A \wedge B|C) = P(A|C)P(B|C)$,
2. $P(A \wedge B|\neg C) = P(A|\neg C)P(B|\neg C)$,
3. $P(A|C) > P(A|\neg C)$, and
4. $P(B|C) > P(B|\neg C)$.

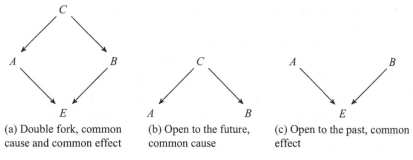

(a) Double fork, common cause and common effect

(b) Open to the future, common cause

(c) Open to the past, common effect

Figure 2.1. Forks as described by Reichenbach (1956).

This says that C raises the probability of A and of B, and that once we know that C or that $\neg C$, A and B are independent. This corresponds to the fork shown in figure 2.1b. The idea is that if we have such a fork, with some particular A, B, and C, and they satisfy the probability relations given above, it means that C is the common cause of A and B and thus it must be earlier than A and B. The fork in figure 2.1a is a result of A and B having both a common cause and a common effect. A fork open to the past, shown in figure 2.1c, would not account for this relationship. For example, if two lamps burn out simultaneously and the room goes dark, the dark room does not account for the lamps burning out. Rather, some earlier common cause such as a burned fuse or problem with a common power supply would account for this.[11] In Reichenbach's initial formulation, A and B must be simultaneous, in which case if there is no common cause one of the events cannot be a cause of the other (since a cause here must be earlier than its effect). Reichenbach is attempting to define causality itself, but since there are many counterexamples to this, the theory is primarily useful as the basis for attempting to find causal relationships. Note though that in practice there can be correlations with no common cause, such as with non-stationary time series. One common example, discussed by Sober (2001), is the case of a pair of monotonically increasing time series – Venetian sea levels and British bread prices. Because of their long term trends, there is no screening off, but no causation either.[12]

An event C is *causally relevant* to another event E if and only if C is earlier than E, $P(E|C) > P(E)$, and there does not exist a set of events S (earlier than or simultaneous with C) such that S screens off C from E.

---

[11] Reichenbach 1956, 157.

[12] For a discussion of some of the limitations of the common cause principle in time series data, along with a more practical restatement of this principle, see Reiss (2007).

That is, there is no other cause screening off C from E, and C raises the probability of E.[13]

One difficulty for this and other probabilistic definitions of causality is posed by cases of causality without probability raising, as exemplified by Simpson's paradox (Simpson, 1951). If C is a cause of E in the general population, we may be able to reverse this relationship by finding subpopulations such that in every such subpopulation C is a negative cause of E. This situation arises when C is correlated with another factor that prevents E. One common example is based on sex bias in graduate admissions at Berkeley (Bickel et al., 1975). In that study the authors found that while in general (looking at the university as a whole), men had a higher rate of admission to the university, within each department there was no correlation between sex and admission rate. Thus, being female did not cause applicants to be rejected, but rather women likely applied to more competitive departments that had lower admissions rates, leading to their overall lower rate of acceptance.

Another common example of this paradox is given by Brian Skyrms (1980). In general, smoking is a positive cause of lung cancer. Consider now what happens if due to air pollution (which we assume here can cause lung cancer), city-dwellers tend to stop smoking in order to not further jeopardize their lungs. Also suppose that due to cleaner air in the country, people there feel freer to smoke given the lack of air pollution harming their lungs. Then, smoking (C) is a positive cause of lung cancer (E), living in the country (V) is a positive cause of smoking, and living in the country is a negative cause of lung cancer. Then, because V is a positive cause of C and a negative cause of E, depending on the ratio of smokers to nonsmokers and the city air quality, since C is correlated with an actual negative cause of E (V), it can be negatively correlated with E although it is a positive cause of it (see figure 2.2). As in the previous case, where being female was associated with a higher probability of admission in each individual department but a lower probability overall, we find that smoking seems to lower the probability of lung cancer when looking at smokers versus nonsmokers, even though it is a positive cause of lung cancer in general. Smoking is correlated with living in the country (and exposure to fresh air), which made it seem to be a negative cause of lung cancer, while nonsmoking was associated with living in the city (and exposure to pollution). Similar examples can be constructed where a drug seems to be effective for men or women alone but is ineffective for people as a whole.

Resolutions for and more in-depth discussion of this issue can be found in Eells (1987b) and Otte (1985).

---

[13] Reichenbach 1956, 204.

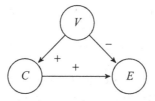

Figure 2.2. Illustration of Simpson's paradox example, with positive edges denoting probability raising and negative ones denoting probability lowering.

2.3.2. Suppes

Many probabilistic accounts of causality (Eells, 1991; Good, 1961a,b; Reichenbach, 1956), exist, but one of the primary developments of this theory came from Patrick Suppes (1970). To weed out spurious causes, Suppes's method seeks earlier causes accounting for the effect. It is assumed that the cause is earlier than the effect and that this temporal ordering is known.

An event A being earlier than an event B could refer to specific times separated by a set distance or could refer to only the ordering of events. Suppes takes the latter view, representing probabilities and events in terms of sets using the notation A_t and $B_{t'}$ to denote event of kind A occurring at time t, and B at time t'. When examining the relationship between smoking and lung cancer, where X is the set of all events, $C_{t'}$ is the subset of X consisting of all events involving smoking at any time t' (where smoking is followed at any later time t by cancer or no cancer), and E_t is the subset of X consisting of all events where people have lung cancer at some time t (preceded by smoking or not smoking at any earlier time t'). The temporal subscripts refer only to the "later" and "earlier" conditions. This will be discussed in finer detail in the next chapter, but note for now that the conditional probability is defined as $P(E_t|C_{t'}) = P(E_t \wedge C_{t'})/P(C_{t'})$. The conjunction $E_t \wedge C_{t'}$ is the intersection of the sets described, consisting of the set of events where smoking is followed by lung cancer.[14] The probability of a set of events is

See section 3.1.1 for details on probabilities.

---

[14] Depending on how finely the events are specified (with this being up to the researcher), and denoting lung cancer by L and smoking by S, the sets may be as follows. All events (X) could be $\{S_1 L_2, S_1 \overline{L_2}, \overline{S_1} L_2, \overline{S_1} \overline{L_2}\}$, where the event space is all combinations of smoking/not-smoking preceding lung cancer/not lung cancer. Then, testing whether $S_{t'}$ causes L_t, the sets are: $C = C_{t'} = \{S_1 L_2, S_1 \overline{L_2}\}$, $E = E_t = \{S_1 L_2, \overline{S_1} L_2\}$. Then, $C_{t'} \wedge E_t = \{S_1 L_2\}$. Another X could specify events more finely, such that some event might denote whether lung cancer occurs after ten years but not after five years, and another lung cancer five years but not ten years after smoking. Then E would be comprised of all of these types of events such that lung cancer happens – regardless of when it happens. In another case, outcomes could be of the form $S_1 L_1 S_2 L_2$. Then, C will contain all events that include S_1 or S_2 while E will contain all those with L_1 or L_2 but the intersection of E_t and $C_{t'}$ should only include those where S is prior to L, such as $S_1 \overline{L_1} S_2 L_2$.

For further details, see the appendix of Suppes (1970).

the sum of the probabilities of the individual events comprising the set, as each is a mutually exclusive outcome. Thus we should think of this as the sum over all ways C can precede E and interpret the temporal subscripts as describing the relationship between times t and t' (e.g., that one is strictly earlier than the other is), not as denoting actual times of occurrence.[15]

Suppes first defines prima facie causes, factors that precede and raise the probability of their effects, before then suggesting how to partition these into genuine and spurious causes.[16]

Definition 2.3.1. An event $B_{t'}$ is a *prima facie* cause of event A_t iff:

1. $t' < t$,
2. $P(B_{t'}) > 0$, and
3. $P(A_t|B_{t'}) > P(A_t)$.

We should interpret this as being for all t and t' where $t' < t$. That is, the probability of A occurring at any time after B is greater than the marginal probability of A occurring at any time. This does not refer to specific values of t and t' but rather describes the relationship between t and t'. In some cases, these causes may later turn out to be false. Even if something meets the criterion of being a prima facie cause, this may be due only to a common cause of it and the effect. Suppes introduces two ways in which something may be a false, or spurious, cause. In each, the idea is that there is some event earlier than the prima facie cause that accounts equally well for the effect, so that once this other information is known, the spurious cause does not have any influence on the effect. Suppes's first definition is as follows.[17]

Definition 2.3.2. $B_{t'}$, a prima facie cause of A_t, is a *spurious cause* in sense one iff $\exists t'' < t'$ and $C_{t''}$ such that:

1. $P(B_{t'} \wedge C_{t''}) > 0$,
2. $P(A_t|B_{t'} \wedge C_{t''}) = P(A_t|C_{t''})$, and
3. $P(A_t|B_{t'} \wedge C_{t''}) \geq P(A_t|B_{t'})$.

While $B_{t'}$ is a possible cause of A_t, there may be another, earlier, event that has more explanatory relevance to A_t. However, condition 2 of the definition above is very strong and perhaps counterintuitive. It means that

An event that is spurious in sense two is spurious in sense one, but the reverse is not true.

---

[15] Suppes gives an example immediately after the introduction of this notation with inoculation and incidence of cholera where A_t is the event of contracting cholera, while $B_{t'}$ is the event of being vaccinated against the disease. It is clear that the temporal subscripts refer only to the temporal order, and not to any particular times (Suppes, 1970, 12).

[16] Suppes 1970, 12.

[17] Suppes 1970, 23.

there exists an event that completely eliminates the effectiveness of the cause for predicting the effect. One way of relaxing this condition is to find not individual events but rather kinds of events. In Suppes's second definition of spurious causes these will be a set of nonempty sets that cover the full sample space and which are mutually exclusive (pairwise disjoint).[18] Thus, only one of these sets can be true at a time and together they cover all possibilities.

Definition 2.3.3. $B_{t'}$, a prima facie cause of A_t, is a *spurious cause* in sense two iff there is a partition, $\pi_{t''}$ where $t'' < t'$ and for every $C_{t''}$ in $\pi_{t''}$:

1. $P(B_{t'} \wedge C_{t''}) > 0$, and
2. $P(A_t|B_{t'} \wedge C_{t''}) = P(A_t|C_{t''})$.

Let us look now at the distinction between these two kinds of spuriousness. One example, given by Otte (1981), is rain (A), a falling barometer (B), and a decrease in air pressure (C). B is a prima facie cause of A since when it occurs the probability that A will follow is increased. However, $P(A|C \wedge B) = P(A|C)$, since given that the air pressure has decreased, the falling barometer does not provide any extra information about the rain. Also, $P(A|B \wedge C) \geq P(A|B)$, since the probability of rain given both a decrease in air pressure and a falling barometer is at least as great as the probability given only the falling barometer. So, B is a spurious cause of A in sense one.[19]

We can also show that B is a spurious cause of A in sense two. Taking the partition π being {decreasing air pressure, non-decreasing air pressure} we then find that the probability of A given $B \wedge C$ is still equal to the probability of A given C and that the probability of A given $B \wedge \neg C$ is equal to the probability of A given $\neg C$. If air pressure is not decreasing, a falling barometer provides no information about whether it will rain. All causes that are spurious in sense two are also spurious in sense one, but the reverse is not true in general. Note however that in the limit, where the barometer reports the air pressure perfectly, it will not be spurious in sense two, as $P(B \wedge \neg C) = 0$ (and the probability must be greater than zero) – though it will still be spurious in sense one.

---

[18] Suppes 1970, 25.

[19] This is a classic example of a common cause, but it is somewhat problematic as we have the thing itself and then our measurement of the thing. In biomedical cases, we usually observe only an indicator for the actual event – a measurement of blood pressure, a set of symptoms pointing to heart failure, and so on.

Finally, Suppes defines *genuine causes* as nonspurious prima facie causes. These definitions allow us to begin to talk about what it means for something to probabilistically cause another thing, but they can be rather limiting. Looking at the definition for spurious causes, the stipulation that $P(A_t | B_{t'} \wedge C_{t''}) = P(A_t | C_{t''})$ means that some causes may not be deemed spurious, despite meeting all the conditions, if there is a small difference in the probabilities on either side of this equality. To address this issue, Suppes introduced the concept of an ε-spurious cause.[20]

Definition 2.3.4. An event $B_{t'}$ is an ε-spurious cause of event A_t iff $\exists t'' < t'$ and a partition $\pi_{t''}$ such that for every $C_{t''}$ of $\pi_{t''}$:

1. $t' < t$,
2. $P(B_{t'}) > 0$,
3. $P(A_t | B_{t'}) > P(A_t)$,
4. $P(B_t \wedge C_{t''}) > 0$, and
5. $|P(A_t | B_{t'} \wedge C_{t''}) - P(A_t | C_{t''})| < \varepsilon$.

This definition means that a genuine cause that has a small effect on the probability of the event being caused will be ruled spurious. The partition, $\pi_{t''}$, separates off the past prior to the possibly spurious cause, $B_{t'}$. Note that there is no set value for ε, other than it being small.

One issue that arises when using these definitions to determine the true cause of an effect is that we may find earlier and earlier causes that make the later ones spurious and the cause may be quite removed from the effect in time (not to mention space). Suppes does not modify the theory to account for this, but introduces the idea of a *direct cause*. This is a concept very similar to screening off and spurious causes, except here we must consider whether there is some event coming temporally between the cause and effect. Note, however, that there is no link between spurious and indirect causes. A direct cause may still be remote in space (and perhaps in time), but this can rule out indirect remote causes.

One of the first problems we encounter with these definitions is in handling causal chains. As discussed by Otte,[21] if there is a chain of causes that each produce their effects with probability one, every member will be spurious aside from the first member of the chain. If another event is added between the last member of the chain and the final effect, and this event produces the effect with some probability $0 < p < 1$, the last member will

---

[20] Suppes 1970, 27.
[21] Otte 1981, 172.

still be spurious, but it will now be the only direct cause of the effect. In many cases, one may find earlier and earlier events to account for the effects, but it is perhaps unsatisfying to say that the only direct cause is spurious and the genuine cause is indirect. It is not obvious whether the first or last link in a chain should be the genuine cause. In this book, I aim to find the most direct causes of an effect as these provide a truer representation of the underlying structure of a system.

Secondly, in the case of overdetermination, where there are two or more possible causes for an effect and all are present, all causes will turn out to be spurious aside from the earliest. Take the case of Bob and Susie who have been armed with rocks to throw at a glass bottle. Bob is standing a little closer to the bottle than Susie is, so Susie aims and throws her rock a little earlier than Bob throws his, but their rocks hit the glass simultaneously, breaking it shortly after impact. It is assumed that once each child aims and throws their rock, it hits the glass with probability one and the glass breaks with probability one (they have excellent aim and a strong desire to destroy glassware). Since Susie threw her rock first, there is an event earlier than Bob's throw and the rocks hitting the glass that accounts for it breaking. This does not quite make sense, as Susie's throw did not set off a chain of events leading to the glass breaking any more than Bob's throw did (and her throw had no effect on his). Why should one be the genuine cause of the glass breaking, simply because it was earlier? This case can also be altered slightly so that one event is clearly responsible, making it a case of preemption. If Susie still throws first but is standing farther away so that now Bob's rock arrives first and breaks the glass before Susie's rock hits it, we would think that Bob's throw caused the glass to break. However, since Susie threw her rock first and the probability of it breaking is unchanged by Bob's throw, Susie's throw is still found as the cause of the glass breaking, even though it was already broken when her rock hit it.

To summarize Suppes's theory, a prima facie cause raises the probability of its effect and is a genuine cause if there are no factors that make it spurious by occurring earlier and fully accounting for the effect. There are two senses in which something may be spurious, which correspond to looking for particular earlier events that explain the effect better than the spurious cause versus making a partition and looking at kinds of events. However, there are open problems in determining exactly how small a difference a cause should make to its effect to be ε-spurious, and it is unclear whether one should indeed call the earliest cause – rather than the most direct one – genuine.

2.3.3. Eells

A second major advance in probabilistic causality comes from the work of Ellery Eells (1991), who proposed separate theories of type and token-level causality. Recall that type causation refers to relationships between kinds of events, factors, or properties, while token causation refers to relationships between particular events that actually occur. While there are practical problems (primarily, unrealistic requirements on knowledge and data) in attempting to use these philosophical theories as the basis for inference, Eells's intention is to provide an alternative account of what causality is – not necessarily how we should find it. This approach gives a new way of measuring the strength of a causal relationship and probabilistically analyzing token causality. While Mackie and Lewis explicitly addressed token causality, this is one of the few probabilistic accounts.

Type-level causation

At the type level, Eells focuses not on finding a single factor that renders a relationship spurious (as Reichenbach and Suppes do), but rather on quantifying the difference a potential cause makes to the probability of its effect. To do this, the probability difference is calculated while holding fixed a set of background contexts, averaging over all of these. A *background context* is a particular assignment of truth values for a set of variables, so with n factors other than the cause, there are 2^n ways of holding these fixed. For a cause, C, those that occur with nonzero probability in conjunction with C and $\neg C$ constitute a background context, so with three factors x_1, x_2, and x_3, one among eight possible background contexts would be $K_i = \neg x_1 \wedge x_2 \wedge c_3$.

Before quantifying the importance of a cause for an effect, Eells defines that C is a *positive causal factor* for E iff for each i:[22]

$$P(E|K_i \wedge C) > P(E|K_i \wedge \neg C), \tag{2.2}$$

where the K_i's are causal background contexts, $P(C \wedge K_i) > 0$, and $P(\neg C \wedge K_i) > 0$. Eells defines negative and neutral causal factors by changing the $>$ in equation 2.2 to $<$ and $=$ respectively. Lastly, C may also have *mixed* relevance for E, where it is not entirely negative, positive, or neutral. This corresponds to C's role varying depending on the context.

---

[22] Eells 1991, 81.

Eells defines that C is *causally relevant* to E if it has mixed, positive, or negative relevance for E – i.e. it is not causally neutral.

Consider how this would work for smoking and lung cancer. The background factors here may be genetic predispositions (G) and asbestos exposure (A). Then, the four possible background contexts are $\{A \wedge G, A \wedge \neg G, \neg A \wedge G, \neg A \wedge \neg G\}$, the set of all possible truth values of this combination. For smoking to be a positive causal factor, the probability of lung cancer (LC) would have to be greater when smoking (S) is present than absent, with respect to each context. This requirement that a causal relationship must hold in all background contents is called *context unanimity*, and is the subject of ongoing debate. Context unanimity is not assumed in this book during inference (discussed in section 4.2.2), since it requires fully specifying every cause in a way that is not realistic. There may be factors that bring about the effect in some scenarios even though they lower its probability in conjunction with other conditions. Genetic factors may determine whether a medication will have its intended effect or will cause certain rare side effects, but in general we would not say that if a drug fails to perform as expected in one case, it should not be considered a cause of survival. Similarly, many of the things that determine whether a cause will raise or lower the probability of an effect are unknown to us at the outset, making it difficult to insist on probability raising across every context. Wearing a seatbelt generally lowers the probability of death from a car accident, but in some cases may injure a person on impact or may prevent them from escaping a vehicle that is on fire. Thus, it will have mixed causal relevance for death from car accidents, even though the majority of the time it is a negative cause.

For further discussion on context unanimity see Dupré (1984, 1990) and Eells (1987a).

In addition to determining *whether* C is causally relevant to E, we may want to describe *how* relevant C is to E. To do this, Eells measures the significance of a factor X for a factor Y with:[23]

$$\sum_i P(K_i)[P(Y|K_i \wedge X) - P(Y|K_i \wedge \neg X)], \qquad (2.3)$$

Average degree of causal significance (ADCS)

where this is called the *average degree of causal significance* (ADCS). The factors held fixed may be at any time earlier than Y, while Suppes's approach would only consider those earlier than X. With $X_{t'}$ and Y_t where $t' < t$, the factors in K_i may be at any time $t'' < t$. However, among other details, Eells omits factors that are causally intermediate between X and Y, so effects of X would be excluded. Thus, as before, the causes inferred may

[23] Eells 1991, 88.

be indirect. While it is not Eells's concern, the large number of relevant factors leads to an enormous number of background contexts, and it is unlikely that most of these would be observed more than once and certainly not with a statistically significant frequency.

Token-level causation

While some theories link type and token causation by relating known type-level causes to single cases or trying to draw type-level conclusions from observations of token-level cases, Eells proposes two unconnected theories. This poses some problems if taken as a methodological recommendation, but the key point is that type-level relationships do not necessitate token-level ones and, whether or not the theories are connected, information about one level is insufficient. Recall the case of a lit match and a house fire, which was discussed in terms of INUS conditions. Regardless of the general relationship between lit matches and house fires, we need to know more about the individual situation to determine whether a lit match caused a particular fire. For example, it is highly unlikely that a match lit days before a fire should be a token cause of it. Even more challenging is a case where a type-level positive cause is a negative token-level cause. Eells's approach allows for these differing roles.

Examples of this type, such as a seatbelt causing death during a car accident, are discussed in depth in section 6.4.3.

Say we aim to determine the relevance of an event x being of type X for an event y being of type Y. Here there are two actually occurring events (specified by their locations in time and space) that are instances of two general types. This could be a particular person, Anne, driving a car while intoxicated and the car crashing along the FDR drive. Then we want to understand what the relevance is of Anne's drunk driving for her car crash that evening. This type of question could be answered by "because of," "despite," or "independently of," corresponding to positive, negative, and neutral causal factorhood as described at the type level. To make these determinations, Eells suggests examining not a single probability, but rather how the probability of the effect changed over time. This so-called probability trajectory details the probability of y being of type Y over time, starting before x is of type X and ending with the actual occurrence of y. Then, it is said that y is of type Y *because of* x if the following are all true:

1. The probability of Y changes at the time x occurs;
2. Just after x the probability of y is high;
3. The probability is higher than it was before x; and
4. The probability remains high until the time of y.

Continuing with the example of Anne, we would deem the car crash occurring at time t to be because of her drunk driving if the probability of the crash increased after she got behind the wheel and remained increased until the crash actually occurred. The probability of the effect changed once the cause occurred, becoming higher than it was before, and did not decrease before the effect finally occurred (which would make it seem that something else must have occurred to raise it again).

Four ways a token event x at time t' can be related to a token event y at time t are:

- y is Y *despite* x if the probability of Y is lowered after $x_{t'}$.
- y is Y *because of* x if the probability of Y is increased after $x_{t'}$ and remains increased until y_t.
- y is Y *autonomously of* x if the probability of Y changes at $x_{t'}$, this probability is high, but then decreases before y_t.
- y is Y *independently of* x if the probability of Y is the same just after $x_{t'}$ as it is just before $x_{t'}$.

Then, x is *causally relevant* to y if it happened either because of or despite x. As at the type level, one must still hold fixed other sets of factors to determine x's contribution to y's probability. These are:[24]

1. Factors that token occur in the particular case, their occurrence is token uncaused by x being X and they are type-level causally relevant to y's being Y holding fixed how things are before these factors actually occur.
2. Factors that token occur in the particular case, are token uncaused by x being X and that interact with X with respect to Y holding fixed what is actually true before x_t.

These factors may occur at any time before y_t and the causal background context is obtained by holding positively fixed all factors of these two kinds.

However, holding fixed these factors does not improve the classification of all relationships. Consider an event z where z occurs at some time after x and before y. If z is causally relevant to y, then we will not have a true understanding of x's significance since we had not considered z intervening, as Eells only holds fixed factors prior to x and not things that may occur and change the scenario after it. In an example given by Eells, there is a patient who is very ill at time t_1, who is likely to survive until t_2 but not until a later t_3. Now assume that at t_1 a treatment is administered that is equally

---

[24] Eells 1991, 345.

likely to kill the patient as the disease is. At t_2 a completely effective cure is discovered and administered and the only remaining chance of death is due to the first ineffective treatment – not the disease. However, the probability of death did not change after the first treatment, so death was token causally independent of it. But, the relation should actually be despite, as the treatment put the patient at unnecessary risk due to its severe side effects (which remain unchanged by the second treatment that cured the underlying disease).

In this example, the second drug is causally relevant to Y (survival) and is not caused by the administration of the first drug. When holding fixed the second drug being given, using the first kind of factor described, the first drug again has no effect on the probability of Y. Using the second kind of factor has no effect in this case, as the two drugs do not interact, so the probability of survival after the first drug does not change dependent on the presence or absence of the second drug.

While Eells's approach is capable in theory of handling cases where a token-level probability is very different from a type-level one, it is unclear how we could glean this type of information. In what cases will we be able to actually separate the factors that were caused by x on a particular occasion from those that were interacting with it? Further, outside of examples in physics, it is unlikely that we could find the probability trajectories. Remember, this is a probability based not on some relationship between type-level probabilities and token-level information but rather how the probability changes over time in a specific scenario.

Eells seeks to elucidate the concept of causality itself, but the counterexamples to his theory suggest that it does not cover all possibilities. On the other hand, such theories may be useful as the basis for inference (suggesting the types of evidence to be amassed) but the stringent requirements on knowledge make this difficult.

To summarize, Eells proposes two probabilistic theories of causality. At the type level, causes must either positively or negatively produce their effects in all background contexts (or be deemed mixed causes if they do both), where these contexts include events earlier than the effect. For the second, at the token level, Eells analyzes how the probability of the token effect changes in relation to the occurrence of the cause.

2.4. Causal Inference Algorithms

The philosophical approaches described so far aim to tell us what it is for something to be a cause, or how we can learn of causes, but to do this from data we need automated methods. Despite the many causal assumptions made in the sciences, comparatively little work has been done to examine the meaning of these assumptions and how we may go about making inferences from a set of data. Much of this work involves field specific methods that are designed to work with particular data types. Computational approaches generally aim to infer causal relationships from data (with significantly less work on extending this to the case of token causality), and can be categorized into two main traditions (along with extensions to these). First, the majority of work on characterizing what can be inferred in general and how it can be inferred has been using graphical models (Pearl, 2000; Spirtes et al., 2000). The theories are technically probabilistic, but it is usually assumed that the relationships themselves are deterministic and the probabilities are due to the limits of what may be observed.[25] Second, Granger (1969) causality, which aims to infer relationships between time series, is not generally considered to be a definition of causality or method of its inference, but was one of the first approaches to include time lags. It has also been used by many researchers in finance and neuroscience, so it will be useful to examine how the approach works and exactly what it is inferring.

2.4.1. Graphical models

Bayesian networks

One of the first steps toward causal inference was the development of theories connecting graphical models to causal concepts, formulated in parallel by Pearl (2000) and Spirtes, Glymour and Scheines (hereafter SGS) as described in (Spirtes et al., 2000).[26] These methods take a set of data and produce a directed acyclic graph (DAG), called a Bayesian network (BN), that represents the causal structure of the system. In these graphs, variables are represented as vertices, and edges between the vertices indicate conditional dependence. The techniques do not require temporal data but rather are designed to take a set of observations (that may or may not be ordered) and produce one or more graphs showing the independence relations that are consistent with the data. During the inference process, edges are directed from cause to effect based on independence rather than temporal ordering in the data.

For a more detailed introduction to Bayesian networks, see Koller and Friedman (2009), Korb and Nicholson (2010), and Neapolitan (2004).

Three main assumptions are needed: the causal Markov condition (CMC), faithfulness, and causal sufficiency. *CMC* says that a variable

---

[25] Other work, by Pearl and others (Halpern and Pearl, 2005; Hopkins and Pearl, 2007; Pearl, 2000), has focused on the development of a statistical theory of counterfactuals that supports queries on known models and determination of the token (actual) cause in such cases.

[26] The notation used here will be primarily that of SGS, but most comments apply to both theories.

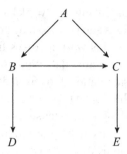

Figure 2.3. Example Bayesian network.

is independent of all of its non-descendants conditional on all of its direct causes (parents). This means that if there is a path in the graph, $X \to Z \to Y$, and it is the only directed path between X and Y, they are independent given Z. The influence of X on Y is entirely mediated by Z, so once it is known, X is no longer relevant for predicting Y. This relates to Reichenbach's common cause principle, described in section 2.3.1, where two events are causally connected if one causes the other or if there is another event that is a common cause of both. With CMC, if two events are dependent and neither one is a cause of the other, then there must be some common causes in the set of variables such that the two events are independent conditional on these common causes. The graphs are not necessarily complete, as there may be causes of some variables or variables intermediate between cause and effect that are left out. Thus, vertices are connected if one is a direct cause of the other, relative to the set of variables in the graph. The graphs are assumed to be complete though in the sense that all common causes of pairs on the set of variables are included.

In the structure shown in figure 2.3, C and D are independent given B, while E is independent of all other variables given C. These independence relations allow the conditional probability of any variable to be calculated efficiently, and represented in a compact way. Without knowledge of the graph, the probability of C conditioned on all variables in the set would be calculated with $P(C|ABDE)$, but using CMC and the graph, we know that C is independent of all other variables given A and B, so $P(C|ABDE) = P(C|AB)$. In general, the probability distribution for a set of variables, $x_1, \ldots, x_n$, can be factored into

$$P(x_1, x_2, \ldots, x_n) = \prod_{i=1}^{n} P(x_i|pa(x_i)) \qquad (2.4)$$

where $pa(x)$ is the parents of x.

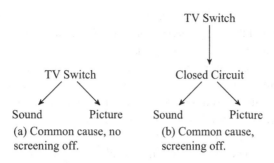

Figure 2.4. Screening off example.

CMC is perhaps the most debated portion of the theory, leading to a multitude of papers criticizing (Cartwright, 2001, 2002; Freedman and Humphreys, 1999; Humphreys and Freedman, 1996) and defending it (Hausman and Woodward, 1999, 2004). The main issue is that depending on how accurately a system is represented, common causes may not always render their effects independent. One example (Spirtes et al., 2000), shown in figure 2.4a, is a television with a switch that does not always turn the TV on. When the TV does turn on, both the sound and picture turn on as well. Thus, even after knowing that the switch is on, knowing that the sound is on still provides information about whether the picture is on as well. Here the picture is not independent of the sound, conditioned on the state of the switch, violating CMC (since there is no edge between picture and sound and the switch fails to screen them off from one another). Adding a variable indicating when there is a closed circuit, shown in figure 2.4b, resolves this. Previously, the picture or sound gave information about the circuit that was not provided by knowledge of the status of the switch. This case was clear with common knowledge about how circuits work, but it is less clear how such a scenario can be resolved in cases where the structure must be inferred from data.

Next, the *faithfulness* condition says that exactly the independence relations in the graph hold in the probability distribution over the set of variables. The implication is that the independence relations obtained are due to the causal structure, rather than coincidence or latent (unmeasured) variables. This is only true in the large sample limit, as with little data, the observations cannot be assumed to be indicative of the true probabilities. There are other cases where faithfulness can fail, though, even with sufficient data. When a cause acts through two paths – say, one where it increases the probability of an effect directly, and one where it increases the probability of a factor that lowers the probability of an effect – there can be distributions where these paths exactly cancel out so that the cause seems to have no impact on the effect and they are independent. Recall the case shown in figure 2.2 that was discussed in relation to Simpson's paradox. There were two paths from living in the country to lung cancer: one where this directly lowered the probability of lung cancer, and another where it raised the probability of smoking, which raised the probability of lung cancer. Probability distributions generated from this structure would be said to be *unfaithful* if the health effect of living in the country exactly balances that of smoking, leading to living in the country being independent of lung cancer. Faithfulness can fail even without exact independence, and in fact one cannot verify exact independence from finite sample data (Humphreys and Freedman, 1996). In practice, one must choose a threshold at which to call variables conditionally independent, so there can be violations of this condition in a wider variety of cases than one may think, such as if the threshold for independence is too low or the distributions come close to canceling out without quite balancing. Biological systems have features designed to ensure exactly this type of behavior, so this can potentially pose a more serious practical problem than it may seem. Another way faithfulness can fail is through selection bias. This is a considerable problem in studies from observational data, as it can happen without any missing causes. As discussed by Cooper (1999), using data from an emergency department (ED), it may seem that fever and abdominal pain are statistically dependent. However, this may be because only patients with those symptoms visit the ED, while those who have only a fever or only abdominal pain stay home.

Finally, *causal sufficiency* means that the set of measured variables includes all of the common causes of pairs on that set. This differs from completeness in that it assumes that the true graph includes these common causes and that they are part of the set of variables measured. If in measurements of the variables in figure 2.3 *A* was not included, this set would not be causally sufficient. Without this assumption, two common effects of a cause will erroneously seem dependent when their cause is not included. When sufficiency and the other assumptions do not hold, a set of graphs that are consistent with the dependencies in the data will be inferred, along with vertices for possible unmeasured common causes. Some algorithms for inferring BNs, such as FCI (Spirtes et al., 2000), do not assume sufficiency and attempt to determine whether there are latent variables, thus aiming to make stronger claims about the relationship between variables (that it is unconfounded).

This section focuses primarily on the general theoretical framework for giving BNs a causal interpretation, but I briefly overview the basic approach to inferring these from data. The main idea is to find the graph or set of graphs that best explain the data, and for this there are two primary methods: (1) assigning scores to graphs and searching over the set of possible graphs while attempting to maximize a particular scoring function; (2) beginning with an undirected fully connected graph and using repeated conditional independence tests to remove and orient edges in the graph. In the first approach, an initial graph is generated and then the search space is explored by altering this graph. The primary differences between algorithms of this type are how the search space is explored (e.g., periodically restarting to avoid convergence to local minima) and what scoring function is used to evaluate the graphs (e.g., one that penalizes larger models to avoid overfitting to a particular dataset). In the second approach, exemplified by the PC algorithm (Spirtes et al., 2000), one begins with a fully connected graph and then iterates through a series of conditional independence tests to determine whether edges can be removed. After removing these edges, the remaining ones are directed from cause to effect. When some edges cannot be directed, the result is a partially directed graph.

The primary criticism of this approach is, as discussed, with regards to its assumptions. While it is not explicitly stated, one assumption is that the variables are correctly specified. This is more critical than one might think. Since BNs do not include temporal information, cases with a strong temporal component will lead to erroneous results if this is not somehow encoded into the variables. However, it is unlikely that without knowing there is a relationship between two variables, we know its timing exactly. In practice, the three primary assumptions (CMC, faithfulness, causal sufficiency) all fail in various scenarios, so the question is whether one can determine whether they hold or if they are true in the majority of cases of interest.

In chapter 7, empirical results quantify the level of this dependence.

Dynamic Bayesian networks

While Bayesian networks can be used for representation and inference of causal relationships in the absence of time, many practical cases involve a lag between the cause and effect. We want to know not only that a stock will eventually go up after certain news, but exactly when, so that this information can be traded on. However, BNs have no natural way of testing these relationships. Instead, dynamic Bayesian networks (DBNs) (Friedman et al., 1998; Murphy, 2002) use a set of BNs to show how variables influence each other across time. There is generally an initial BN depicting

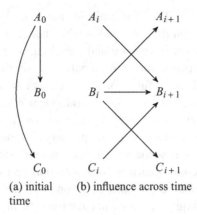

(a) initial   (b) influence across time
time

Figure 2.5. Example DBN with one graph showing the initial state of the system (time zero), and then a second DBN that shows how variables at any i are connected to those at the next time $i + 1$.

the connections between variables at some time t and then a set of BNs showing the system at time $t + 1, t + 2$, and so on, with connections across time slices indicating dependence of a variable on itself or another variable across time. The simplest case, a system that is stationary and Markov, is shown in figure 2.5. That system has an initial state and then a DBN with two time slices, showing how variables at time t_i influence those at t_{i+1}. Recent work has extended DBNs to non-stationary time series, where there are so-called changepoints when the structure of the system (how the variables are connected) changes. Some approaches find these times for the whole system (Robinson and Hartemink, 2010), while others find variable specific changepoints (Grzegorczyk and Husmeier, 2009).

Like BNs, though, there is no DBN-based method for testing complex relationships. Variables can be defined arbitrarily, but there is no structured method for forming and testing hypotheses more complex than pairwise ones between variables. One could not automatically determine that smoking for a period of 15 years while having a particular genetic mutation leads to lung cancer in 5–10 years with probability 0.5. Since each connection at each time slice is inferred separately (finding c at time t causes e at $t + 1, t + 2$, and so on) this leads to significant computational complexity. Relationships between all variables at all lags in a range being tested are assessed simultaneously (leading to a score for the entire graph), requiring searching over a large sample space (all pairs of variables connected in all possible ways across a range of times). As a result, one must use heuristics, but these can be sensitive to the parameters chosen and overfit the data.

Even more critically, few relationships involve discrete lags and, even in cases where the timing is precise, it is unlikely that it would seem that way from observational data. Some researchers choose specific timepoints and create variables that group events occurring in a time range, but again one would need to know the timing of relationships before knowing of the relationships.

2.4.2. Granger causality

Clive Granger (1969, 1980) developed a statistical method to take two time series and determine whether one is useful for forecasting the other. Granger did not attempt to relate this to philosophical definitions of causality but rather proposed a new definition that is most similar to correlation. However, it is one of the few methods that explicitly include time and has been used widely in finance (Granger, 2007) and neuroscience (Bressler and Seth, 2011; Ding et al., 2006). It has also been used by physicists to model information flow (Hlavackova-Schindler et al., 2007). Thus, it will be useful to discuss the basic idea and its limitations, as well as some misconceptions about the approach. It is also included in the empirical comparisons in chapter 7.

The notation used here is as follows. $X_1(t)$ denotes the value of variable X_1 at time t, while $X_1^*(t)$ is the set of measurements of X_1 up to time t (i.e., $X_1(t), X_1(t-1), \ldots, X_1(1)$). $W^*(t)$ is the set of all possible knowledge up to time t (including both X_1 and X_2), though in practice it is a vector of explanatory variables. Then, Granger (1969, 1980) defined:

Definition 2.4.1. X_2 *Granger-causes* X_1 if

$$P(X_1(t+1)|W^*(t)) \neq P(X_1(t+1)|W^*(t) - X_2^*(t)). \tag{2.5}$$

As this is not exactly causality, it has come to be called Granger causality, although it is sometimes referred to as Wiener-Granger causality as Granger's work built on ideas from Wiener (1956). Granger's definition takes temporal priority as a given and does not make claims about how much of a difference X_2 makes to the probability of X_1 (or whether this difference is positive or negative). X_2 may not be the best or only predictor of X_1, rather it is simply found to be informative after accounting for other information.

This definition has been debated in both philosophy (Cartwright, 1989) and economics (Chowdhury, 1987; Jacobs et al., 1979), with many counterexamples showing that it is neither necessary nor sufficient for causality (Hoover, 2001).[27] Granger did not dispute this, but instead argued that the primary advantage of the approach is that it is easy to understand and pragmatic.[28] Since the focus of this book is also on practical methods, my discussion will focus on such concerns.

One cannot truly use all possible variables over an infinitely long timescale, so later work focused on making this approach feasible. While there are a number of methodological choices (e.g., linear versus nonlinear methods), the primary distinction is between bivariate and multivariate tests. When researchers say they are using a Granger test, it is usually the bivariate test that is meant. It has the advantage of being simple and computationally efficient, though it does not capture the intention of the original definition, which is to use all information. In the bivariate test, only two time series are included: that of the effect, X_1, and the cause, X_2. One bivariate method is to use an autoregressive model with the two variables, where if the coefficients of the lagged values of X_2 are nonzero, then X_2 is said to Granger-cause X_1. An m-lag autoregressive model takes lagged values of a time series up to $t - m$ when calculating the value of a variable at time t. Each lagged value is weighted by a coefficient, so that a variable may depend more strongly on recent events than those that are more temporally distant. More formally, X_1 can be represented as the following m-lag linear autoregressive model:

$$X_1(t) = \sum_{j=1}^{m} A_{11}(j)X_1(t - j) + \sum_{j=1}^{m} A_{12}(j)X_2(t - j) + \varepsilon_1(t). \qquad (2.6)$$

The m lags mean that the values of X_1 and X_2 at times $t - 1, t - 2, \ldots, t - m$ influence that of X_1 at time t. The coefficient $A_{11}(j)$ is how much the value at t depends on $t - j$. Here A_{kl} means the influence of X_l on X_k, so that A_{11} is the dependence of X_1 on itself and A_{12} is that of X_1 on X_2. According to Granger's original definition, m would ideally be infinite, though in practice it is much smaller. The so-called error term, ε, is assumed to be a random variable, usually with mean zero. Using this, Granger causality can be tested by whether nonzero values for A_{12} lead to a smaller variance in the error term ε_1 than when these are zero (and whether this reduction is statistically significant). There are many implementations of this including the granger.test function in the MSBVAR R package, and the Granger causal connectivity analysis (GCCA) MATLAB toolbox (Seth, 2010).

---

[27] One of the more amusing studies showed that in fact eggs Granger-cause chickens (Thurman and Fisher, 1988).

[28] Granger 2007, 290–291, 294.

As Eichler (2009) has discussed, despite the popularity of this bivariate approach, it does not capture Granger's original definition. Further, it cannot distinguish between causal relationships and correlations between effects of a common cause. This can be seen in equation 2.6. If X_1 and X_2 have a common cause, X_3, and these effects do not always occur simultaneously, then $X_2^*(t-1)$ will provide information about when X_3 has occurred and will thus significantly improve the prediction of X_1. A more accurate approach is the multivariate one, which includes other variables in the model of each time series. Using a vector autoregressive model with variables $v \in V$, now instead of a single variable $X_V(t)$ is a vector representing the measurement of all variables in V at time t. The system is represented as:

$$X_V(t) = \sum_{j=1}^{m} A(j) \times X_V(t-j) + \varepsilon_V(t). \qquad (2.7)$$

Here A is a $V \times V$ matrix of coefficients and ε_V is a vector of error terms. Using this representation, X_2 Granger-causes X_1 if at least one of $A_{12}(j)$ is nonzero.

While this comes closer to causal inference than the bivariate test does, it has practical problems. Such a model quickly becomes computationally infeasible with even a moderate number of lags and variables. Using a model of order 20 with 20 variables leads to a summation over twenty 20×20 matrices. Outside of finance (where influence is often assumed to drop off steeply as m increases) many areas of work involve influence over long periods of time, such as in epidemiological studies, but these would be prohibitively complex to test. Similarly, even if there were only a few lags, much work involves dozens to hundreds of variables. To illustrate the complexity of this approach, the multivariate test was applied to the same set of data as the approach discussed in this book. That method took 2.5 hours to test relationships between a set of 26 variables with a lag of 20–40 time units and 100,000 events. By contrast the GCCA Matlab toolbox implementation of the multivariate test used all 8GB of RAM on the PC, and was finally stopped after running for 48 hours without finishing. The same method was implemented in R, but required more than the available RAM. Thus, while the multivariate test has been shown to perform better in comparisons (Blinowska et al., 2004), it is easy to see why the bivariate test continues to be used so widely. Nevertheless, researchers should be aware of its limitations.

Chapter 7 gives empirical results on the accuracy and time complexity for the bivariate test.

As with DBNs, there is no intrinsic method of representing complex factors such that their causal roles may be inferred automatically from the data. We may want to test not only whether there is a relationship between unemployment and a bull market, but perhaps:

$$(a \wedge b)Uc \rightsquigarrow^{\geq t_1, \leq t_2}_{\geq p} d,$$

which could be interpreted to mean that after a bear market (a) and increasing unemployment (b) both become true and persist until unemployment reaches 20% (c), then within 1 (t_1) to 2 (t_2) months, there will be a bull market (d) with probability p.

Finally, one seeming advantage of Granger's approach is that it can deal with continuous variables, not just discrete events (or discretized time series). Much data in economics and finance is of this form, and information may be lost by binning such variables or treating them as binary (such as only increasing or decreasing).[29] However, graphical models have been extended to deal with hybrid systems that mix continuous and discrete variables (Dondelinger et al., 2010; Lauritzen and Wermuth, 1989). Similarly, the approach of this book has been extended to continuous variables, with a measure of causal significance based on conditional expected value and a new logic that allows representation of constraints on continuous variables (Kleinberg, 2011). Thus, there are other approaches that can be applied to handle continuous-valued time series.

---

[29] This is not always true, though, as discretization can be helpful with noisy and error-prone time series.

3

Probability, Logic, and Probabilistic Temporal Logic

3.1. Probability

Whether we want to determine the likelihood of a stock market crash or if people with a given gene have a higher risk of a disease, we need to understand the details of how to calculate and assess probabilities. But first, what exactly are probabilities and where do they come from? There are two primary views. The *frequentist* view says that probabilities relate to the proportion of occurrences in a series of events. For example, the probability of a coin coming up heads being $1/2$ means that with a large number of coin flips, half should be heads and half tails. The probability then corresponds to how often something will occur. However, we also discuss the probability of events that may only happen once. We may want to know the probability that a recession will end if a policy is enacted, or the chances of a federal interest rate change on a particular date. In the frequentist case, we can get close to inferring the true probability by doing a large number of tests, but when an event may only occur once, we must instead rely on background knowledge and belief. There is another interpretation of probability, referred to as the *Bayesian* or *subjectivist* view. Here the probabilities correspond to degrees of belief in the outcome occurring. In this case, one must have what is called a *prior*, on which the belief is based. For example, if you bet that the Yankees will beat the Mets in the World Series, you are basing this on your knowledge of both teams, and given that information, which team you think is likelier to prevail. How closely the subjective probability corresponds to the actual probability depends heavily on the prior, and can differ between individuals. In the following sections, I review some basic concepts in probability that are needed for the following chapters. Readers seeking a more thorough introduction should consult Jaynes (2003), while readers familiar with these details may move on to the next section on logic.

For more detail on theories of probability see Gillies (2000).

3.1.1. Basic definitions

We will begin with some basic concepts in probability. First, probabilities are defined relative to the set of possible outcomes, called the *sample space*. For a single coin flip, there are only two outcomes – heads and tails – with these outcomes being equally likely and each having probability $1/2$. The sample space can be represented as a set, with events defined as subsets of this set. If we flip a coin two times in a row, the set of all possible outcomes (the sample space, represented by the symbol Ω) is:

$$\Omega = \{HH, HT, TH, TT\} \tag{3.1}$$

where H means heads and T means tails. Then if we are interested in the event of exactly one tail, there are two such outcomes: $\{HT, TH\}$. Here all outcomes are equally likely, so we can find the probability of an event by taking the number of favorable outcomes as a fraction of all outcomes. For exactly one T, this is $2/4$. We write the probability of an event x as $P(x)$, where P is the function that assigns this probability.

In general, the outcomes in the sample space can have varying probabilities (this will be the case if a coin is biased toward heads or tails), but there are some properties that a probability function must have. First, the value of a probability must be greater than or equal to zero and less than or equal to one. An event with probability zero is usually considered impossible, although this is not the case when there is an infinite number of events. Second, the probabilities of all events in the sample space must add up to one. This ensures that the probability that some outcome in the set will occur is one. Finally, if events are mutually exclusive (meaning they cannot both occur), the probability of either event occurring is the sum of their individual probabilities. For example, the event of flipping both heads and both tails cannot be true at the same time. Thus, if we want the probability of either HH or TT, this is $P(HH) + P(TT)$. On the other hand, events such as increasing unemployment and decreasing interest rates are not mutually exclusive, as one occurring does not preclude the other from occurring, so the probability of either happening needs to be calculated differently.

These three rules are known as Kolmogorov's axioms (Kolmogorov, 1956). More formally, relative to a sample space Ω and a set S that contains subsets of Ω, a probability function P must satisfy:

1. $P(A) \geq 0$ for all A in the set S. $P(A)$ is the probability of event A.
2. $P(\Omega) = 1$.

3. For any A and B in S, if A and B are mutually exclusive, then:

$$P(A \vee B) = P(A) + P(B). \qquad (3.2)$$

We use $A \vee B$ to denote "A or B" and $A \wedge B$ to denote "A and B." In terms of sets, these correspond to union ($\cup$) and intersection ($\cap$) respectively. If A and B are mutually exclusive, then $P(A \wedge B) = 0$. Figure 3.1 illustrates these operations along with a few others that are discussed shortly.

Equation (3.2) gives the probability of $A \vee B$ for the special case where A and B are mutually exclusive (disjoint). In general this probability is:

$$P(A \vee B) = P(A) + P(B) - P(A \wedge B). \qquad (3.3) \qquad \textit{Addition rule}$$

This is known as the *addition rule*. As shown in figure 3.1a, the area $A \wedge B$ is contained in both A and B, so if we simply add $P(A)$ and $P(B)$, it will be counted twice. In the mutually exclusive case, $P(A \wedge B)$ is zero and can be omitted. Thus to find the probability of increasing unemployment or decreasing interest rates, we can sum their individual probabilities and then subtract the probability of both occurring.

It is also useful to be able to calculate the probability of the negation of an outcome. Going back to flipping a coin twice, let A be the event HH (heads twice in a row). Now if we are interested in the probability that A does not occur, we want the probability of all the other events that can happen: HT, TH, and TT. However, since this means the entire set Ω minus the A events, and we know that $P(\Omega) = 1$, we can simply subtract the probability of A from one to get the probability of not A. Since A and $\neg A$ are disjoint:

$$1 = P(A) + P(\neg A), \qquad (3.4)$$

and thus:

$$P(\neg A) = 1 - P(A). \qquad (3.5) \qquad \textit{Complement rule}$$

This means, for example, that the probability that someone does not have the flu is one minus the probability that they do have the flu. See figure 3.1e for an illustration of the complement.

Two other concepts needed are dependence and independence of events. If I flip a coin twice, the outcome of the second flip is unrelated to the outcome of the first flip. This is an example of events that are *independent*. That means that if we want to know the probability of H (denoted by A) followed by T (denoted by B), it is simply:

$$P(A \wedge B) = P(A)P(B). \qquad (3.6)$$

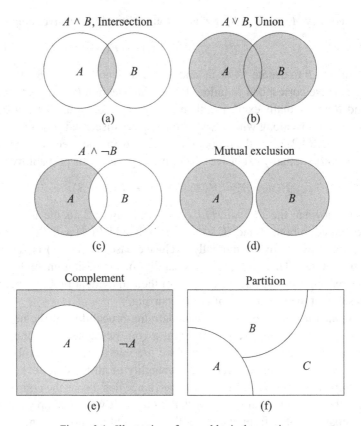

Figure 3.1. Illustration of set and logical operations.

Imagine the full sample space as a rectangle containing the circles showing where A and B are true in figure 3.1a. Then $P(A)$ tells us if we pick a random point in the rectangle what the chances are that point will be inside the circle marked A. When A and B are independent, whether a point is in A has no bearing on whether it is also in B, which has probability $P(B)$. For example, it being Wednesday would not change the probability of a patient having a heart attack.

However, if we are interested in the probability that someone smokes and has lung cancer, these events will likely be *dependent*. In that case, we must calculate the probability using the *multiplication rule*:

Multiplication rule

$$P(A \wedge B) = P(B|A)P(A). \tag{3.7}$$

The intuition is that now, if a point is in A, whether it is also in B is no longer random. This could also be stated as $P(A \wedge B) = P(A|B)P(B)$.

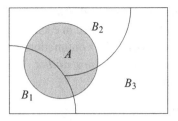

Figure 3.2. Partition of sample space, general case.

If we compare this to the equation for the independent case, we see that when A and B are independent it implies:

$$P(B|A) = P(B). \tag{3.8}$$

Recalling the coin flipping case, this says that the probability of tails is unchanged by the prior flip being heads. In another case, this might be the probability of a particular politician being chosen as vice president, given who the nominee is. Clearly this will differ significantly between candidates. The notation $P(B|A)$ means the probability of B given A and is called the *conditional probability*. In general (regardless of whether the events are independent), this is defined as

$$P(B|A) = \frac{P(A \wedge B)}{P(A)}. \tag{3.9}$$

Conditional probability

Next we can use disjoint events to help calculate the probability of an outcome. We may not have direct measurements of $P(A)$ (the probability that a disease is fatal) but we might know the probability of death when it is treated by a drug ($A \wedge B$) and when it is not ($A \wedge \neg B$). Thus, if we have a partition of the sample space, such as B and $\neg B$, we can calculate the probability of A as follows:

$$P(A) = P(A \wedge B) + P(A \wedge \neg B). \tag{3.10}$$

This corresponds to using the shaded areas of figures 3.1a and 3.1c to find the area of A. A *partition* is defined as a group of disjoint sets whose union is the entire sample space. See figure 3.1f for a depiction of a set partition. With an arbitrary partition $B_1, B_2, \ldots, B_n$ that covers the entire sample space, the probability of A is:

$$P(A) = P(A \wedge B_1) + P(A \wedge B_2) + \cdots + P(A \wedge B_n). \tag{3.11}$$

With $n = 3$, this is illustrated as shown in figure 3.2.

Intuitively, since the partitions are disjoint (they do not overlap), we are adding the portion of A that is contained in each of the B_i's. More generally, using equation (3.7) to rewrite the conjunctions in terms of conditional probabilities, this is the *law of total probability*. With a set $B_1, B_2, \ldots, B_n$ that partitions the sample space:

Law of total probability

$$P(A) = P(A|B_1)P(B_1) + P(A|B_2)P(B_2) + \cdots + P(A|B_n)P(B_n) \quad (3.12)$$

$$= \sum_{i=1}^{n} P(A|B_i)P(B_i). \quad (3.13)$$

The resulting probability of A is also called the *marginal probability*, and the process of summing over the set $B_1, \ldots, B_n$ is called *marginalization*.

In some cases, it is convenient to calculate a conditional probability using other conditional probabilities. For example, A might be the event of having a disease and B a diagnostic test being positive (with $\neg B$ meaning the test is not positive). Then we want to know the probability that a patient has the disease given a positive test result. Since tests may have false positives (where the result erroneously indicates the patient has a disease) or false negatives (where the test fails to identify the patient's illness), this is a frequent practical problem. In this case, we have prior information on the probability of each of these occurrences. Observe that in equation (3.7), $P(A|B)P(B) = P(B|A)P(A)$. Rearranging this, we find:

Bayes' theorem

$$P(A|B) = \frac{P(B|A)P(A)}{P(B)}. \quad (3.14)$$

This is known as Bayes' theorem (also called Bayes' rule or Bayes' law). Recall also that $P(B) = P(B|A)P(A) + P(B|\neg A)P(\neg A)$. This is one of the key theorems used throughout probabilistic causal inference, in which relationships are described using variants of the conditional probability of the effect given the cause. In the beginning of this chapter, I briefly mentioned the idea of Bayesian probabilities, where the probability of an outcome takes into account prior beliefs. In this formulation, B is taken to represent a person's prior knowledge (referred to as the prior distribution, or just prior). Then $P(A|B)$ is the *posterior probability* of the hypothesis A given the evidence B, where $P(A)$ and $P(B)$ are the *prior probabilities* of A and B, and $P(B|A)$ is called the *likelihood*.

This is useful for formally taking into account a frame of reference. Say you read a paper about a randomized trial that showed praying for patients' recovery 10–16 years after their initial hospital stay resulted in them having a shorter stay, and that this result was statistically significant. Most doctors would not take this information and then hire teams of people to pray for the recovery of their past patients. In fact, such a study was indeed done, and showed that this temporally and spatially remote prayer intervention did yield shorter hospital stays (Leibovici, 2001), but there has been (as far as I know) no sudden upsurge of prayer in hospitals. The randomized controlled trial conformed to current standards and the results would normally be accepted given the usual convention of rejecting the null hypothesis at a significance level of 0.05 (the study achieved 0.04). Yet no matter how low the *p*-value, this conflicts with many potential beliefs (that the present cannot affect the past, that there should be a physical connection between the patient and treatment, and that prayer is not an effective treatment to name a few). This disconnect can be accounted for by incorporating beliefs on the efficacy of such an intervention, showing that these are so low that essentially no study, no matter what the significance level, would change them.

3.2. Logic

The inference and explanation approach discussed in the rest of this book is based on a probabilistic temporal logic, but before we can discuss its details, we need to begin with a review of propositional logic followed by an introduction to modal and temporal logic.

3.2.1. Propositional and modal logic

The previous discussion of probability made use of some logical operators and their set theoretic equivalents, but did not discuss their details. Propositional logic allows us to combine a set of symbols, called atoms, using the connectives $\wedge$ (conjunction, and), $\vee$ (disjunction, or), $\neg$ (negation, not), $\rightarrow$ (material implication), and $\leftrightarrow$ (material biconditional, equivalence) to form sentences that may be true or false. We can construct statements such as:

I am a vegetarian (v) and I like broccoli (b)
$v \wedge b$

which is true in the case where both "I am a vegetarian" and "I like broccoli" are true. Similarly,

I will take the bus to work (b) or I will walk to work (w)
$b \vee w$

is true if either b is true or w is true. The negation $\neg b$ is true in the case that I do not take the bus. Finally, implication allows for statements such as:

> If the grass is wet (g), then either the sprinklers were on (s) or it is raining (r)
> $g \rightarrow (s \vee r)$.

This statement is then true if either the grass is not wet ($\neg g$) or if $s \vee r$ is true (meaning that it is raining or the sprinklers were on). The statement $p \rightarrow q$ is thus equivalent to $\neg p \vee q$. This is because if p is true, then q must be true. Equivalence, $p \leftrightarrow q$, simply stands for: $p \rightarrow q$ and $q \rightarrow p$. This is also referred to as "if and only if," and written as iff. If p is "I am wearing running shoes" and q is "I am running" then this is true, since these are either both true or both false as I only go for a run in my running shoes and I only wear my running shoes to run. Instead, if p were "bringing an umbrella" and q "not getting wet," $p \leftrightarrow q$ would be false since I can buy a new umbrella or wear a raincoat.

The statements described so far have been facts with a single truth value. However, we may wish to distinguish between things that must be true and those that could be true. Modal logics extend these types of statements to describe whether a formula is "necessary" (denoted by $\square$) or if it is simply "possible" (denoted by $\lozenge$). For example, we can write

> It must be that either Barack Obama (b) or John McCain (m) is the 44th President of the United States
> $\square(b \vee m)$

and

> It is possible that Al Gore (g) was the 43rd president of the United States
> $\lozenge g$.

Instead of the propositional case where statements were either true or false, the use of possibility and necessity in modal logic means that we can describe what *could* have been or *must* be or *may* be in the future. Truth values of statements are then determined relative to a set of possible worlds, where a possible world is simply a collection of propositions that are true in the world. Then with a set of worlds, W, we can define necessity and possibility as:

Possible worlds are also discussed in chapter 2.

> $\square p$ is true if p is true in each world in W.
> $\lozenge p$ is true if there is at least one world in W where p is true.

One of the possible worlds, called the *actual world*, represents what is actually true. Some possible worlds will be accessible from the actual world, while others will not. Not all worlds accessible from the current world have the same truth values for propositions, but all of these valuations would be considered to be in the realm of possibility. For example, a world in which it rains tomorrow is possible, but one where $2 + 2 = 5$ is not. Possibility and necessity are usually defined relative to a particular world: if all worlds accessible from it satisfy a statement, then it is necessary while if there is at least one accessible where a statement holds, then it is possible. This means that a formula can be false in the actual world, but still possible.

3.2.2. Temporal logic

In some cases, the truth value of a formula may be time dependent. For example, at one point it was possible that Al Gore would be the 43rd president of the United States, but this is no longer possible once a different person has been elected as the 43rd U.S. president. While I am not currently tired, I will *eventually* be tired and go to sleep. Someone who is born will *always* die. For a gun to be a useful weapon, it must remain loaded *until* it is fired. Temporal logic, introduced by Arthur Prior in the 1960s (Prior, 1967), modified modal logic to describe *when* formulas must hold, or be true. In the 1970s Amir Pnueli built upon these ideas to develop computational methods for checking these formulas in computer systems (Pnueli, 1977).

In general, temporal logics can express whether a property is true at, say, the next point in time, or at some future timepoint, although there are also different ways of thinking about the future. In branching time logics, such as computation tree logic (CTL) (Clarke et al., 1986), the future may be along any number of possible paths (sequences of states). This means it is possible to express whether a property should hold for *all* possible paths (in every possible future, I will eventually eat and sleep) or if there simply *exists* a path where it is true (it is possible that in some futures, I will eventually study physics again). In contrast, in linear time logics such as linear temporal logic (LTL), from each state there is only one possible path through time. The logic used in this work is a branching time one, so I will only review CTL before moving on to probabilistic extensions of this logic. The goal of temporal logic has been to reason about computer systems to determine if they satisfy desirable properties or can guarantee that they will avoid serious errors. For this reason, temporal logics are usually interpreted relative to specifications of systems that are encoded by graphs called Kripke structures, which describe how the systems work in a structured way (Kripke, 1963). In chapter 5, the interpretation of formulas relative to observation sequences is discussed. For example, we may try to understand a microwave by testing whether a model of it satisfies some properties

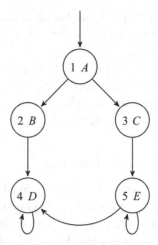

Figure 3.3. Kripke structure.

(e.g., is it possible for food to cook with the door open?). Such properties are verified by testing the states a system can occupy (e.g., determining if there is a path to cooked food that does not go through a state where the door is closed). When using observations, the task is more similar to trying to learn the properties of the microwave by watching people use it. Here we are seeing only a subset of the possible states and possible paths through the system, and will not observe low probability sequences without a very long sequence of observations.

More formally, a Kripke structure is defined by a set of reachable states (nodes of the graph), labels (propositions) that describe the properties true within each state, and a set of edges denoting the transitions of the system (which states can be reached from other states) (Clarke et al., 1999). The system in figure 3.3 begins in state 1, where A is true, and can then transition to either state 2 or state 3. Note that once the system is in state 4, it can only keep transitioning to this state via the self loop.

Definition 3.2.1. Let AP be a set of atomic propositions. A Kripke structure M over AP is a four tuple $M = \{S, S_0, R, L\}$ where:

- S is a finite set of states,
- $S_0 \subseteq S$ is the set of initial states,
- $R \subseteq S \times S$ is a total transition relation, such that $\forall s \in S, \exists s' \in S$ s.t. $(s, s') \in R$, and
- $L : S \to 2^{AP}$ is a function that labels each state with the set of atomic propositions that are true within it.

The function R being a total transition function means that for every state, there is at least one transition from that state (to itself or to another state). The function L maps states to the truth value of propositions at that state. Since there are AP propositions, there are 2^{AP} possible truth values for these propositions and L maps each state to one of these. In the structure shown in figure 3.3 the states in S (using s_n to denote state n) are $\{s_1, s_2, s_3, s_4, s_5\}$ and the set of initial states, S_0, is $\{s_1\}$. The transitions comprising R are:

$$\{(s_1, s_2), (s_1, s_3), (s_2, s_4), (s_3, s_5), (s_4, s_4), (s_5, s_4), (s_5, s_5)\}.$$

This means, for example, that s_5 can transition to itself, while it cannot transition to s_1. The set of atomic propositions is $\{A, B, C, D, E\}$ and L maps, for example, s_3 to C. Notice that there is at least one transition possible from each state. Thus, a path in the Kripke structure is an infinite sequence of states. A path, denoted by π, is a sequence of states ($\pi = s_0, s_1 \ldots$) such that for every $i \geq 0$, $(s_i, s_{i+1}) \in R$. This says that the series of transitions described by the sequence is possible. Then, π^i is used to denote the suffix of path π starting at state s_i. So, $\pi^2 = s_2, s_3, \ldots$ and so on.

To find the properties that are true in these systems, we need a formal method of representing the properties to be tested. There are a number of temporal logics that each express slightly different sets of formulas, but we begin with CTL as it is the simplest such logic en route to our final destination of probabilistic temporal logic. CTL allows expression of properties such as:

See Clarke et al. (1999) for an in-depth introduction to temporal logic and model checking.

For all (A) paths, at all states (G), the sky is blue (b).
AGb

There exists (E) a path where eventually (F) food in the microwave will be cooked (c).
EFc

There exists (E) a path where at the next time (X) the subway doors will open (s).
EXs

Notice that in all cases we begin by stating the set of paths the formula pertains to (all paths, A, or at least one path, E). We then constrain the set of states that must satisfy the formula – all states along the paths (G), at least one state at some point (F), or the next state (X). Finally, we can also describe the temporal relationship between two propositions:

There exists (E) a path where food in the microwave is cooked (c) until (U) the door is opened (o)
$EcUo$

or,

> For all paths (A), a door remains closed (c) unless (W) it is opened (o).
> $AcWo$

What has been described by example is that formulas in CTL are composed of paired path quantifiers and temporal operators. Path quantifiers describe whether a property holds A ("for all paths") or E ("for some path") starting at a given state. The temporal operators describe where along the path the properties will hold. This means that while AGf is a valid CTL formula, $AGFf$ is not, since F is not paired with one of A or E. More formally, the operators are:

- F (finally), at some state on the path the property will hold.
- G (globally), the property will hold along the entire path.
- X (next), the property will hold at the next state of the path.
- U (until), for two properties, the first holds at every state along the path until at some state the second property holds.
- W (weak until, also called unless or release), for two properties, the first holds at every state along the path until a state where the second property holds, with no guarantee that the second property will ever hold (in which case the first must remain true forever).

Now we describe how formulas in the logic are constructed (the syntax of the logic). First, there are two types of formulas: path formulas, which are true along specific paths, and state formulas, which are true in particular states. Then, where AP is the set of atomic propositions, the syntax of state formulas is given by:

- If $p \in AP$, then p is a state formula.
- If f and g are state formulas, then so are $\neg f$, $f \vee g$, and $f \wedge g$.
- If f is path formula, then Ef and Af are state formulas.

Path formulas are specified by:

- If f and g are state formulas, then Ff, Gf, Xf, fWg, and fUg, are path formulas.

The set of possible combinations of CTL operators is: AX, EX, AF, EF, AG, EG, AU, EU, AW, and EW. However, each can be expressed in terms of EX, EG and EU (a minimal set of operators).

- $AXf \equiv \neg EX(\neg f)$
- $EFf \equiv E[\text{true}\, Uf]$
- $AGf \equiv \neg EF(\neg f)$
- $AFf \equiv \neg EG(\neg f)$

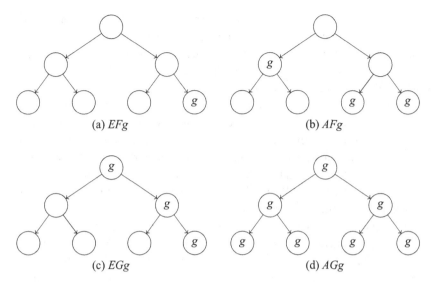

Figure 3.4. Illustrations of CTL formulas.

- $A[fUg] \equiv \neg E[\neg gU(\neg f \wedge \neg g)] \wedge \neg EG\neg g$
- $AfWg \equiv \neg E[(f \wedge \neg g)U(\neg f \wedge \neg g)]$
- $EfWg \equiv \neg A[(f \wedge \neg g)U(\neg f \wedge \neg g)]$

Figure 3.4 illustrates the most common operators in terms of computation trees. Note that each tree continues infinitely beyond the states shown. Rather than depicting the structure of the system, these show how the future may unfold. For example, the computation tree associated with the system in figure 3.3 is shown in figure 3.5.

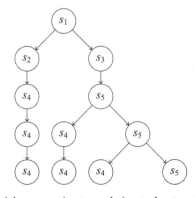

Figure 3.5. Partial computation tree relating to the structure of figure 3.3.

Once we can represent how a system behaves and express properties of interest, we need a method of determining when these properties are satisfied. In the microwave example, once we have a model and method for constructing formulas such as that there is no path to cooked food where the door does not eventually close, we want to determine if this is satisfied by the microwave model. This is exactly the goal of model checking, which allows one to determine which states of a system satisfy a logical formula. If the initial states of the system are in that set of states, then the model satisfies the formula. Assume that there is a Kripke structure $M = \{S, S_0, R, L\}$ and a CTL formula. Say we want to determine whether M satisfies $AG(f \wedge g)$. We work from the innermost formulas, first finding states where f and g are true, then labeling them with these formulas. The next step is to label states that are already labeled with f and g individually with the conjunction $f \wedge g$. The basic principle is that states are labeled with subformulas that are true within them, and in each iteration more complex formulas are analyzed. During this process, there are six main cases: f, $\neg f$, $f \vee g$, EXf, $E[fUg]$, and EGf (all other formulas can be expressed in terms of those). The notation used is that satisfaction of state formula f at state s in Kripke structure M is represented by $M, s \models f$ and satisfaction of path formula g by path π in Kripke structure M is represented by $M, \pi \models g$.

The rules for labeling states with the formulas in the previous six cases are as follows. Recall that all states begin labeled with the propositions true within them due to the labeling function, L. A state is labeled with $\neg f$ if it is not labeled with f, a state is labeled with $f \vee g$ if it is labeled with either f or g, and a state is labeled with EXf if the state has a transition to a state labeled with f. That is, EXf is satisfied at state s_1 if $\exists s_2$ such that $(s_1, s_2) \in R$ and $M, s_2 \models f$. The final two cases are slightly more complex. For a formula $h = E[fUg]$, we first find states labeled with g, and then for each such state where there is a path to those states where each state on the path is labeled with f, it is labeled with h. As the formulas are built incrementally beginning with those of size one, the states satisfying f and g have already been labeled at this point. For example, let us check this formula in the structure shown in figure 3.6.

Initially, states s_2 and s_3 are labeled with f, and states s_2 and s_5 are labeled with g. We begin with states s_2 and s_5 as both are labeled with $j = fUg$. Note that this means the formula can be true without f ever holding. Next, we label states s where $M, s \models f$ and $(s, s') \in R$ where $M, s' \models j$. States satisfying f that can transition to states known to satisfy j are labeled with the until formula. Here this is true for s_3. Finally, states

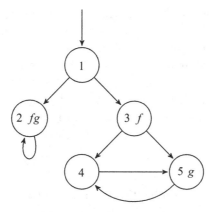

Figure 3.6. Kripke structure for model checking example.

not labeled with j but that can transition to such states are labeled with h, since there is a path from them to a state where this holds. The initial state, s_1, is labeled with h and thus the structure satisfies the formula.

Finally, for $g = EGf$ we are attempting to find if there is a path such that eventually f will always hold. Since each state has at least one transition, this requires that there is a transition to a strongly connected component where each state in the component is labeled with f. A strongly connected component (SCC) of a graph is a set of vertices such that for any pair (v,u) in the set, there is a path from u to v and from v to u. While

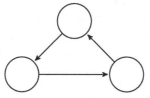

is an SCC,

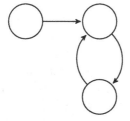

is not (though it contains an SCC). Note that a self loop is a trivial SCC.

Finally, let us discuss the complexity of this approach to checking formulas. Where $|X|$ denotes the size of set X, labeling states with some formula where all of its subformulas have already been processed takes time $O(|S| + |R|)$. For a formula of size $|f|$ (where this is the number of propositions and operators in the formula), the complexity is $O(|f| \times (|S| + |R|))$. This is because each iteration is $O(|S| + |R|)$ and the algorithm begins with the innermost formula, working outward, so when we get to formula f, every component of f has already been checked, and there are at most $|f|$ subformulas of f.

3.3. Probabilistic Temporal Logic

CTL allows us to answer questions about various futures and to determine what is possible, what must occur, and what is impossible. While it may be useful to know that a train will eventually arrive using a model of the subway system, most riders would want to know the time bounds on when the next train will arrive, and how likely it is that it will come in the specified interval. Probabilistic computation tree logic (PCTL) allows precisely this type of reasoning, so that one could determine that with probability greater than 0.98, a train will arrive in 2–10 minutes after the last one has left the station. It extends CTL by adding deadlines – so that instead of a property holding eventually, it must hold within a particular window of time, and quantifies the likelihood of this happening by adding probabilistic transitions to the structures used. There are a variety of logics that quantify both time and probability, but in this work I build on that introduced by Hansson and Jonsson (1994). For a more detailed survey of PCTL, see (Ciesinski and Größer, 2004) .

PCTL allows statements such as "ordering a pizza leads to a delivery in 20–30 minutes with at least probability 0.4." As with CTL, formulas are defined relative to a Kripke structure but here probabilities are added for each transition. Probabilistic Kripke structures (Clarke et al., 1999; Kripke, 1963), also called discrete time Markov chains (DTMCs), are directed graphs with a set of states, S, that are labeled with the properties true within them via a labeling function that maps states to the set of atomic propositions of the system. There is an initial state from which paths through the system can begin and a transition function that defines, for each state, the set of states that may immediately follow it and the probability of each of these transitions. This is a total transition function, which means that each state has at least one transition to itself or another state in S with a nonzero probability. The sum of the transition probabilities from any state is 1, meaning that at each timepoint a transition must be made – the system cannot simply remain in the state.

More formally, a probabilistic Kripke structure is a four tuple: $K = \langle S, s^i, L, \mathcal{T} \rangle$, such that:

- S is a finite set of states;
- $s^i \in S$ is an initial state;
- $L : S \rightarrow 2^{AP}$ is a labeling function assigning atomic propositions (AP) to states;
- $\mathcal{T}$ is a transition probability function, $\mathcal{T} : S \times S \rightarrow [0, 1]$, such that:

$$\forall s \in S : \sum_{s' \in S} \mathcal{T}(s, s') = 1.$$

Note that this is a Kripke structure with a transition function that tells us which transitions are possible and the probability with which they will occur. The sum of the transition probabilities from a state must equal one, as at each timepoint a transition must be made (either to a different state or to the same state). Finally, $L(s)$ is used to denote the labels of a particular state, s.

As in CTL, there are two types of formulas: path formulas and state formulas. State formulas express properties that must hold within a state, such as it being labeled with certain atomic propositions (e.g., is a state s labeled with rain?), while path formulas refer to sequences of states along which a formula must hold (e.g., for some sequence of states, will it eventually rain?). The formulas are comprised of atomic propositions $a \in AP$, propositional logical connectives (such as $\neg, \wedge, \vee$), and modal operators denoting time and probability. Then, the syntax of the logic tells us how valid PCTL formulas can be constructed.

1. All atomic propositions are state formulas.
2. If f and g are state formulas, so are $\neg f$, $f \wedge g$, $f \vee g$, and $f \rightarrow g$.
3. If f and g are state formulas, and t is a nonnegative integer or ∞, $f U^{\leq t} g$ and $f W^{\leq t} g$ are path formulas.
4. If f is a path formula and $0 \leq p \leq 1$, $[f]_{\geq p}$ and $[f]_{>p}$ are state formulas.

The second item of the preceding says that state formulas can be combined and negated to make new formulas, with $\neg, \wedge, \vee$, and $\rightarrow$ defined in the usual manner as: negation, conjunction, disjunction, and implication. In the third item are the until (U) and unless (weak until) (W) operators. In this context, "until" means that the first formula must hold at every state along the path until a state where the second formula becomes true. The formula above, $fU^{\leq t}g$, means that f must hold until g holds at some state, which must happen in less than or equal to t time units. Unless is defined the same way, but with no guarantee that g will hold. If g does not become true within time t, then f must hold for a minimum of t time units. Following this, we can construct state formulas, such as $j \lor (r \land i)$, which could mean "job growth or recession and inflation." We can also construct path formulas describing a relationship such as "a drug (d) is administered until a person stops seizing (s), which happens in less than 10 minutes":

$$dU^{\leq 10}s. \tag{3.15}$$

To include these types of temporal statements in state formulas, we must add probabilities to the unless and until path formulas. For example, $[fU^{\leq t}g]_{\geq p}$ (which may be abbreviated as $fU^{\leq t}_{\geq p}g$), means that with probability at least p, g will become true within t time units and f will hold along the path until that happens. This until formula with its associated probability defines a state formula, where the probability of the formula is calculated by summing the probabilities of the paths from the state, where a path's probability is the product of the transition probabilities along it. Continuing with the drug example, we can now say that either a drug stops seizures in 10 minutes, which happens with at least probability 0.6, or a coma (c) is induced:

$$(dU^{\leq 10}_{\geq 0.6}s) \lor c. \tag{3.16}$$

Let us look at how the probabilities are calculated by going through an example. Take the following structure, where the start state is indicated with an arrow and labeled with a.

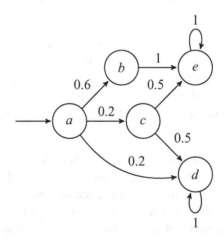

Remember that each state has at least one transition, but this can be satisfied by a self loop with probability one, as is true of the states in the previous diagram labeled with d and e. A path, σ, through the structure is then an infinite sequence of states, and is written $\sigma \equiv s_0 \rightarrow s_1 \rightarrow \cdots s_n \cdots$. We can also take the prefix, say of length n, of path σ. This is denoted by $\sigma \uparrow n$ and defined by:

$$\sigma \uparrow n = s_0 \rightarrow s_1 \rightarrow \cdots s_n.$$

Then the probability of a path (denoted by μ_m and called the μ_m-measure) is the product of the transition probabilities, and the probability of a set of paths from a state is the sum of the probabilities over the set of paths from the states that satisfy the formula. For the preceding prefix, this is: $\mathcal{T}(s_0, s_1) \times \cdots \times \mathcal{T}(s_{n-1}, s_n)$. Now, looking at the preceding structure let $\sigma = a \rightarrow b \rightarrow e \rightarrow \cdots e \cdots$, and let us take $\sigma \uparrow 2$. The probability of this path is then $\mathcal{T}(a, b) \times \mathcal{T}(b, e)$, which is 0.6×1. Now say we are calculating the probability of the set of paths of length two from a to e. There are two such paths: one through b and one through c. The probability of this set of paths is the sum of the individual path probabilities: $0.6 \times 1 + 0.2 \times 0.5 = 0.7$. Then, for a particular state, a probabilistic formula such as $[f]_{\geq p}$ is satisfied if the sum of the path probabilities of the set of paths satisfying the formula is at least p. A structure K satisfies a state formula if the initial state satisfies it.

Let us now discuss the truth values of PCTL formulas more formally. The satisfaction relation $s \vDash_K f$ means that state formula f is true in state s in structure K. Then, $s \vDash_K a$ (state s satisfies atomic proposition a) iff $a \in L(s)$. Relations for $\neg, \wedge, \vee$, and $\rightarrow$ are defined as usual. The path satisfaction relation $\sigma \vDash_K f$ means that the path σ satisfies the path formula f in model K. Then, we have the following path relations:

- $\sigma \vDash_K f U^{\leq t} g$ iff $\exists i \leq t$ such that $\sigma[i] \vDash_K g$ and $\forall j : 0 \leq j < i : (\sigma[j] \vDash_K f)$ (strong until);
- $\sigma \vDash_K f W^{\leq t} g$ iff $\sigma \vDash_K f U^{\leq t} g$ or $\forall j : 0 \leq j \leq t : (\sigma[j] \vDash_K f)$ (weak until);
- $s \vDash_K [f]_{\geq p}$ if the μ_m-measure of the set of paths σ starting in s for which $\sigma \vDash_k f$ is at least p;
- $s \vDash_K [f]_{> p}$ if the μ_m-measure of the set of paths σ starting in s for which $\sigma \vDash_k f$ is greater than p.

We will also make use of the standard modal operators as shorthand for their PCTL equivalents, defining PCTL operators analogous to the CTL path operators A ("for all paths") and E ("for some future path") and temporal operators G ("holds for entire future path") and F ("eventually holds").

- $Af \equiv [f]_{\geq 1}$
- $Ef \equiv [f]_{>0}$
- $Gf \equiv f W^{\leq \infty} \text{ false}$
- $Ff \equiv \text{true } U^{\leq \infty} f$

One final operator that will be useful is "leads-to." This is defined by Hansson and Jonsson (1994) as:

$$f \leadsto_{\geq p}^{\leq t} g \equiv AG[f \rightarrow F_{\geq p}^{\leq t} g]. \tag{3.17}$$

This means that for every path from the current state, states where f hold lead, through some series of transitions taking time $\leq t$, with probability p, to states where g holds. As defined in equation (3.17), leads-to considers the case where f and g are true at the same state as one that satisfies this formula. Instead, it will later be necessary stipulate that there must be at least one transition between f and g. In addition to being important for the temporal priority condition for causality, this is also in keeping with how one naturally reasons about the term "leads to." The expectation if someone says "one thing led to another" is that there was some sequence of events connecting "one thing" and "another" and that they are not co-temporary. Thus, we aim to construct formulas such as:

$$f \leadsto_{\geq p}^{\geq r, \leq s} g, \tag{3.18}$$

which is interpreted to mean that g must hold in between r and s time units with probability p (where $0 \leq r \leq s \leq \infty$ and $r \neq \infty$). If $r = s$, this means it takes exactly r time units for g to hold. In appendix B.3, it is shown how this minimum time can be added to the leads-to operator.

3.3.1. PCTL model checking

Model checking in the probabilistic case is similar to that for CTL, labeling states with subformulas true within them, beginning with all states labeled with the propositions true within them. This section describes how formulas can be checked relative to a model, but in many cases we will have only observations of a system, not a model of how it functions. In chapter 5,

I discuss how PCTL formulas can be checked against such observations without first inferring a model. The labeling rules for states are:

A state is labeled with $\neg f$ if it is not labeled with f.
A state is labeled with $f \wedge g$ if it is labeled with both f and g.
A state is labeled with $f \vee g$ if it is labeled with f or with g.
A state is labeled with $f \rightarrow g$ if it is labeled with $\neg f$ or with g.

The other cases reduce to a small set: $f U^{\leq t} g$, combined with $[f]_{\geq p}$, and $[f]_{>p}$. In the case where the probability and time do not take extreme values (0 or 1 and ∞ respectively), $f U^{\leq t}_{\geq p} g$ is checked as follows, with the $> p$ case being the same except that states will be labeled with the formula if the calculated probability is strictly greater than p.

Proposition 3.3.1 (Hansson and Jonsson (1994)). *Assume that the states satisfying f and g are labeled with these formulas. Then, for $t \neq \infty$, the μ_m measure for the set of paths σ from s for which $\sigma \models_K f U^{\leq t} g$ is given by $P(t, s)$, where this is defined to be 0 if $t < 0$ and is otherwise given by:*

$$
P(t, s) = \begin{cases} 1 & \text{if } g \in \text{labels}(s), \\ 0 & \text{if } f \notin \text{labels}(s), \quad (3.19) \\ \sum_{s' \in S} \mathcal{T}(s, s') \times P(t - 1, s') & \text{otherwise.} \end{cases}
$$

The labeling algorithm follows from this recursion, labeling state s with $f U^{\leq t}_{\geq p} g$ if $P(t, s) \geq p$. The complexity of the resulting algorithm (remembering that all subformulas have already been checked) is $O(t \times (|S| + |E|))$. This is the same as the earlier complexity for a CTL formula where all subformulas have been checked, with an added factor of t. Checking whether a structure satisfies formula f, as before, depends on the size of f and is at most $O(t_{max} \times (|S| + |E|) \times |f|)$, where t_{max} is the maximum time parameter in f.

Faster algorithms, linear in $|S|$, exist for the cases where p takes the values 0 or 1 regardless of the value of t. In the case where the probability is not 0 or 1, and $t = \infty$, a different approach is required, as the one given would not terminate. There states in S are divided into a few subsets: S_s, R, and Q. S_s contains states labeled with g, Q contains states not labeled with f or with g as well as those from which it is not possible to reach a state in S_s, and R is the set of states for which the probability of reaching a state in S_s is 1.

Proposition 3.3.2 (Hansson and Jonsson (1994)). *Assume that in structure K, states satisfying f and g have been labeled with these formulas. Then,*

Some accounts of runtime verification include Chan et al. (2005), Kim et al. (2001), and Leucker and Schallhart (2009).

Formulas using W can be defined in terms of U formulas.

with Q and R defined above, the μ_m-measure for the set of paths σ from s for which $\sigma \vDash_K fU^{\leq\infty}g$ is given by the solution to $P(\infty, s)$:

$$\mathcal{P}(\infty, s) = \begin{cases} 1 & \text{if } s \in R; \\ 0 & \text{if } s \in Q; \\ \sum_{s' \in S} \mathcal{T}(s, s') \times P(\infty, s') & \text{otherwise.} \end{cases} \qquad (3.20)$$

Solving with Gaussian elimination gives a complexity of $O((|S| - |Q| - |R|)^{2.81})$. Algorithms for finding Q and R are described in appendix B, where I also reformulate until formulas to allow for a lower bound on the associated timing, as needed when using the leads-to operator to represent causal relationships.

4

Defining Causality

4.1. Preliminaries

The first few chapters of the book reviewed causality (highlighting some primary approaches to reasoning about and inferring it), probability, and logic, so that readers without expertise in these areas could follow the later discussions. The remainder of the book is devoted to developing a new approach that builds on probabilistic causality and temporal logic to infer complex causal relationships from data and explain the occurrence of actual events (called token causality, and the subject of chapter 6). The first task is to determine exactly what causes will be inferred and how these fit in with other theories of causality and causal inference. This chapter will focus on conceptual differences, while chapter 7 contains experimental comparisons against other inference methods. When discussing causality or causal inference, it is important to be precise about the meaning ascribed to the term "causal." Many fields (including epidemiology, biology, economics, and politics) have developed their own criteria and conventions for what evidence is needed to substantiate a causal relationship. It is common to draw causal conclusions in biology from few experiments where a gene is suppressed (knocked-out) and one tests whether a given observable trait (phenotype) is present in the absence of the knocked-out gene. When the trait is absent the usual explanation is that the gene causes it, but this does not mean it is the sole cause (it may be only one of a set of necessary conditions) nor does it mean that the presence of the trait indicates non-causality. Presence of the phenotype in the absence of the gene may be due to backup mechanisms, or a relationship that is more complex than the pairwise one being studied. Biomedical research yields frequent reports of environmental factors that cause cancer or foods that are positively associated with heart disease, but these reports often contradict one another over time or are later found inconclusive. Inferences are always relative to specific datasets and current knowledge and may change as these do.

A clear understanding of the link between causality and methods for testing it is critical, particularly if the results are to form the basis for potentially costly and invasive diagnostic tests or years long drug discovery processes.

Before suggesting a method for finding causes, it must be clear exactly what is being found. This chapter focuses on the target of the inference approach being developed: what is being inferred and when can we infer it? This type of question has primarily been the domain of philosophy, so the discussion here will draw heavily on and refer frequently to this work.

4.1.1. What is a cause?

The term "causes" is used often in daily life (with meanings such as brings about, is responsible for, and produces) and is at the core of many areas of research (from finding the causes of historical events to tracing disease outbreaks). However, despite centuries of work on what causes are and how they are connected to their effects, it is difficult to even define causality in a non-circular way. While there are many theories for reasoning about and recognizing causality (some of which were described in chapter 2), there is still no unified definition for the concept or theory of its inference that can handle all possible cases and counterexamples.

This book is focused on practical methods for finding out about causes (not defining what they intrinsically are), but it is important to understand that there are two distinct lines of work and sets of goals in the causality literature. There is the question of what causes are (a metaphysical concern) and that of how we can recognize them (an epistemological concern). Work in metaphysics addresses the necessary features of a causal relationship (e.g., must a cause be earlier than its effect? does a cause always raise the probability of its effect?) and its components (e.g., can omissions be causal? *Note a subtle* can there be causation at a distance?). Epistemology instead addresses how *distinction:* we can come to know about these relationships. Hume (1739), for example, *epistemology* tackled both areas, with contiguity, temporal priority, and necessary con- *is about what* nection being essential parts of the relationship, and observation of these *can be* regular sequences of events being how we can learn of the relationships. *known, while*

methodology While many theories refer to causation as a relation between two events, *is the set of* there is controversy about the components of this relation (including their *tools used to* type and number) and how they are connected. Causes have been primarily *make these* argued to be objects (Hume, 1748), events, and processes (Salmon, 1980a), *inferences.* though there is also disagreement about how to define events (Davidson, 1998; Kim, 1976). As discussed earlier in this book, philosophers have given probabilistic (Eells, 1991; Good, 1961a; Suppes, 1970), process oriented (Dowe, 2000), and mechanistic (Glennan, 1996; Machamer et al., 2000) descriptions (among others) of the connection between cause and effect, but each one has counterexamples. Some examples can be reasoned about with all theories, suggesting that there is some intersection between them, but there are others that can only be handled by a subset of the approaches, casting doubt on whether it is even possible to have a single unified theory of causation. This has some bearing on epistemology as it seems likely that if there is no single relationship to be inferred, there may be many ways one can learn of causal relationships and a set of methods that are each suited to different situations may be needed. The goal of this work is not to solve such debates, but rather to make it clear which assumptions are well accepted and which are still unsettled, and to further discuss why the assumptions are made and how they affect the proposed theories.

As a result of the failure to uncover a unified theory of causality, there is an increasing movement toward "causal pluralism" (Godfrey-Smith, 2010; Hitchcock, 2007), though there is a plurality of pluralisms: metaphysical (Psillos, 2010), conceptual (Anscombe, 1971; Cartwright, 2007b; Hitchcock, 2003), evidential (Russo and Williamson, 2007), and methodological (Russo, 2006) among others. There could be different underlying notions at work, different ways of establishing causal claims, or different inference methods needed. The work in this book is not tied to any particular metaphysical idea of causality (regardless of whether there is one or many, or if causality is a mental construct).[1] Even if there is truly only one concept, there may be several ways of recognizing this relationship, especially since each method is only a heuristic that sheds light on some of its underlying unmeasurable qualities. Think of mathematics, where there may be many methods for proving the same theorem, such as by induction, contradiction, or exhaustion. The theorem itself is unchanged, but there are many ways of providing evidence for the claim. Similarly, it may turn out that causality is one thing, but instances of it can be supported using mechanisms, probabilistic evidence, or counterfactual arguments. This view is called evidential pluralism (Russo and Williamson, 2007) and is closest to current scientific practice (a similar position is argued for by Joffe (2011)). Much as there are different statistical tests that apply to different situations, we likely need a toolbox of methods for causal inference that can be

Advocates of one form of pluralism (e.g., evidential) may still argue for other types of monism (e.g., metaphysical) (Williamson, 2006).

---

[1] Much as this work builds on philosophical foundations, though, philosophers focused on metaphysical issues may be able to build on the results of this computational work to potentially draw metaphysical conclusions, particularly when it comes to testing and verifying their assumptions.

drawn from depending on the problem at hand. The method advanced in this book is in keeping with this idea, as it is not intended as a definition of causality or method for recognizing all of its possible manifestations. Rather, the proposed approach will be a practical one for reliably inferring causal relationships from time series data.

Causal relata

Instead of causes being defined as events in the sense of things that occur at a particular point in time and space, it is desirable to allow that a cause could be a property ("the scarf being red caused the bull to charge") or fact – and not necessarily the event of a change in property (i.e., the scarf did not become red, it had the property of being red before and after the bull charged). This book will remain agnostic as to what sorts of things have the capability to cause others (leaving open, for example, the possibility of mental causation) and will only restrict what sorts of things are examined and tested as potential causes for the sake of computational feasibility. The algorithms developed here will aim to infer relationships that can be described using temporal logic formulas. In these logics, there is a base level of atomic variables that can be known to be true or false. How these are defined is a primarily methodological issue: propositions taken to be basic in one study may be higher level abstractions in others. One study may separately measure people's weights and heights, retaining these as binned variables (such as $w_1 = 150$–200 pounds, $h_2 = 5'5"$–$6'$) while another study may classify people as being underweight, normal weight, or overweight. The data gathered allow us to infer properties of the system, such as whether being overweight seems to cause diabetes (or if both have a shared cause), but whether or not being overweight has the capability

Other logics such as PCTLc (Kleinberg, 2011) can be used to represent relationships with continuous and discrete variables.

to cause such conditions directly is a separate question.[2] Causes here will be referred to alternately as formulas and factors, but may be properties, omissions, facts, mental states, and so on. In the simplest case, they are propositions but (as discussed in chapter 3) temporal logic allows a rich representation of the temporal relationship between events. This logical formalism will be quite useful for efficient automated testing of a wide variety of relationships, but it cannot express every conceivable relationship

[2] While this work does not concern itself with which factors have the capacity to produce various effects, the question of what has this capacity has been debated by others. For more on capacities (or causal powers), see Cartwright (1989, 2007a).

that may be of interest. For example, the logic used in this book, an adapted version of PCTL, would need to be augmented to describe properties such as constraints on continuous variables or spatial relationships.

One relationship that can be represented (and thus tested) in this logic is: "a student not doing homework and not going to class until failing multiple classes causes the student to be expelled from school." There is no single event causing expulsion, nor is it caused by a conjunction of events. There are properties and actions of a student that must continue for some time – long enough for a third property to become true. While it is perhaps also true that failing multiple classes causes expulsion, representing the relationship in this way gives more insight into exactly how one must fail to be expelled. This cannot be represented in the same way by a causal chain since not doing homework and not attending class (where this could be satisfied by missing one class and one homework assignment, maybe due to illness) does not cause failure of multiple classes, as in many cases students skip both with no ill effects. It is also possible that different causes lead to expulsion with different probabilities. Note that "not doing homework" is neither an event nor an action, though it is a property of the student that can be easily represented ($\neg$ *homework*). This is also an illustration of why we should allow causation by omission (it is possible) and how simple it is to represent logically. Omissions will not be specifically discussed any further, as with logical formulas they only amount to negations of properties. If a relationship cannot be represented in this manner, this does not mean it is not causal but rather that it is outside the scope of this method and may be inferred by other means.

See equation 4.1 for the formal representation of this relationship.

4.1.2. How can causes be identified?

Given several potential explanations for how and why a phenomenon occurs, how can we determine which of these are causal? Every study begins by selecting the variables that will be measured or which parts of an existing dataset to use. This narrowing is necessary due to the expense of data collection and the computational complexity of analysis. With a set of data on patients and their health status, we must make judgments about which variables to include in a study based on whether they may plausibly impact health. It is unlikely that one would consider whether each patient was born on an even or odd day, but why is that? Common sense tells us that this has no bearing on health, but many cases are less straightforward. For this reason, there are two initial criteria that will help weed out non-causes from causes. This is not to say that these are features essential to actually being a cause, but rather that they are exhibited in enough cases (and cases of interest) that they are useful as indicators for causality.

First, in this approach a cause must precede its effect in time. This is in keeping with the philosophical foundations described in chapter 2, particularly those of Hume and Suppes. While there is no inherent reason that cause and effect could not be simultaneous, one could not distinguish between cause and effect when this is always the case. Such a case is also likely to be an artifact of the granularity of measurements, so that if these were made on a finer timescale, the cause would be found to be earlier than the effect. In general, the cases that are considered are those consisting of observations of a system over time, so there is already information on the temporal order of events and we should make use of it. While other methods for inference (such as those by Pearl and SGS) do not require time course data and infer the direction of the causal relationship and its existence, this comes at the expense of much stronger claims about the way the data have been generated and how the conditional independence of cause and effect is estimated. In general, inference from non-temporal data (such as cross-sectional studies) involves using background or mechanistic knowledge to find the time ordering of relationships to distinguish cause from effect. This work aims to make inferences in cases where few if any of the assumptions needed to do this without such knowledge hold: not all common causes have been measured, the data are noisy, relationships are nonlinear, and common causes may not fully screen off their effects.

We know that it is possible to make useful inferences in such messy cases with relationships more complex than "event *c* causes event *e*." This is something humans are quite good at, and which untrained juries do every day. Similarly, doctors manage to diagnose patients when given inaccurate, incomplete, and conflicting information. While the success of these infer- ences depends extensively on prior beliefs and background knowledge (as well as common sense), one might also imagine that much of this may be amenable to automation given enough data (and data of the right type). One bottleneck is the preponderance of counterexamples and arguments against theories of causality and methods for causal inference that do not act as expected in all possible cases, including those of far fetched examples. The question should instead be why we would expect automated methods to perform better than humans. When the field of artificial intelligence was beginning, one of its main goals was to be able to automate the type of rea- soning people do, to create a machine with the intelligence of a human that could solve problems. The ultimate test of this is the ability of a machine to

See Hausman (1998), Papineau (1992) and Reichenbach (1956) for more discussion of the direction of the causal relationship and the direction of time.

How people learn and reason about causality is the subject of much work in psychology. For a small sample, see Gopnik and Schulz (2007) and Sloman (2005).

hold a conversation that is indistinguishable from that of a human partner (the Turing test). However, what was found is that it is extremely difficult to replicate how humans think (Moor, 2003). Expert systems tried to translate human knowledge into rules and facts, but the success of these methods depends highly on the quality of the experts and their ability to articulate what they know and how they know it (Yoon et al., 1995). Many judgments are uncertain and subjective, relying on intuition, and cannot be stated in terms of facts (Davis, 1989). While machines have not surpassed human reasoning, they have instead excelled at other tasks, such as identifying complex patterns in massive datasets. The goal of computational inference should not be to replace the need for human judgment and decision making, but to help sift through the massive datasets we now face to draw a person's attention to a smaller set of relevant data that they can make sense of. We cannot hope to make causal inferences in a completely error free manner if even human judgment about causality can differ. If we can make inferences in even most of the cases that can be handled by someone examining all information manually, then we should consider the method a success.

There is a yearly Turing Test competition, but as of 2011, judges remain unconvinced.

The second criterion used here is that potential causes alter the probabilities of their effects. This is a primary component of probabilistic theories of causality, such as that of Suppes (1970). I will mostly refer to probability raising, as probability lowering (negative) causes – those that inhibit their effects – can be defined in terms of their complement (where $P(E|C) < P(E)$, $P(E|\neg C) > P(E)$) in order to keep things in terms of probability raising. There may still be cases where a cause is so weak that the difference it makes to the probability of its effect is not perceptible, though it is still a cause (perhaps there are other factors required for it to cause the effect or it is stronger in some small set of cases while being weak in general). This assumption can be defended by noting that if the cause has so little influence on the effect, it will not be helpful for either of our stated purposes (prediction and explanation), and if it makes so little difference there must be other causes that account better for the effect and it would be more fruitful to first explore those. Requiring probability raising (or lowering, incorporating negative causes by formulating them as positive causes using their complement) is a methodological choice and not a conceptual necessity. As Cartwright (1979) notes and was discussed earlier, there are other instances of causality without a change in probability, for example when two paths by which a cause produces an effect cancel out. The main point is that we seek factors that on the whole alter the probability of an effect and then will go about quantifying how much they do so relative to other possible explanations. Thus, while a cause itself does

An example where the cause is not obvious even with full knowledge of the scenario is described in section 6.3.4.

not have to impact the probability of an effect, the ones investigated here do. On the off chance that the effect is produced by only rare causes whose number approaches infinity, we would likely regard such an effect as simply random.

What is meant by "causal" in this book, then, is implicit in the way causality is identified. At least some of the time, causes are things that precede and alter the probability of their effects. This is what will be meant by the terms "causal" and "causes" throughout the rest of this book, albeit with some qualifications. As there may be many spurious causes that seem to raise or lower the probability of events that they do not cause, we need methods for distinguishing between these and actual causes.

4.1.3. Requirements for a definition of causality

We use the temporal ordering of cause and effect and the idea of making a difference to the probability of an effect to help identify causes. Here we look in more detail at what is required in terms of these conditions and their representation.

Probability & time

While the temporal priority condition and its motivation have been discussed, simply stating that a cause is earlier than an effect is not enough, we want to represent and know the amount of time between cause and effect. Consider what happens if inference focuses solely on the production of networks representing conditional independencies. If we have two datasets with the same conditional independencies between variables (represented by edges connecting appropriate vertices), but where the relationships occur over varying timescales, we will not see any difference between them. If the information gleaned from a system ends at the presentation of the system as such a network, we lose vital temporal information.

For example, cigarettes in the UK have warnings such as "smoking kills" and "smoking causes fatal lung cancer" in large type. Without any other details, we must make decisions on whether or not to smoke based on implicit assumptions: that smoking will cause death before something else would, that it will always cause death, and that it will cause our death in particular. In and of itself "smoking kills" is no more informative than "birth kills" as with probability one, everyone who is born dies. Now imagine one pack of cigarettes says "smoking kills: within 2 years" and another says "smoking kills: in 80 years." Without information on the relative probabilities one may assume they were equal and would choose the second package. We need to be able to find and explicitly represent when the effect will occur after a cause of it occurs. This will also be useful when we later attempt to use these relationships to explain token cases. If a person begins smoking and then dies the day after, we would likely say that there must be some other cause of death. Without any further temporal information in the causal relationship, however, this intuition cannot be captured.

We have still made no reference to the probability of death nor to the duration that one must smoke for in order for death or cancer to occur. The first case described above could be a 0.01% chance with the latter being 50%. Further there are likely other factors that affect this timing, such as environmental exposures and genetic mutations. This additional information and the way that it will affect the decision-making process shows the need for a more detailed description of causality. When we describe a causal relationship we need to include its probability, the time over which it takes place, and whether there are other events and properties required for the effect to be caused.

Expressing causality

The next question is how exactly to represent the relationships to be inferred. Many causal relationships are complex and have a critical temporal component, but efficient testing of arbitrarily complex relationships requires a structured method for representing them. Other methods leave this representation to the user, who must then create indicator variables to stand in for concepts such as "x happens 10–16 days after y," but this precludes efficient inference and is unsustainable when creating hypotheses involving multiple factors at a time. For instance, we want to be able to make statements such as "not doing homework and not attending class until multiple classes are failed will lead to expulsion within two semesters with probability greater than 0.6," and be able to test whether such an assertion is true.

As described in chapter 5, a natural method for reasoning about such information is with a probabilistic temporal logic. Philosophical theories of causality and methods based on graphical models allow causes and effects to be defined arbitrarily by users, but this does not easily lead to methods for specifying and testing these arbitrarily complex relationships. If one wanted to test whether a particular rate of birth control usage causes prostate cancer after a minimum of 15 years with probability 0.2 (due to excess estrogen in the water supply), there would be no convenient way of expressing this using an arrow between two nodes, and in the absence of some standardization, methods for testing these sorts of statements would need to be written for each individual case. Formulating relationships using a well-defined logic allows for testing methods to be built on existing frameworks. Let us briefly discuss how the problem of causal inference relates to that of model checking to provide context for the following definitions (inference is discussed in depth in chapter 5).

The general problem is, given a set of time series data from a system in which we hypothesize there may exist a causal structure, how can we infer the underlying relationships that characterize this structure? When observing a system over time, what we see is one possible path through it. Unlike the usual case of model checking, we do not have the structure but rather aim to understand its functioning by observing its behavior. For example, we can take barometer measurements over time and record the weather conditions, the day of the week, and the season. Thus, at one timepoint we might observe that on a Tuesday in the winter, the barometer is falling rapidly and there is a storm, and at another timepoint we might see that on a Thursday in the summer the barometer is steady and there is no rain. These collections of propositions specify two possible states the system can be in: {(barometer-falling-rapidly, storm, Tuesday, winter), (barometer-steady, ¬rain, Thursday, summer)}. These observations yield the frequency with which the system occupies these states.

The set of propositions for the system is: {rain, storm, barometer-falling-rapidly, barometer-steady, Thursday, Tuesday, summer, winter}, and a state can be labeled with a combination of these. If a state is not labeled with a proposition, such as rain, it is considered to be labeled with its negation (i.e., ¬rain). It is also possible to make the labeling probabilistic, so that "barometer falling" may be false due to the barometer being broken with some small probability. The two separate probabilities – one due to the actual probability of the system, the other due to lack of knowledge about the system – would be explicitly captured in that case. In the approach here, these are implicitly combined into one measure.

Note that we may not observe all states, especially those that occur with a low probability. The observations only provide some set of those that are possible. As they have a time order, though, they indicate transitions between the states and their frequency. A state is simply a collection of properties that are true and a transition between two states, s_1 and s_2, means that it is possible for the system to be in an s_1 state at some time t_1 and to then be in an s_2 state at time t_2, where $|t_2 - t_1| = 1$ time unit, and this unit size may be defined by the scale of the measurements. The probability of this transition can be inferred (increasingly accurately as the number of observations tends toward infinity) based on the frequency with which it is observed in the data. Thus, we can potentially reconstruct or redescribe this structure consisting of states and transitions between them from the data. However, in practice this problem is not trivial. It is possible, though, to query the data directly. Then we can ask questions about what properties either a structure or a set of observations satisfies. Here that means finding out whether it satisfies various causal relationships, which will be done by building on work from model checking and runtime verification (testing properties from observation sequences).

Let us return to the prior example, where "a student not doing homework and not going to class until they fail multiple classes causes the student to be expelled from school," and see how this may be represented as a PCTL formula. The propositions are doing homework (h), class attendance (c), failure of two or more classes (f), and expulsion (e). Then, the relationship is:

The syntax and semantics of PCTL are discussed extensively in section 3.3 and dealt with relative to traces in chapter 5.

$$[(\neg h \wedge \neg c)U_{\geq p_1}^{\leq \infty} f] \rightsquigarrow_{\geq p_2}^{\geq 1, \leq t} e, \qquad (4.1)$$

where t is the maximum amount of time it will take for expulsion to occur. This is a powerful approach to representing relationships, and testing these has been well-studied, leading to efficient methods (complexity is discussed in detail in the next chapter).

As another example, consider how one might describe that when a brain is deprived of oxygen (o) for 4–6 minutes this leads to irreversible brain damage (d) within 1–2 hours with probability 0.5:[3]

$$[oW_{\geq p}^{\geq 4, \leq 6} \textit{false}] \rightsquigarrow_{\geq 0.5}^{\geq 60, \leq 120} d. \qquad (4.2)$$

On the other hand, brain damage from carbon monoxide poisoning (c) may take longer to develop, so that relationship may be something like:

$$[cW_{\geq p}^{\geq 4, \leq 6} \textit{false}] \rightsquigarrow_{\geq 0.5}^{\geq 1, \leq 2} d \qquad (4.3)$$

where this means that carbon monoxide poisoning induced oxygen deprivation (c) for 4–6 minutes leads to brain damage in 1–2 weeks. Relationships like this can be modeled more finely, with the mechanisms by which carbon monoxide poisoning leads to hypoxia. This too can be represented in a straightforward manner, allowing us to eventually infer and compare causal relationships across timescales.

---

[3] Weak until, where the second part of the formula may never hold, can be used to specify durations. With $fW^{\geq a, \leq b} \textit{false}$, f has to hold for a–b time units since no times satisfy *false*.

4.2. Types of Causes and Their Representation

4.2.1. Prima facie causes

While most of the work of causal inference is in identifying spurious causes, the set of potential causes to be explored is still constrained by specifying minimal conditions for causality. For some c and e, to identify c as a possible cause of e, c must be temporally prior to e and must change the probability of e. Prima facie (potential) causes are those that satisfy these basic requirements. Recall that when we describe a cause c and effect e, both may be arbitrarily complex logical formulas. In the following examples, I will just refer to c and e but note now that there are no conditions on them other than that they must be valid PCTL state formulas. In this chapter, examples are generally relative to structures, since we have not yet discussed the problem of inference from data.

First, the temporal priority condition of the causal relationship is specified in terms of the time that elapses between cause and effect, rather than the occurrence times of the cause and effect. If c occurs at some time t and e occurs at a later time t', the relationship is characterized by the time that elapses between them, $|t' - t|$. To state that after c becomes true, e will be true with probability at least p in $|t' - t|$ or fewer time units – but with at least one time unit between c and e (so that e occurs in a particular time window after c) – one may write:

This is a leads-to formula, which means that, unlike "until", c may occur only once with e following in the specified window afterward.

$$c \rightsquigarrow_{\geq p}^{\geq 1, \leq |t'-t|} e.$$

Satisfying this formula requires at least one and potentially many transitions between c and e, as long as the sum of probabilities of the paths between c and e taking at least one time unit is at least p. The transitions are assumed to each take one time unit, but there is no restriction on the definition of a time unit. If we only want to say that c is earlier than e, the lower bound will be 1 and the upper bound ∞. In most cases, we aim to infer the timing of this relationship. Then, the bounds in the second condition that follows (1 and ∞) can be replaced with any arbitrary r and s where $1 \leq r \leq s \leq \infty$, and $r \neq \infty$. Section 5.3 discusses how to infer these times in an automated way with minimal prior knowledge.

The probabilistic nature of the relationship between cause and effect can be described in terms of the probability of reaching c and e states, and of the paths between c and e states. We need to specify that c must occur at some point and that the conditional probability of e given c is greater than the marginal probability of e. More formally, prime facie, or potential, causes, are defined as follows.

Definition 4.2.1. Where c and e are PCTL formulas, c is a *prima facie* cause of e if there is a p such that the following conditions all hold:

1. $F_{>0}^{\leq\infty} c$,
2. $c \leadsto_{\geq p}^{\geq 1, \leq\infty} e$, and
3. $F_{<p}^{\leq\infty} e$.

These conditions mean that a state where c is true will be reached with nonzero probability and the probability of reaching a state where e is true (within the time bounds) is greater after being in a state where c (probability $\geq p$) is true than it is by simply starting from the initial state of the system (probability $< p$). When making inferences from data, this means c must occur at least once, and the conditional probability of e given c is greater than the marginal probability of e (usually calculated from frequencies). Since, as noted, negative (probability lowering) causes can be defined in terms of their complement (so that if c lowers the probability of e, $\neg c$ raises its probability), the definition here and in the following discussion is in terms of positive, probability raising, causes. However, one could explicitly allow for these by reformulating definition 4.2.1 so that the probability is not higher, but just different.

The conditions stated in definition 4.2.1 are based on Suppes's conditions for probabilistic causality (definition 2.3.2) and, in fact, these are equivalent.

Theorem 4.2.1. *Assume there is a structure* $K = \langle S, s^i, L, \mathcal{T} \rangle$ *representing the underlying system governing the occurrences of the events. Then the conditions for causality given in definition 4.2.1 are satisfied if and only if the conditions for causality given by Suppes in definition 2.3.2 are satisfied.*

See appendix B.2 for the proof.

As an example, take the structure in figure 4.1. I use the term "causal structure" in this book to denote this type of structure, where this is the underlying one governing the behavior of the system. The goal is generally to infer its properties from a set of data (observations of the system moving through a set of states over time), but for the moment assume it is given. Unlike models such as causal Bayes nets, the arrows between states in these structures have no causal interpretation. They only imply that it is possible to transition from the state at the tail to the state at the head with some nonzero probability (that is used to label the edge). There may also be multiple states with the same labels. For instance, there could be two states labeled with

This is a probabilistic Kripke structure as described in section 3.3.

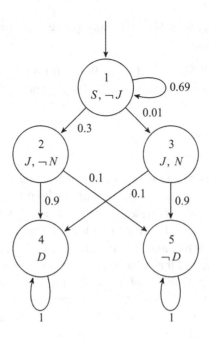

Figure 4.1. Example structure containing states with their labels and transitions with their associated probabilities. s_1 is the initial state.

identical sets of propositions that are reached by different paths and that have different paths possible from them. It follows then that we can evaluate properties true for every state with a certain label, and those that hold only when other sets of conditions leading up to (or occurring after) those states are true. Thus, this type of model fundamentally differs from Bayesian networks, where each variable is represented by one node with incoming and outgoing edges (and lack thereof) representing (in)dependencies. In this chapter, I use the convention that diagrams with circular nodes represent such structures, while those with no borders around the nodes illustrate only temporal ordering (with the node at the tail being earlier than that at the head and the length of the arrow usually being proportional to the amount of time between the nodes) and some probabilistic dependence.

We will now go through the calculation of probabilities to show how one may determine prima facie causality from a structure (inference from data is dealt with in the next chapter). Readers who wish to skip these details may continue on to section 4.2.2. This example is discussed in full when examining token causality in chapter 6, but for the moment say we aim to find the cause and probability of death (D) for a suicidal person (S) who jumps from a building (J) that may (N) or may not ($\neg N$) have a net. This case is probabilistic, so a person may also survive this jump attempt ($\neg D$). In this very simple example, we will only test the minimal conditions for potential causality – that the causes occur at least one time unit before their effects (which may take an infinite amount of time to occur) and change their probabilities. The states are numbered for reference, and labeled with literals (non-negated or negated atomic propositions) $S, J, \neg J, N, \neg N, D,$ and $\neg D$. The transitions in the graph are also labeled with their probabilities.

With $c = J \wedge \neg N$ and $e = D$ we will test whether c is a prima facie cause of e. To do this, we need to know two things: whether the probability of c is greater than zero, and whether the probability of e given c's earlier occurrence differs from the marginal probability of e. We know that c meets the first condition of definition 4.2.1, since s_2 satisfies c, and the probability of reaching s_2 from s_1 is greater than zero. Specifically, $\mathcal{T}(s_1, s_2) = 0.3$, but the probability of reaching s_2 from s_1 is actually greater than this due to the cycle at s_1. Remember that s_2 may occur at any time. Thus, the cycle at s_1 may be revisited multiple times before a transition to s_2. The system has paths of infinite length (a person can remain suicidal, without jumping, for an arbitrarily long period of time), so computation of the probabilities requires a little more work than may be obvious. This section only gives an overview of the process, but more details of the algorithm can be found in appendix B.3 (see theorem B.3.2 and the related algorithms B.1 and B.2).

To determine whether c alters the probability of e, we first need the marginal probability of e. Recall the model-checking methods from chapter 3, where for a path formula it was possible to find a state where it held and then work backwards, finding states that could transition to these satisfaction states. With an infinite upper bound on the timing, though, this could lead to an infinite loop in the computations. Instead we can deal with sets of states. These are those that have no path to a state where e is true or where e is not currently true (set Q) and where the probability of reaching a state where e holds is 1 (set R). A third set is needed when using a lower bound with the leads-to operator (set P, states where e is true or there is a path to e that is shorter than the minimum time window). A state can be in both P and R in cases where every path from it leads to a state where e holds, but where some of these paths are shorter than the minimum time on the leads-to formula.

The probability of e is calculated as follows. The sets are: $P = \{\emptyset\}$, $Q = \{s_5\}$ and $R = \{s_4\}$. Set P is empty, because there is no minimum time bound here. The only state from which it is not possible to reach s_4 is s_5, so this state is in Q. Finally, all other states could potentially end in s_5, so the only state where success is guaranteed (and thus the only member of set R) is s_4. The probability of e occurring at any time, represented by the probability of $F^{\geq 0, \leq \infty} e$, is given by $P(\infty, s_1)$, since s_1 is the initial state of the system. The temporal operator F means "finally," so with an infinite upper time bound it is satisfied from a state if there is some path that eventually leads to a state where e is true. The probability of this satisfaction is the probability of the set of paths from that set to the state (or states) where e holds. Remember that the probability of a set of paths is defined as the sum of the probabilities for each path from s_1, where each is defined recursively as the product of the transition probability from s_1 and the path probability from the state transitioned to.

$$P(\infty, s_1) = T(s_1, s_1) \times P(\infty, s_1) + T(s_1, s_2) \times P(\infty, s_2)$$
$$+ T(s_1, s_3) \times P(\infty, s_3).$$

There were two probabilities in the previous equation that must be calculated, and these are defined analogously to the probability from s_1:

$$P(\infty, s_2) = T(s_2, s_4) \times P(\infty, s_4) + T(s_2, s_5) \times P(\infty, s_5)$$
$$P(\infty, s_3) = T(s_3, s_4) \times P(\infty, s_4) + T(s_3, s_5) \times P(\infty, s_5)$$

Then, s_4 and s_5 are in the previously defined sets, so:

$$P(\infty, s_4) = 1, \text{ since } s_4 \in R$$
$$P(\infty, s_5) = 0, \text{ since } s_5 \in Q$$

Now these results can be substituted into the previous equations:

$$P(\infty, s_2) = 0.9 \times 1 + 0.1 \times 0 = 0.9$$
$$P(\infty, s_3) = 0.1 \times 1 + 0.9 \times 0 = 0.1$$
$$P(\infty, s_1) = 0.3 \times 0.9 + 0.01 \times 0.1 + 0.69 \times P(\infty, s_1)$$

Finally, we can solve for $P(\infty, s_1)$:

$$0.31 \times P(\infty, s_1) = 0.271$$
$$P(\infty, s_1) = \frac{0.271}{0.31} \approx 0.87$$

Thus, the probability of e is < 0.88 and ≈ 0.87. Finally, the probability of $c \rightsquigarrow^{\geq 1, \leq \infty} e$ is exactly 0.9 (there is only one path from a state where c holds to a state where e holds and it is the transition between states s_2 and s_4). Since $0.9 > 0.88$, c being prior to e raises the probability of e and it is a prima facie cause of e.

4.2.2. Insignificant causes

Intuitions

As discussed in section 2.3, the conditions for prima facie causality are insufficient to distinguish between causes and non-causes, and the primary difference between probabilistic theories of causality is in how exactly they make this distinction. The two main types of methods are those based on information and those based on manipulation. Information-based theories such as those already discussed in this book use the idea that a cause provides some information about an effect that cannot be gained in other ways, and set about finding evidence for this. Manipulation theories hold that a cause is a way of bringing about an effect, and can be understood in terms of how the probability or value of the effect changes when manipulating the cause to be true (Woodward, 2005). One approach is not inherently superior to the other – there are counterexamples to both manipulation and information based methods and neither subsumes the other. Since manipulation is not possible in many cases (particularly those discussed in this book), it is undesirable to require it. It would not make sense to insist that probability raising be understood in terms of manipulations or suggest that the addition of manipulations could provide more robust results since it is simply not possible to intervene on stock markets, political systems, and humans in the ways one would need to for this to be broadly applicable.

Methods that aim to infer causal relationships from observational data – because it is readily available or because manipulations are costly, infeasible, or unethical – generally use some variant of the information-based approach. Thus, the distinguishing feature between them is how to quantify the information provided about the effect. As many approaches are based on comparing probabilities in the presence and absence of the cause, there is debate on what else should be included in this comparison. The basic idea is that of holding fixed some set of information and then seeing how likely the effect is when the cause is present and absent relative to that set of information. Before discussing the details of a new measure for causal

See Fitelson and Hitchcock (2011) for a comparison of measures of causal strength.

significance, I review some prior methods and discuss the desiderata for quantifying causal influence.

Consider the following set of relationships (an abstraction of a DTMC):

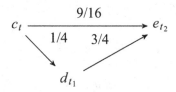

This is a subset of a full system that we may have a model of or observe. Here c can cause e in two time units through two paths, directly or through d: 1/4 of the time c causes d at $t + 1$, 9/16 of the time it causes e directly at $t + 2$, and 3/16 of the time it does neither. Now assuming the marginal probability of e is much lower than 1/4 (remember this is not a DTMC and c is not the label of the start state), how might we determine how significant c and d are for e?

One approach is to find the earliest cause that best accounts for the effect. This is Suppes's method (as described in section 2.3.2), which says that a cause is spurious if there is other information that predicts the effect at least as well and, once this information is known, the probability of the effect is unchanged by knowledge of the spurious cause. In the preceding example this would erroneously call d spurious since c occurs earlier than it and $P(e|c \wedge d) = P(e|c)$. Similarly, using Granger causality one would also fail to find d as a cause of e since the probability of e is unchanged once information about d is included. This is incorrect since d is in fact a cause of e and accounts for e exactly as well as c does. Further, d brings about e more quickly than c does and with a higher probability (3/4 versus 9/16 when c causes e directly). In Suppes's approach, though, as long as there is one such c for which the relevant conditional probabilities are equal (or near equal, using his looser notion of ε-spuriousness), d would be labeled as spurious.[4] In this case, d is not only useful for predicting e but is known to actually cause it. If we included other variables in the example there would be many other cases where d makes a significant difference to e's probability. It is not similarly possible for c to be spurious in Suppes's approach since the only other factor that could make it seem so is d and d occurs later than c. This is contrary to the approach taken here, which

---

[4] With ε-spuriousness, the primary question is what value to use for ε.

aims to infer the most direct causes of an effect, relative to the set of factors measured.

Since attempting to find a single factor that renders a possible cause irrelevant can lead to anomalous results, another approach is assessing the average significance of a cause for its effect. The idea is to measure overall how well a possible cause predicts its effect. One method of this type is Eells's average degree of causal significance (ADCS), as described in section 2.3.3. First, when evaluating the significance of a cause Eells holds fixed events occurring at any time prior to the effect, rather than only those prior to the cause.[5] Second, instead of only comparing against individual factors, Eells holds fixed contexts comprised of all relevant factors held fixed in all possible ways. The result is a quantity denoting how significant each cause is for its effect, though one must still determine how to interpret these values. Unlike Suppes's approach this measure can be positive or negative, allowing a more nuanced notion of causal relevance. There is also mixed relevance, where the probability difference is positive in some contexts and negative in others and may average to zero despite strong influence in both directions. However, there are practical problems if this is taken as a methodological recommendation. The set of contexts grows exponentially in the number of variables (n variables means 2^n contexts), so it is rare to have enough data to see each occur with a meaningful frequency and testing all contexts is a nontrivial computational task. In a case such as analyzing gene expression data, where there may be thousands of variables, it is simply not possible to construct this set of contexts (let alone to do so for each possible cause whose significance must be computed). As with ε-spuriousness, there is the same question about how to determine which values of the ADCS should be considered significant. While Eells's approach is not computationally feasible, we can build on the intuition of using an average significance, rather than finding a single factor that makes a cause spurious, adapting this to suit the needs of methodology.

In this book, the goal is to develop a general method applicable to a variety of types of observational time series data. This means the metric must allow for computational efficiency and have reasonable data requirements. Beyond these practical concerns, though, how should a measure of causal significance behave?

The underlying idea is to assess how much a possible cause tells us about an effect, as compared to other possible factors that may account for it.

---

[5] He excludes causally intermediate factors, as the aim is to include factors relevant to the effect but not those to which the possible cause is causally relevant.

First, the calculated values for causal significance should be proportional to how informative or effective a cause is for an effect, so that a sole necessary and sufficient cause of an effect has a significance of one, while a cause that is necessary but not sufficient should have a lower value, since other information could still help predict the effect.[6] Intuitively, this means that other causes will need to be taken into account, since one could only determine that a cause is unnecessary by finding other causes of the same effect. Second, it should identify the most direct causes of an effect, so that if in the example above c only caused e through d (severing the direct link from c to e), we would only find the causal relationships between c and d and between d and e. This is because we are not attempting to assign responsibility or blame or make metaphysical judgments, but rather to understand the workings of a system to allow for effective prediction and interventions. A more direct cause yields more effective strategies for bringing about the effect, with no loss of information as the other links of the chain will also be inferred (so that one may use knowledge of the relationship between c and d, and d and e to use c to control e). This is in line with the goals of other computational methods and biomedical work, where understanding the details of the chain is important for planning interventions since if it is possible to control d it is a more likely candidate than c for controlling e. Finally, the metric should distinguish between causes of infrequent events (that may raise an already small probability by a small amount) and causes that make a large difference to more frequent events. Since the goal is to understand the workings for a system, and have some hypotheses for how to begin to interact with it, a cause that raises the probability of an event from 0.0001 to 0.0003 is much less interesting and useful than one that raises a probability from 0.1 to 0.3. As a result, the metric will concentrate on absolute probability differences rather than ratios such as the log-odds ratio (Fienberg, 1980).

Measuring causal significance

Taking inspiration from the approaches described, a new measure will be developed that addresses the desiderata previously outlined. Since spuriousness implies falsity, I will refrain from using this terminology as I do not intend to imply that the prima facie causes that will be abandoned are

---

[6] There is a significant amount of work in psychology on modeling causal judgments. Though all measures are heavily debated, there is some evidence that both structure and strength factor into this.

necessarily false, only that they are of low import. Instead, let us now discuss how to determine which of the prima facie causes are insignificant.[7] To do this, each cause will be compared, pairwise, against each other possible explanation of the same effect (its other prima facie causes), yielding an average difference in probabilities. The idea is to determine whether there are other factors that may be more informative about an effect. These other factors may occur at any time prior to the effect – they may be before, after, or co-temporary with the cause being evaluated. To evaluate the significance of a cause c for an effect e in light of another factor, x, we hold x fixed and then determine how much c changes the probability of e.

$$P(e|c \wedge x) - P(e|\neg c \wedge x). \tag{4.4}$$

However, there will be many other factors to be compared against and we do not seek only one factor that makes a cause insignificant, but rather aim to determine overall how much c raises or lowers the probability of e.

The general approach is to calculate the average difference in the probability of an effect for each of its prima facie causes, in relation to all other prima facie causes of the same effect. If the probability of the effect does not differ substantially when a potential cause is present or absent, then it may be insignificant. By holding fixed only the set of prima facie causes, we are not comparing against factors that are independent of or negatively correlated with e (or which never co-occur with c or $\neg c$). We assume that the probabilities are representative of the true probabilities.[8] More formally, where X is the set of prima facie causes of e, the significance of a cause c for an effect e is defined as:

However, the complement of a negative cause may indeed be included.

$$\varepsilon_{avg}(c, e) = \frac{\displaystyle\sum_{x \in X \setminus c} \varepsilon_x(c, e)}{|X \setminus c|} \tag{4.5}$$

where:

$$\varepsilon_x(c, e) = P(e|c \wedge x) - P(e|\neg c \wedge x). \tag{4.6}$$

The relationships between c and e, and x and e have associated time windows and are of the form $c \leadsto^{\geq r, \leq s} e$ and $x \leadsto^{\geq r', \leq s'} e$. Thus, the probabilities above refer to e's occurrence in the overlap of these windows.

---

[7] For the moment, significance and insignificance refer to causal significance and insignificance. Later on we will need to choose a threshold for when these values are statistically significant. This is discussed in depth in section 5.2.1.

[8] When testing from data it is further assumed that these probabilities can be accurately inferred from the data as it grows infinitely large (that is, it is ergodic) and that the relationships do not change over time.

For $P(e|c \wedge x)$, c and x must each occur so that e's occurrence may be a result of either. For $P(e|\neg c \wedge x)$, x occurs prior to e, which occurs in the window $[r', s']$ after x, but c does not occur at such a time that its window overlaps with x's. For more details on these timings and how they fit in with inference from time series data and frequency-based probability calculations, see section 5.2.1.

For each prima facie cause, this measure assesses its average potency as a predictor of its effect. These scores are used to determine which are causally (and later, statistically) significant. The full time subscripts are included here, since it is important to observe that one may evaluate the significance of a cause for an effect across multiple timescales. These subscripts will be dropped when the problem is clear without them as they can become unwieldy.

Definition 4.2.2. Where $c \leadsto_{\geq p}^{\geq r, \leq s} e$, a prima facie cause, c, of an effect, e, is an ε-*insignificant cause* of e if $|\varepsilon_{avg}(c_{r-s}, e)| < \varepsilon$.

What does the value of $\varepsilon_{avg}(c_{r-s}, e)$ mean? When it is positive, it means that c occurring has a positive influence (proportional to the magnitude of ε_{avg}) on e's occurrence. When it is negative, then c's absence is more informative about e than c's presence is, as the probability of e is greater after c's absence (and as a corollary c is a negative cause of e). Small values of this measure may mean that c is simply a statistical artifact. In other cases, c may indeed be a real cause, but one that only makes a small difference to e. In both cases, c is discarded as a cause of e: in the first case because it is not a real cause and in the second because despite being a real cause it makes little difference (and will not be that useful for prediction or explanation). As discussed in the previous section, the probability difference is more appropriate for these purposes than the log-odds ratio, as we aim to distinguish between factors that perturb a small probability and those that make an effect significantly more likely. It is not assumed that ε_{avg} will be exactly equal to zero for spurious causes. This is due to many factors such as noise and strongly correlated data, and in fact these scores will be normally distributed in the absence of causal relationships (this is shown empirically in chapter 7). If ε_{avg} is exactly equal to zero, one cannot conclude that c neither increases nor decreases the probability of e, as its positive and negative influences could cancel out.

Two differences between this approach and others are which factors are held fixed, and how the differences are averaged. First, holding fixed all prima facie causes means that it does not require excessive background knowledge and can find the most direct causes. The set of factors may be at any time before e (they can be before, after, or at the same time as c) and there is no restriction other than that they are prima facie causes of the effect, so they may be causes of or caused by c. Some factors may turn out to be causally intermediate (effects of c and causes of e). These intermediate factors are not held fixed in some other methods, as doing so can lead to finding that c does not cause e.[9] Aside from that it is not a direct cause and should not be inferred, without background knowledge we could not know which factors are intermediate and should be excluded. At this stage we only know the prima facie causes, and have not yet determined what c's actual causes and effects may be. It would not make sense to not condition on a factor that later turns out to be an insignificant effect of c because it seemed at first that it may be a genuine one. This work aims to be parsimonious in its assumptions and does not suppose any knowledge of which factors are relevant or not. Conditioning on the set of prima facie causes (those that are potentially relevant) achieves this. We later examine structures where a cause may be mistaken for being genuine based on it being an early link in a causal chain. We instead avoid such mistakes by conditioning on all prima facie causes of the effect (including the erroneous one's direct effects). When the timings of relationships are also inferred from the data – without prior knowledge – holding fixed all prima facie causes is what enables one to test a set of windows (where some may be far too large) without finding in a causal chain, $c \rightarrow d \rightarrow e$, that c causes e.

While a change in probability is not strictly necessary for causality, limiting the set X to only prima facie causes (rather than say all factors in the system) improves computational complexity while still enabling identification of erroneous causes. A factor that is independent of or negatively correlated with e should not be able to make a cause seem insignificant by better explaining the effect. If some x is independent of e and it does not interact with c with respect to e, then $P(e|c \land x) - P(e|\neg c \land x)$ will be equal to $P(e|c) - P(e|\neg c)$.[10] It may be possible for x to interact with c with respect to e, while remaining independent of e, but examples of this form usually involve c being an actual cause of e where x somehow reduces c's efficacy (such as an antidote to a poison that is harmless on its own). Not conditioning on x may overstate c's average significance, but would not lead to finding a causal relationship where one does not exist.

---

[9] One exception is that Cartwright suggests holding fixed effects of c that were not actually caused by c on that particular occasion (Cartwright, 1989, 95–96). It is unclear how one might glean such information. See also Eells and Sober (1983).

[10] This may also be the case when x only appears independent of e due to its positive and negative influence canceling out.

Next is the case where x is not a prima facie cause because $P(e|x) <$ $P(e)$. Intuitively such a factor should not be able to make c seem insignificant, as it does not provide more information about the occurrence of e than c does. Thinking of the types of factors that may account better for an effect, x may cause both c and e or there may be a chain where c causes x and x causes e. If c being a prima facie cause of e is fully explained by x being a common cause of both, though, x will also be a prima facie cause of e.[11] If x is in between c and e in a causal chain, and this is the only reason c is a prima facie cause of e, then x will once again be a prima facie cause of e (since c cannot raise the probability more than x does). So in both of these cases, x will already be in the set of prima facie causes. Note also that when generating a set of hypotheses here we generally use propositions and their negations, so that if x lowers the probability of e, $\neg x$ raises the probability and in fact will be a prima facie cause and thus in the set compared against.

A factor x that is negatively associated with an effect may also be a positive cause of it in conjunction with other factors. For example, if c is a reasonably effective treatment for a disease, perhaps x is a treatment that leads to poor outcomes on its own, but works very well in combination with other treatments (which may or may not include c). But x still cannot provide more information about e than c does. If x does interact with c to bring about e (perhaps with an even higher probability than c alone), then the righthand side of the difference in equation (4.6) will still be quite small (since x alone is negatively associated with e and presumably cannot cause it without c) while the lefthand side will be the same as or larger than $P(e|c)$. If instead x causes e in conjunction with some set of factors (that does not include c) and is independent of c given e, then it still cannot make c seem insignificant, and it is not problematic to exclude it from the calculations.

Finally, c's impact on e's probability is averaged over all of the differences. This means that c may raise the probability of e in some situations and lower it in others, but its overall impact must be positive to be identified as a cause. Whether to require context unanimity (that a cause must raise the probability of its effect in all contexts or lower it in all contexts) has

---

[11] There can be cases where x causes c and e directly, but also strongly lowers the probability of e by causing a preventative of it. However, in those cases c will not be initially found as a prima facie cause of e. More far-fetched examples can be constructed, but remember, the goal here is not to create the only counterexample-free theory of causal inference, but to create a method that works well in the majority of cases of interest.

been debated in the literature on causality, with Eells going so far as to say that "average effect is a sorry excuse for a causal concept."[12] However, this work does not assemble the full set of background contexts (all variables held fixed in all possible ways), and it does not make sense to require that *c* raise *e*'s probability with respect to each other prima facie cause of it. With two causes where each is active just in case the other is not, this would mean that neither is a cause as neither would raise the probability with respect to the other. The idea of background contexts was abandoned earlier, since even with all possible data and all relevant factors included, each context would be specified by more and more features and would be narrowed down to the point of fully specifying individuals (if it occurs at all). Further, even with all background contexts, unanimity would require us to identify the right populations so that those where the cause prevents the effect or is irrelevant for it are excluded. As Dupré (1990) has discussed in detail, this is a problem for practice as we do not normally have such information, so this requires quite a lot of causal knowledge before one can assess the efficacy of a cause.[13] It seems reasonable that if *c*'s role changes, there must be something else that determines whether it will have a positive or negative influence, but just because there is some way of preventing *c* from causing *e* or turning *c* into a negative cause of *e* does not diminish the fact that it is a genuine positive cause in other cases. In the calculations here, *c* must still change the probability of *e* overall. For each case in which it has negative significance, there must be a positive case that offsets the amount of negative influence.

Thus, if *c* has an ε_{avg} that exceeds ε, then it has an overall significantly positive role and if we do not know the other factors that make a difference, the best estimate is to say that *c* causes *e*. If $|\varepsilon_{avg}(c, e)| < \varepsilon$, then knowing *c* alone does not help us to predict *e*. This is not to say that *c* does not cause *e* (there may be other conditions that in conjunction with *c* are significant positive causes), but rather that *c* alone is not significant for *e* and does not give us enough evidence to predict whether *e* will occur. This is another reason why I eschew the language of spuriousness, since, among other possible explanations, an ε-insignificant cause may be a component of a significant cause and it is nonsensical to say that a significant cause is comprised of spurious causes. However, causes that are insignificant on their own could be significant in combination.

---

[12] Eells and Sober 1983, 54.
[13] This could include mechanistic knowledge, so that knowing how currently available birth control pills work tells us that the right population to study is women.

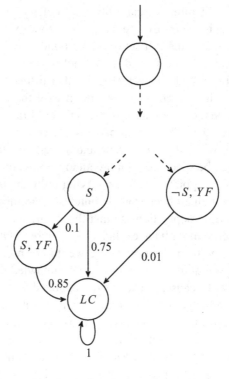

Figure 4.2. Smoking (*S*), yellow fingers (*YF*), and lung cancer (*LC*).

Examples

We will now work through two examples to illustrate how this measure is calculated. First, as a simple example of testing for insignificance, consider a set of data on smoking (*S*), yellow stained fingers (*YF*), and the incidence of lung cancer (*LC*) in people who smoke and have stained fingers. Now, assume smoking and staining of fingers occur prior to the development of lung cancer, though we will keep this first example abstract to avoid overcomplicating matters. Then, both *S* and *YF* are likely to be prima facie causes of *LC*. However, the difference $P(LC|YF \wedge S)$ $- P(LC|\neg YF \wedge S)$, which tests *YF*'s contribution to *LC*, will likely be nearly zero (accounting for the possibility of another reason for stained fingers being a cause of lung cancer). This scenario is shown in figure 4.2. In that structure, transition probabilities from a state sometimes add to less than one, indicating states not shown, but where none of these hidden states are labeled with *S*, *YF*, or *LC*. Then:

$$\varepsilon_S(YF, LC) = P(LC|YF \wedge S) - P(LC|\neg YF \wedge S) = 0.85 - 0.75 = 0.10,$$

and

$$\varepsilon_{YF}(S, LC) = P(LC|S \wedge YF) - P(LC|\neg S \wedge YF) = 0.85 - 0.01 = 0.84.$$

Thus, YF is presumably an ε-insignificant cause of LC as here there are only two possible causes and $\varepsilon_S(YF, LC)$ is very small, while $\varepsilon_{YF}(S, LC)$ is much higher. Consider what would happen if there were other causes of lung cancer that did not lead to YF, such as asbestos, air pollution, or radon exposure. Would we still be able to find that YF is insignificant with these and other variables in the system? The answer is yes. The value for ε_{avg} may be positive (remember these are not zero with no causal relationships, but are normally distributed), but will always be much less than that for S, since S can occur and lead to LC without YF but when YF occurs when not caused by S, LC does not follow. This is shown experimentally in chapter 7 where data with a similar structure is simulated.

As a second example, let us more abstractly revisit the case of a poison and antidote. The probability of death (D) within 30 minutes of poisoning (O) is quite high, perhaps 0.8, so that $P(D|O_{\leq 30}) = 0.8$. However, there is a very effective antidote (A) such that when given within 10 minutes of poisoning, the probability of death is reduced to 0.001. This is the same as the probability of death from the antidote in the absence of the poison, as it has occasional side effects. Thus, $P(D|A) = P(D|A \wedge O) = P(D|A \wedge \neg O) = 0.001$. Both O and A will be prima facie causes of D, assuming 0.001 is greater than the marginal probability of death. When holding fixed A, we find:

$$P(D|O \wedge A) - P(D|\neg O \wedge A) = 0. \qquad (4.7)$$

It seems that O makes no difference to D. Including other variables in the comparison (as we normally have many measurements), would remove this problem. This is one reason that we do not seek a single factor that renders a cause insignificant, but rather average over a set of alternative explanations. For example, we may hold fixed factors such as that someone has recently eaten (as this may have some effect on how quickly the poison works). The average significance allows us to find whether overall O makes a difference to D, while not being hampered by one factor that fully removes its efficacy.

4.2.3. *Just so causes*

What is a prima facie cause whose ε_{avg} is greater than the threshold? Some ε-insignificant causes may turn out to be genuine while others that seem significant may be spurious due to factors such as the choice of ε (which may be too strict or lax) as well as the data not being representative of the underlying probabilities. For this reason, I refer to the prima facie causes that are not ε-significant as "just so" (or ε-significant) causes.

Definition 4.2.3. c, a prima facie cause of an effect, e, is an ε-significant or *just so* cause of e if it is not an ε-spurious cause of e.

What can be claimed about these just so causes? There is good reason to believe that these are genuine and that the ε-insignificant ones are spurious, but without further investigation, the degree of this belief is proportional to one's confidence in how representative and complete the data are. One must also apply statistical methods to choose an appropriate value for the ε threshold. Methods for controlling false discoveries (how often a spurious cause is called significant) in large-scale testing focus on controlling the rate at which this happens relative to all discoveries (very conservative approaches control the probability of making even one false discovery) at a user defined threshold. Thus, there is a small probability that each cause called statistically significant may turn out to be insignificant, but this can be controlled at a level that is acceptable for a given application. One of the advantages of evaluating each relationship and its significance individually is that one incorrect discovery will not affect the others or propagate errors. Instead, methods that assess how well a graph explains a dataset or which conduct independence tests iteratively may find that one incorrect inference affects later tests.

The just so causes inferred are useful for prediction and may potentially be useful for influencing the system or explaining the occurrence of the effect in particular instances. To go beyond statistical significance, though, requires experimental validation of the relationships. Controlled experiments where one attempts to alter a system's behavior by altering the cause are the usual approach to doing this. However, as has been discussed in counterexamples to interventionist theories of causality, one cannot always infer that the continued presence of the effect after removing a cause means the relationship was spurious (since there may be backup mechanisms, especially in biology) and forcing a cause to be true will not always produce the effect (as one may have omitted the conditions needed for the cause to be effective and it can be difficult to manipulate individual variables in isolation). In some areas this may still be done, but there are others where due to ethical, financial, or other restrictions, one cannot conduct any conceivable experiment. In these cases, finding just so causes can be a valuable inference, and one may continue collecting observational data to determine whether the relationships continue to hold or may be refuted.

4.2.4. Genuine causes

Thus far, I have provided primarily negative definitions, focusing on what cannot be inferred or what is not truly causal. Let us now turn our attention to positive claims: what are genuine causes and under what conditions are just so causes genuine? In one sense, if we know the underlying structure of a system (the probabilistic Kripke structure representing its functioning), it would not seem to matter whether something is a cause or not. We can see exactly how the system works, what the probabilities of any possible path through it are, and can come up with our own hypotheses about how to change and predict its future behavior. After all, understanding these inner workings from observations is precisely our goal. This position is perhaps unsatisfying philosophically as it implies that there is no need for a notion of causality once there is a fully specified model.

While we do want to understand how the system works (usually by deciphering its rules from observational data), a completely detailed model does not necessarily provide the information we seek. State labels only indicate the truth value of propositions, so that when examining factors that precede an effect, these are not limited to those actually required to cause it. Thus we would be back to data mining, finding frequent patterns, which may lead to incorrect choices for intervention. We aim to find a compact representation of the system, allowing us to succinctly describe and better understand it. A model of lung cancer that details every step from smoking to development of disease at the level of molecules and cells is at the wrong level of detail for an epidemiological study that aims to understand the relative risk of lung cancer after smoking. One may wish to know that this chain of events can connect smoking and lung cancer, but knowing the chain itself is not always necessary. This type of reasoning relates to mechanistic theories of causality, which involve elucidating the connection between cause and effect.

If we want to explain the occurrence of an effect, we do not necessarily want to specify every detail, including information that is only marginally relevant. Causal relationships can provide these succinct descriptions and improve understanding of how a system will behave as a result of interventions. In most cases, we will not be given a model and will not attempt to infer one, but rather will test logical formulas directly in the data. As will become clear when we discuss inference, it is easier to find the formulas best characterizing the system than it is to find the entire structure. In the structure of figure 4.2, what is the best way to predict whether someone will get lung cancer or explain the occurrence of lung cancer? In a more complex structure, it would be ideal to find succinct relationships such as "smoking causes lung cancer in 10–20 years with probability 0.2." We now want to determine what needs to be true about the structure in order for the best explanation to be the genuine one.

Assumptions

There may be many genuine causes of an effect that each cause it to varying degrees. Particularly in the case of probabilistic causality, it is better to think of causality as being along a continuum rather than as being a partition into genuine and spurious classes. There may be weak genuine causes as well as strong ones, and statistical tests will rarely divide the possible causes cleanly into sets of spurious and genuine causes. The ε_{avg} values for spurious causes will instead have a normal distribution, with the values for genuine causes deviating from this. Thus, we need to choose a threshold at which to call something both causally and statistically significant. Second, while we are not committing to a manipulability or interventionist view of causality, a primary intuition is that a genuine cause is often one that can be manipulated to bring about the effect. While it is not always possible to achieve this experimentally, the idea is that in other cases one may be observing an artifact, but if the cause is genuine then if one could force a change in the cause (making it true, or changing its value) this should change the effect with the probability associated with the relationship.[14] What assumptions must be made about the system to make such a statement?

Manipulability theories say that causes are things that can be intervened upon to alter effects. See Pearl (2000) and Woodward (2005) for further reading.

From the prior definitions, just so causes are candidates for genuine causality though these are not exhaustive as, for example, the value chosen for ε may be too high. Remember that the current goal is to describe relationships relative to a structure K using logical formulas (conditions for successful inference and a discussion of how to infer the relationships from data are dealt with in the next chapter). As before, it is assumed that this is the correct underlying structure. This implies that any states reached with nonzero transition probabilities in K are possible states of the system, and that the transition probabilities are the actual ones. However, this does not mean that K contains every part of the whole. If we were studying

---

[14] Even though we cannot manipulate factors such as people's gender or ethnicity, the idea is that if we could do so and these were causes, then the effects would occur. In practice, it is rarely possible to manipulate one variable in isolation. In medicine each intervention may have multiple effects, not all of which are desirable. For example, if a statin lowers cholesterol but also causes vitamin D deficiency, doctors may prescribe both a statin and a vitamin supplement at the same time, anticipating this effect.

the human body, we may model the workings of the elbow or digestive tract, without specifying a whole body. We cannot simply amputate the functioning of the elbow and still understand it, but rather must keep some information from the larger whole to create a self-contained system for study.

This means that if we want to find genuine causes and not only just so ones, all common causes should be included. If they are not, then the just so causes may simply be indicators for genuine causes. Take smoking, yellowed fingers, and lung cancer. Smoking likely causes both yellowed fingers and lung cancer, while the two effects play no causal role in either smoking or with one another. Suppose that only yellowed fingers and lung cancer are measured and the measurements are over time. It is possible then that someone who has smoked enough to yellow their fingers will be more likely to develop lung cancer than if this was not the case. If the yellowing of fingers somehow occurs at a regular time before lung cancer, we may find yellowed fingers just so cause lung cancer. While this is not the true causal relationship, yellowed fingers could still be a useful predictor of lung cancer and it may be possible to use this information as an indicator for the stage of the disease. In other words, just so causes are primarily useful for prediction, but their true role can only be determined through background knowledge (as we know it is not possible for yellowed fingers to cause lung cancer given what we know about physiology) or experimentation. Distinguishing between just so and genuine causes allows us to be explicit about the level of support for a causal relationship (and implies what it can be used for as well).

The primary question is: how can we know that we have enumerated all common causes? This is at the crux of the issue as knowing that common causes are included means being able to take pairs of formulas and say whether they have a common cause. Problematically, this implies that there is background knowledge, otherwise the algorithms would have no starting point. Indeed, Nancy Cartwright (1989) summarizes this situation as "no causes in, no causes out." This view is shared by Pearl[15] and others (Robins and Wasserman, 1999; Woodward, 2005), though disputed by Glymour et al. (1999). But how can we acquire this "old" causal knowledge in the first place? One strategy Cartwright gives is to conduct perfectly randomized experiments, thus controlling for all unknown factors. That we only need to include common causes, and not every other cause of the effect, is suggested

---

[15] Pearl (2000, 60) suggested "Occam's razor in, some causes out." Cartwright (1989, 72) is in fact against this simplicity assumption.

as greatly simplifying matters (Papineau, 2001), but it still does not address how we can build this background causal knowledge.[16] There must always be a level of causes that are not subject to these inference rules, on which all other inferences can be based. This is dissatisfying, as there is no well defined base case for this recursion. If we do not trace everything back to its underlying physics, it seems that there must be some matter of opinion or belief in the causal relationships. If we cannot build these relationships from some lower level laws, it must be that asserting there is no common cause of two factors is really saying that I *believe* that there is no common cause of them or that I have *confidence* that the experiment was conducted such that all common causes were included. We should be explicit about the amount of intuition and judgment required. Research often involves secondary analysis of observational data. It is obvious that if we do not measure smoking, we will not discover that smoking causes lung cancer, but whether yellowed fingers are found to genuinely cause lung cancer (as that dataset would suggest), depends on whether we already know enough about lung cancer to know that it and yellowed fingers have a common cause. If we already have that information, it seems unlikely that we would conduct such a study, but perhaps only maintain a strong belief that such is the case while continuing to examine alternatives.

Thus, a just so cause *is* genuine in the case where all of the outlined assumptions hold (namely that all common causes are included, the structure is representative of the system and, when data is used, a formula satisfied by the data will be satisfied by the structure). Our *belief* in whether a cause is genuine, in the case where it is not certain that the assumptions hold, should be proportional to how much we believe that the assumptions are true.

4.3. Difficult Cases

While causal inference algorithms can be tested on simulated data, where the ground truth is known, the same cannot be done for philosophical theories of causality. As a result, counterexamples have proliferated, and researchers argue whether or not a theory can handle these conceptually. In this section, classic counterexamples to theories of causality are ana-lyzed to show that the proposed approach can handle most of them.[17] There are a few canonical test cases that apply to most theories (redundant

---

[16] There are approaches such as FCI for inferring the presence of hidden common causes or when there is an unconfounded relationship in a BN. However, these have not performed as well in practice as in theory (Entner and Hoyer, 2010) and BNs are hampered by their inadequate representation of time and complexity.

[17] In chapter 7, this approach is evaluated empirically on simulated and actual data in a variety of domains.

causation, transitivity, cycles) along with others specific to probabilistic theories (determinism, causation without probability raising, probability raising without causation). Some of these are most plausibly discussed as objections to token-level theories of causality, and are thus discussed in chapter 6. The following examples focus on type-level inferences that may be made from a structure or using the inference method described in chapter 5. These are discussed in the context of the broader goals of this book (inference and explanation relative to time series data) with the aim of making it clear what the approach advanced can and cannot do. This is a critical point as all theories of and methods for inferring causality fail to handle some scenarios, so researchers must be aware of these differences when choosing methodologies for their work.

4.3.1. Determinism

In deterministic cases, an effect occurs with probability one as a result of a cause, leading to difficulties for probabilistic theories of causality. Such scenarios sometimes involve more complex issues such as multiple causes that each lead to the effect with probability one, but for now take a simple case with one very effective cause of an effect.

> Each morning, Alex and Keith wake at 7 am and begin drinking their daily cup of coffee at 7:15 am. Alex is a mathematician who believes coffee is critical to creating elegant proofs, so he is diligent about maintaining the machine and ensuring a steady supply of coffee and milk. Once he finishes reading the newspaper and begins making coffee, this process never fails and results in him drinking coffee in exactly 5 minutes.

Here, drinking coffee (D) can only occur when coffee is made and making coffee (M) always results in drinking coffee, so M is both necessary and sufficient for D. This situation could be represented by the probabilistic Kripke structure (DTMC) in figure 4.3a, where all transitions have probability 1 and intermediate transitions detailing the 5-minute long coffee-making process are denoted by the dashed arrows. Once the system is entered, coffee is always produced and then drunk, so the probability of drinking coffee (D) here at some point, $P(D)$, is 1.

Now, say we wanted to use this structure to find out what causes coffee drinking within this system. One might have a hypothesis such as $M \leadsto^{\geq 5, \leq 5} D$, but in fact M would not even be a prima facie cause of D. Remember that the notation $P(D|M_5)$ means the probability of D given that M occurred 5 time units beforehand. This subscript is sometimes omitted when it is clear. Since $P(D) = 1$ and $P(D|M_5) = 1$, there is no change in probability. As a result, it is not possible to use this approach with such a structure to find

Section 5.3 discusses how to find the timings of relationships without such prior knowledge.

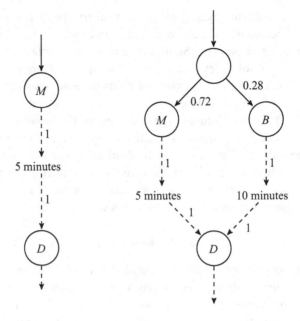

(a) *M* is necessary and sufficient for *D*.

(b) *M* and *B* are sufficient but not necessary for *D*.

Figure 4.3. Deterministic case where all paths lead to coffee.

any causal relationships. It may seem that there should be some causes, since we can posit that if the coffee machine failed there would be no coffee drinking afterward. Just because the mechanisms have never failed in the past, though, does not mean that this will never happen in the future. If one day the machine broke or the coffee shop had a fire while Keith was buying coffee, there would be no coffee, but there is no way of inferring that from this specification. However, without such background knowledge we would be unable to distinguish this case from other strong noncausal regularities (such as day following night). All that can be known is that it is a property of this system that all paths lead to *D* in exactly 5 minutes after *M*.

Observe though that this structure represents the functioning of a process that is executed once per day. It can be thought of as being part of some larger system, and may be better captured through inference using data from the same scenario (the assumption being that this model is not accurately modeling the system). While this has not yet been discussed in detail, the probabilities during inference from data come from frequencies of

See section 5.1 for details on checking formulas in data.

occurrence in the data. The probability of D is the fraction of timepoints labeled with D out of all timepoints in a set of observations. Thus, $P(D)$ would certainly be less than one, so now M does indeed raise the probability of D in 5 minutes, as $P(D|M_5) = 1$ and $P(D) < 1$. There are no other variables in this simple system, so the set X of other potential causes of D is empty and it is not yet possible to calculate $\varepsilon_{avg}(M_5, D)$. However, if other variables were added to the system then $\varepsilon_{avg}(M_5, D)$ would be one, since M is both necessary $(P(D|\neg M_5) = 0)$ and sufficient for D $(P(D|M_5) = 1)$.

So far we have examined one cause that is necessary and sufficient for its effect. Now let us alter the scenario so that M is still sufficient, but no longer necessary for D.

> Continuing with the simple coffee example, on some mornings Keith now picks up coffee from a nearby shop. He does not spend time reading the newspaper, so the slightly longer coffee procurement process (10 minutes, to be exact) still concludes with drinking coffee at 7:15 am. Further, Keith is always aware of when the coffee shop is open and closed, so this process never fails and thus results in coffee with probability one.

This is illustrated in figure 4.3b, where coffee is either made (M) or bought (B) (never both at once) and both actions result in drinking coffee (D) with probability one. This is a case of two sufficient causes, where neither is necessary since there is always a backup. While the coffee example may seem simplistic, this type of scenario is common in biology, where there can be two mechanisms that produce a result and either is active just in case the other is not. For example, only a fraction of the genes in yeast are essential for it to survive, but it has many copies of these genes. They are not active at the same time, but there are mechanisms so that if one copy becomes damaged or inactive, another will take over. Other more complex mechanisms also exist, where one cause of an effect silences another when it is active, so if it is knocked out, the other will no longer be silenced and will become active. Such cases pose difficulties for counterfactual theories of causality, since either one would cause the effect if the other did not, so the effect depends counterfactually on neither. This type of scenario, where there are two possible causes of an effect, but only one process begins and runs to completion, is called early preemption. At the type level, it is not necessary to treat this case separately, since the goal is to determine only whether it can be found that both causes are in fact causes in the long run (over many observations, or from a Kripke model of the system).

As in the previous example, there are again no prima facie causes relative to the structure in figure 4.3b, since the probability of D is one and cannot be raised. Using an observation sequence (series of timepoints with the propositions true at each), one may try to calculate the ε_{avg} values for

$M \rightsquigarrow^{\geq 5, \leq 5} D$ and $B \rightsquigarrow^{\geq 10, \leq 10} D$. While the set X is no longer empty as it was before, ε_{avg} cannot be calculated. Take the case of M, which is:

$$P(D|M_5 \wedge B_{10}) - P(D|\neg M_5 \wedge B_{10}). \qquad (4.8)$$

This has not yet been discussed (see section 5.1 for details), but when using data, these probabilities are defined in terms of frequencies as:

$$\frac{\#(D \wedge M_5 \wedge B_{10})}{\#(M_5 \wedge B_{10})} - \frac{\#(D \wedge \neg M_5 \wedge B_{10})}{\#(\neg M_5 \wedge B_{10})} \qquad (4.9)$$

where $\#(x)$ is the number of timepoints that satisfy x. As shown in the equation, remember that there are time constraints on all occurrences so that using the time windows associated with M and B, $M_5 \wedge B_{10} \wedge D$ is when both M and B occur such that the time windows overlap and D occurs during that overlapping time. However, $M \wedge B$ never occurs (and will not be observed) so the related probability and thus the difference is undefined. As before, if there were other variables measured, though, the ε_{avg} values could be calculated and, in the limit, these would tend toward the relative proportion of cases of coffee drinking that each cause accounts for.

Thus, whether deterministic causes can be found from a structure depends on how it is modeled, and in particular how closely it corresponds to actuality in terms of the probabilities of events. In the case of inference from data, deterministic causes that are both necessary and sufficient as well as those that are only sufficient can be inferred.

4.3.2. Redundant causes

Another case that can pose difficulties is when there are multiple causes that would have brought about an instance of an effect. This is called redundant causation. In some cases, all causes might occur while in others there might only be a backup cause that would have sprung into action had the first cause failed. Two specific cases of this type are usually discussed: *preemption*, where only one of the causes is actually responsible for the effect; and *overdetermination*, where multiple causes occur such that any may have caused the effect. Terminology varies considerably, and overdetermination is sometimes referred to as symmetric overdetermination, with preemption being asymmetric overdetermination (there overdetermination is used synonymously with redundant causation). Within preemption there are early and late flavors. In the early case, only one cause actually occurs, while in the late case the preempted cause or causes do actually occur and their associated processes run to completion (but the effect has already occurred when they do so). The meaning of "preemption" is usually late preemption. The example in the previous section where coffee was either made or bought is a case of early preemption, where only one process occurs before each instance of coffee drinking. If instead Keith was delayed due to a robbery at the shop, so that by the time he got back Alex was already drinking coffee, that would be a case of late preemption. These cases are usually discussed in the context of token causality (and are discussed in depth in chapter 6), and are particularly problematic for counterfactual theories of causality (since the effect would have occurred without one of the causes as the other would have taken over), but it is useful to see how this impacts inference.

At the type level, systematic overdetermination is not problematic, as it is simply a case of multiple causes of an effect that frequently (or in the extreme case, always) co-occur. Each will be found to be prima facie and just so causes of the effect. With a firing squad where each member shoots simultaneously, such that any of them would have caused death, we will correctly find that all members firing cause death. The timing from shooting to death will also be correctly identified. Similarly, early preemption, where the backup cause does not actually occur, is not an impediment to inference. This is simply a case where there are multiple causes of an effect that are mutually exclusive. There are multiple execution methods – firing squad, lethal injection, and electric chair – that all result in death of an inmate, but only one of these is used at a time (though one may be attempted after the failure of another).

Systematic late preemption would mean that two or more causes regularly precede the effect, but only one is actually responsible for it. To impede inference it would have to be the same cause that is preempted each time. There may be cases with a set of factors sharing a common cause and common effect. If these all frequently co-occur, then they frequently overdetermine the effect as well. There may be many cases where one preempts the others, but it is not systematic in that it is not the same one preempting the others each time.[18] In the firing squad example, consider one member consistently shooting before the others, so that her bullet is the fatal one, but despite this happening every time, the other shooters still always shoot and their shots would have brought about death had hers missed. Such a case is rather unlikely, but even so, this method would correctly infer that the actual and preempted causes are both causes of the effect, but might incorrectly find the timing associated with the preempted causes. Using the running coffee example, perhaps Keith buys coffee each morning even

---

[18] In chapter 7, an example with such a scatter-gather graph is shown to be correctly inferred.

though Alex also makes coffee and starts drinking it before Keith returns. In this case D (drinking coffee) occurs before B (buying coffee) could have caused it, but without this prior knowledge one would infer that B leads to D in less than 10 time units. This can be remedied by modeling the system more finely, such as adding variables indicating that coffee must be ready before it is drunk. This is similar to the commonly used example of Bob and Susie throwing rocks at a glass bottle (discussed in section 2.3.2), where in some cases Susie throws earlier but is standing further away (so her rock hits after Bob's does even though she throws first). There, indicators can be added for when the rocks hit the glass to account for cases when a rock hits a bottle that is already broken.

4.3.3. Transitivity

In some cases, there is a series of causes (called a causal chain) such that x_1 causes x_2, x_2 causes x_3, and so on until some final x_n, which causes the effect e. Theories that include transitivity say that a cause of a cause of an

For further discussion on the transitivity of causation, see Eells and Sober (1983).

effect causes the effect, even though it does so indirectly. I do not attempt to resolve whether causality is indeed transitive, but rather aim to make clear whether and how this is captured in the definitions set forth. The next section shows that the desired inferences can indeed be made. Here the goal is to infer the most direct causes relative to a set of variables, so with $x_1 \rightarrow x_2 \rightarrow \ldots \rightarrow x_n$ relationships between each x_i and x_{i+1} should be inferred. Inferences of a causal relationship between any x_i and x_{i+j} where $j \neq 1$ will be considered incorrect (false discoveries when quantifying the results).

Transitivity is thus only captured indirectly here in terms of the degree of abstraction in modeling or measurement. It is unlikely that one would be able to measure or model every single link between cause and effect. In a study on the health effects of smoking, one would record smoking behavior and incidences of lung cancer, heart disease, and other conditions but would not include every individual biological process in between (particularly as many of these links are not yet discovered). Thus, there may be a hidden chain of processes linking cause and effect, but the causes inferred will be the most direct relative to the set of variables. Similarly, if the hypotheses tested include only overly distant time windows, one might again find only an indirect cause. If each x_i in the previous chain causes the next x_{i+1} in exactly 1 time unit, but relationships between all pairs of variables are tested with a window of exactly 2 time units, one would erroneously infer that x_i causes x_{i+2}, while missing the relationship between x_i and x_{i+1}.

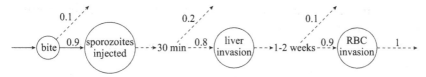

Figure 4.4. Abstraction of the *Plasmodium falciparum* liver stage. Stages are abbreviated with *B* (bite), *S* (sporozoite injection), *L* (liver invasion), and *R* (RBC invasion).

Even though the variables and measurements are at the right time granularity, the hypotheses tested are not. In section 5.3, an algorithm for inferring causal relationships and their timings without prior knowledge is discussed, and it will avoid this problem by ensuring that the full time space is covered, so this potential difficulty is not serious.

4.3.4. Causal chains

The previous section discussed what types of inferences we aim to make when faced with causal chains, arguing that judgments about the transitivity of causality are outside the scope of inference methods. In this section, it is demonstrated that we will indeed find the most direct relationships.[19]

> When an infected mosquito bites a human, it injects sporozoites (undeveloped forms of the malaria parasite) into the blood stream. Within about half an hour, these reach the liver, where they invade its cells. They remain there for 1–2 weeks, multiplying before they then move on to invade red blood cells.

This chain of events is shown in figure 4.4, which also shows the timings between stages using dashed edges (these stand for multiple transitions taking the indicated time).[20] This process is probabilistic, as each stage could be interrupted or could fail before leading to the next one, but this is the only path from mosquito to blood stream. Antimalarials commonly target the blood stage, but newer drugs are being developed to stop the infection during the liver stage, before symptoms even set in. People with sickle cell anemia also have blood cells that resist invasion. As a result, each stage is necessary for the next one, but not sufficient for it.[21] Since the transition probabilities from each state must add to one, transitions to states outside the chain are indicated with dashed arrows along with their

---

[19] In chapter 7, it is shown experimentally that this can be done using the method described here.

[20] The example was simplified by using *Plasmodium falciparum*, where sporozoites do not lay dormant in the liver as they do with *Plasmodium vivax*.

[21] Probabilities have been added to the figure to enable calculation, but they are only for the purposes of being able to carry out the calculations (not for modeling malaria).

probabilities. It is assumed that none of these states are labeled with the propositions shown.

Say we test three hypotheses for causes of red blood cell (RBC) invasion (R):

$$B \leadsto^{\geq 1, \leq 2} R \tag{4.10}$$

$$S \leadsto^{\geq 1, \leq 2} R \tag{4.11}$$

$$L \leadsto^{\geq 1, \leq 2} R. \tag{4.12}$$

Here we have the initial bite (B), injection of sporozoites (S), and invasion of the liver (L). The timings in all cases are 1–2 weeks, but if the transition between L and R were on the order of minutes, the hypotheses would be specified as the sum of the transition time from the possible cause to R. Since 1–2 weeks is much larger than all other terms, we ignore these details. Here S and L are prima facie causes, but B will not be as $P(R_{1-2}|B) = P(R)$ relative to the system shown in figure 4.4. The significance of S and L for R is calculated as follows. First, $\varepsilon_{avg}(L_{1-2}, R)$ is defined as:

$$\varepsilon_{avg}(L_{1-2}, R) = \frac{\varepsilon_{S_{1-2}}(L_{1-2}, R) + \varepsilon_{B_{1-2}}(L_{1-2}, R)}{2}. \tag{4.13}$$

Dispensing with the temporal subscripts as these can become unwieldy, the components of this are:

$$\varepsilon_S(L, R) = P(R|L \wedge S) - P(R|\neg L \wedge S)$$

$$\varepsilon_B(L, R) = P(R|L \wedge B) - P(R|\neg L \wedge B).$$

Using the usual ratio formulation, these are expanded as:

$$\varepsilon_S(L, R) = \frac{P(R \wedge L \wedge S)}{P(L \wedge S)} - \frac{P(R \wedge \neg L \wedge S)}{P(\neg L \wedge S)}$$

$$\varepsilon_B(L, R) = \frac{P(R \wedge L \wedge B)}{P(L \wedge B)} - \frac{P(R \wedge \neg L \wedge B)}{P(\neg L \wedge B)}.$$

With the numbers from the figure, these become:

$$\varepsilon_S(L, R) = \frac{0.9 \times 0.8 \times 0.9}{0.9 \times 0.8} - \frac{0}{0.9 \times 0.2}$$

$$\varepsilon_B(L, R) = \frac{0.9 \times 0.8 \times 0.9}{0.9 \times 0.8} - \frac{0}{0.9 \times 0.2 + 0.1}.$$

Finally, plugging these differences back into (4.13) gives:

$$\varepsilon_{avg}(L, R) = \frac{0.9 + 0.9}{2}$$

$$= 0.9.$$

This simply gives the probability of R given L_{1-2}, since neither S nor B can cause R except through L. As a result, ε_{avg} for S_{1-2} and B_{1-2} will be undefined, as L also does not occur except through S and B, and probabilities such as $P(R|\neg S_{1-2} \wedge L_{1-2})$ will be undefined.[22] We will not find S and B to be insignificant, but rather cannot assess their roles. However, L is not insignificant, as we would correctly assume.

Since there was only one path from B to R in the previous case, let us look at an abstract example where members of the causal chain have other causes. Take the following case:

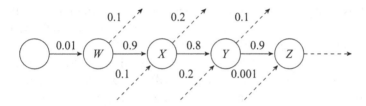

Here W causes X, X causes Y, and Y in turn causes Z. In each case, this happens in exactly one time unit. In addition, X, Y, and Z can also be triggered (with much lower probabilities) by factors outside the chain, making their causes within it no longer necessary for their occurrence. The convention used in the figure is that dashed edges stand for one or more transitions to or from states outside the figure, where none of these other states have the labels used in the figure or a path back to the states in the figure (and can thus be ignored for the following computations). The edge labeled 0.2 into the node labeled Y means that all other possible ways Y can occur (without going through X) together have probability 0.2. The probability of Z other than when preceded by Y is very low, so W_3, X_2, and Y_1 are prima facie causes of Z, since $P(Z|Y_1) = 0.9$, $P(Z|X_2) = 0.72$, and $P(Z|W_3) = 0.648$. Subscripts are omitted from the following calculations,

---

[22] The standard definition of a conditional probability in terms of the ratio of marginal probabilities is used here.

and some intermediate steps are skipped (since these were illustrated in detail in the previous example).

$$\varepsilon_{avg}(Y, Z) = \frac{\varepsilon_x(Y, Z) + \varepsilon_W(Y, Z)}{2}$$

$$= \frac{(0.9 - 0) + (0.9 - 0)}{2} = 0.9$$

$$\varepsilon_{avg}(X, Z) = \frac{\varepsilon_Y(X, Z) + \varepsilon_W(X, Z)}{2}$$

$$= \frac{(0.9 - 0.9) + (0.72 - 0)}{2} = 0.36$$

$$\varepsilon_{avg}(W, Z) = \varepsilon_Y(W, Z) + \varepsilon_X(W, Z)$$

$$= \frac{(0.9 - 0.9) + (0.72 - 0.72)}{2} = 0.$$

Thus, if these are the only factors in the system, they have been correctly ranked with Y being the most important and X being second in importance, which is consistent with how we would think about the problem. If you could find out whether X is true or whether Y is true, it would be more useful to know Y if the goal is to predict Z. It might seem problematic that W is irrelevant for Z, but remember that the goal is to infer direct causes. When making inferences from data, we will correctly find the three causal relationships (between W and X, X and Y, and Y and Z), which is the goal. Nevertheless, one should not be disturbed by the idea of W being insignificant for Z, even if some consider it a cause of X. In fact, saying that W does not cause Z, but rather causes X, which in turn causes Y, which causes Z is a much truer representation of the system. The timings and probabilities in this case were also chosen adversarially. If one tested relationships between pairs of variables in one time unit (i.e., $X \rightsquigarrow^{\geq 1, \leq 1} Z$), the example would have been trivial as only Y would have been at all relevant for Z. This example describes a "worst case" where the timings are chosen exactly to coincide with the chain for maximum spurious correlation. In chapter 7, experimental results on these types of structures shows that in practice the most direct causes can be inferred – even in cases where the timing is initially unknown.

4.3.5. Cycles

One feature of the structures and logic used is that due to the total transition function there must be at least one cycle in the graph (either that or an infinite number of states, which is not allowed here).[23] In contrast, graph-based inference methods, such as those based on Bayesian networks, generally specify that the structure must be a DAG (directed acyclic graph), but this is limiting in that the probabilities in such a graph only convey the probability of the effect happening at some point after the cause. Instead, biological systems often exhibit repeated behavior or have cycles that maintain homeostasis in the face of perturbations. Even though the prevalence of feedback is well-known, this type of structure has eluded most reasoning and inference approaches.[24]

Instead of a single trial, it is often useful to think of a scenario as ongoing, where there may be many opportunities for the cause to occur and to bring about the effect. Take the structure in 4.1, where the propositions are: being suicidal (S), being dead D (where $\neg D$ means alive), jumping from a building J, and existence of net below area being jumped from N ($\neg N$ means there is no such net). In the figure shown, it is specified that a person who is dead remains dead but that one who survives an attempted suicide somehow becomes immortal and remains not dead forever. If all three self loops are removed, we end up with a familiar DAG and avoid such problems. However, it would be better to augment the graph as follows (shown in figure 4.5), resulting in a graph with cycles that behaves as expected. We should keep the self loop at s_4, so as not to allow resurrection in this example. At s_5 we should add an edge to s_1 with nonzero probability, as there is some chance that a person who survives a suicide attempt will become suicidal again. This means changing the probability on the self loop, to make sure the sum of the transition probabilities at s_5 is one. We should also allow a transition from s_5 to s_4, in consideration of the possibility that the person may die of other causes. The goal at the moment is not to reconstruct the most accurate structure representing suicide by jumping from buildings, but rather to illustrate the expressiveness of PCTL as opposed to other frameworks and the desirability of cycles in a causal structure.

With no other modifications, we see that given an infinite amount of time, a person who becomes suicidal will eventually succeed in their attempts.

---

[23] This may be trivially satisfied by adding a sink state with a self loop in cases where cycles are not desired.

[24] Other approaches have focused on inferring cycles (Hyttinen et al., 2010; Richardson, 1996; Schmidt and Murphy, 2009; Spirtes, 1995), but this has received much less attention than the acyclic case and the algorithms face limitations in terms of the amount of data required or their computational complexity. The approach here naturally allows cycles and finding them is no more challenging than inferring a chain of causes.

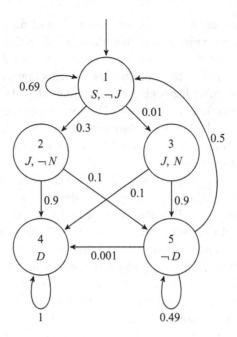

Figure 4.5. Example structure containing states with their labels and transitions with their associated probabilities. s_1 is the initial state. This is an altered version of figure 4.1.

This is a result that could not be achieved without cycles in the graph. However, it is not particularly useful to assume that a person has infinite time to kill himself. Thus, we can add an upper bound and ask whether a person who becomes suicidal will successfully kill themselves within x units of time. Such a question is easily represented and posed in the framework presented, but has no analogue in the graphical models previously described. For instance, one may test hypotheses such as $S \leadsto^{\geq 2, \leq 50} D$, or $J \wedge \neg N \leadsto^{\geq 1, \leq 200} D$.

Instead of determining the likelihood of suicide given various amounts of time, let us examine a biological cycle. The progression of malaria from mosquito bite to red blood cell invasion was used earlier as an example of a causal chain, and after the invasion the system exhibits interesting cyclical behavior.

During the liver stage, sporozoites reproduce, creating thousands of merozoites. When these enter the bloodstream, they invade the red blood cells (RBCs), where they again multiply during a 48-hour cycle. Finally, the RBCs burst, releasing a new set of merozoites that go on to invade RBCs. Instead of reproducing in this asexual cycle after invasion of an RBC, some merozoites undergo sexual

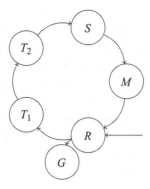

Figure 4.6. Abstraction of the malaria (*Plasmodium falciparum*) blood stage.

differentiation, producing gametocytes. If an uninfected mosquito then bites the infected human, these gametocytes will transmit the infection and produce the sporozoites that will infect the next person bitten by that mosquito.

Here there are actually two cycles. There is the blood stage reproductive cycle (shown in figure 4.6), and then the larger cycle, from bite to liver to blood to infection of a new mosquito and back to the initial bite. Focusing on the blood stage, the question is whether this cycle could be inferred from data using the proposed method. Since the cycle is quite long, this process has been abstracted and the timings omitted. In an actual experiment, we may make repeated measurements over multiple runs of this cycle, where each set may terminate with some probability, or may continue through multiple cycles. This is illustrated in the following five observation sequences.

R T_1 T_2 S M R G

R T_1

R T_1 T_2 S M R T_1 T_2

R T_1 T_2 S M R

R G

The key point is that through the repeated observations of the system's functioning and a constrained time window between cause and effect, it is possible to infer the cycle. The preceding sequences contain measurements over a total of 25 timepoints. R occurs a total of 8 times, leading to a frequency-based probability of 8/25 (or 0.32). The conditional probability of R 1–2 time units after M is 1, so clearly M is a prima facie cause of R. It will have a high value of ε_{avg} since the only path to R is through M, so all probabilities when M is false will be zero. As with causal chains where each member has only one cause (the preceding member), only the most direct cause can be assessed due to undefined probabilities in the other cases. However, this yields the correct result as only the immediate links are found.

5

Inferring Causality

Thus far, I have discussed the types of causes that will be identified, how they can be represented as logical formulas, and how the definitions hold up to common counterexamples. This chapter addresses how these relationships can be inferred from a set of data. I begin by examining the set of hypotheses to be tested, the types of data one may make inferences from, and how to determine whether formulas are satisfied directly in this data (without first inferring a model). Next, I discuss how to calculate the causal significance measure introduced in the previous chapter (ε_{avg}) in data, and how to determine which values of this measure are statistically significant. I then address inference of relationships and their timing without prior knowledge of either. The chapter concludes by examining theoretical issues including the computational complexity of the testing procedures.

5.1. Testing Prima Facie Causality

Chapter 4 introduced a measure for causal significance and showed how probabilistic causal relationships can be represented using probabilistic temporal logic formulas. This representation allows efficient testing of arbitrarily complex relationships. In this chapter, I adapt standard PCTL model checking procedures to validate formulas directly in a set of time series data without first inferring a model (as this can be computationally complex or infeasible in many cases).

5.1.1. The set of hypotheses

The initial hypotheses are first tested to determine which meet the conditions for prima facie causality, being earlier than and raising the probability of their effects. These are a set of formulas of the form:

$$c \rightsquigarrow^{\geq r, \leq s} e, \tag{5.1}$$

111

where c and e are PCTL state formulas, $1 \leq r \leq s \leq \infty$, and $r \neq \infty$. To form this set, the simplest case is when we have some knowledge of the system and either explicitly state the formulas that may be interesting or use background information to generate the set. Data on risk factors for disease may include gender, race, and age group, but we can avoid generating formulas for scenarios that are mutually exclusive or which cannot change, so that while a person may be of multiple races, these cannot change over time and there are also constraints such that a person cannot be simultaneously elderly and a child. Similarly, we may not know the exact connection between neurons in a particular scenario, but may have background knowledge on the timing between one firing and triggering another to fire. Here we could choose to generate increasingly large formulas and stop at some predefined size. Another approach is to determine this threshold based on whether the quality of causal relationships is continuing to increase using the associated ε_{avg} measures (as, assuming the scores are the same, there is generally a preference for simpler explanations). With limited data, we could begin by determining what types of formulas may be found in them (at satisfactory levels of significance) based on formula size, length of the time series, and the number of variables. However, efficient hypothesis generation in general remains an open problem. The initial hypotheses include time windows, but these need not be known a priori and section 5.3 discusses in depth how to infer the timing of relationships in a way that converges toward the true timings. When timings are unknown one can use this approach to test formulas with a set of associated time windows, iteratively perturbing these for the significant relationships to determine their true boundaries.

5.1.2. The set of data

Taking the set of hypotheses and determining which members are prima facie causes means testing first whether the relationships are satisfied in the data and second whether this probability is higher than the marginal probability of the effects. Assume that the data consist of a series of timepoints with measurements of variables or the occurrence of events at each. A subset of one dataset (which may have any number of timepoints and variables) might look like:

	t_1	t_2	t_3
a	1	0	1
b	0	0	1
c	1	1	0

Here there are observations of three variables at three timepoints. At each timepoint, each variable is measured and is either true or false, but in other cases we will need to choose how to handle non-observations. For example, when analyzing electronic health records, when there is no mention of diabetes in a patient's record we would generally assume that the patient is not diabetic even though this is never explicitly stated.[1] On the other hand, questions about a patient's social history (e.g., alcohol use and smoking) are not always asked or answered, so we cannot infer that a patient with no mentions of past or present smoking has never smoked (leaving aside whether the answers given are truthful). Thus this distinction is a methodological choice that depends not only on the domain but also the characteristics of the particular variable. In this book, the default assumption will be that non-occurrence is interpreted as false, as this is appropriate in the types of cases studied here. In the preceding example, the set of atomic propositions in the system is $\{a, b, c\}$. Here a proposition occurring (being true) is denoted by 1, and not occurring (being false) by 0. At t_1, a and c are true. Another way of describing this is to say that the system is in a state where a and c are true.[2] Each observation yields a state the system can occupy, and the temporal order of these observations shows possible transitions between states. We assume there is some underlying structure, which may be very complex and include thousands of states, and we are observing its behavior over time.

There are two main types of data. The first is a long sequence of times, which is one of many partial runs of the system. The second is a group of (usually shorter) observation sequences (also called traces in model checking). Cases like this can arise in medical domains, where there are sets of patients observed over time. While one long run may initially seem equivalent to many shorter runs, there are some important distinctions. To understand these, consider the structure shown in figure 5.1. Say we then observe the sequence $P, Q, S, T, \ldots, T, S, \ldots$ and do not know this underlying model (as is normally the case). With only this one trace (beginning from the start state, s_1), we will never see the transition from s_1 to s_3 (i.e., P, R) and will not know that it is possible. However, with a large set of short traces, as the size of this set increases (assuming no bias in the sample),

---

[1] In practice this is more complicated, as true diagnoses are omitted for a variety of reasons.

[2] This work assumes that variables are either discrete or have been binned so they relate to propositions that are true or false in order to represent the relationships using PCTL. In other work, I have extended PCTL to continuous variables with the logic PCTLc and developed methods for assessing the impact of causes on continuous-valued effects (Kleinberg, 2011).

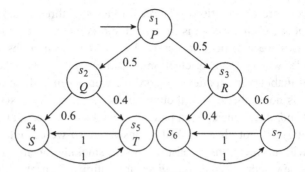

Figure 5.1. Example of a probabilistic structure that might be observed.

we will get closer to observing the actual transition probabilities so half the traces will begin with P, Q and the other half with P, R.

In practice many systems, such as biological systems, have cyclic patterns that will repeat over a long trace. While the true start state may only be observed once, other states and transitions will be repeated multiple times. In such a system, we can then infer properties from one long trace. However, when the system is nonrecurrent, inference may require a set of traces sampled from a population. If there are properties related to the initial states of the system and they do not occur again, they cannot be inferred from a single trace. When one has control over the data collected, it is worth noting the differences between the two types.

5.1.3. Intuition behind procedure

Before discussing how to test logical formulas in data, let us discuss an example that illustrates the general idea. Say we are testing $c \leadsto_{\geq p}^{\geq 1, \leq 2} e$ for some p and we observe the sequence c, a, cd, f, e, ac, eb. This can be represented as the following sequence of states and transitions:

Now we must determine whether the probability of the formula, given this observation, is at least p. Thus, the part of this sequence that we are interested in is:

Since the underlying structure is not known and will not be inferred here, (consider that for a set of 1,000 stocks that only go up or down, there are 2^{1000} possible unique states and there may be multiple states with the same labels), we view all instances of c as possibly leading to e, regardless of what the current underlying state is (there may be no path, or there could even be a deterministic path). At this point, any time where c is true seems identical. That means that the previous sequence looks like the following set of paths:

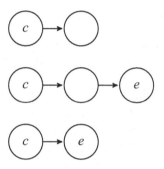

and would seem to be generated by the following (partial) structure:

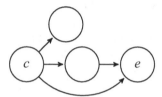

The probability of the leads-to formula being tested is the probability of the set of paths leading from c to e (within the specified time limit), which is defined by how frequently those paths from c are observed. Thus, with a trace of times labeled with c and e, and a formula $c \leadsto^{\geq 1, \leq 2} e$, the probability of this formula is the number of timepoints labeled with c, where e also holds in at least one and fewer than two time units, divided by the number of timepoints labeled with c. In this example, the probability is estimated to be $2/3$. The trace is then said to satisfy the formula $c \leadsto^{\geq 1, \leq 2}_{\geq p} e$ if $p \leq 2/3$.

Alternatively, one could begin by inferring a model. Then, satisfaction of formulas and algorithms for model checking are exactly that of Hansson and Jonsson (1994). However, model inference is a difficult task and may include development of phenomenological models and abstractions of the true structure. When inferring a model, there is again the problem of a nonrecurrent start state. The probabilities inferred will also not necessarily correspond to the true probabilities of the structure. Further, it is unknown whether, as the number of observations tends toward infinity, the inferred model approaches the true structure. Since we are generally interested in a set of properties that is small relative to the size of the underlying structure, we focus on inferring the correctness of those properties. In other cases, for a relatively small structure one may wish to begin by inferring a model.

5.1.4. Satisfaction of a formula

Testing the set of hypotheses for prima facie causality means testing whether (and with what probability), each relationship in a set of formulas is satisfied by the data, which may be either one long time series or a set of shorter ones. The approach to testing formulas in data developed in this book differs from others built on PCTL (Chan et al., 2005) as we must deal with 1) long traces that cannot be broken up into shorter traces based on knowledge of the start state (as it is not assumed that there is a model) and 2) short traces whose first observations vary and are not indicative of the start state. Thus, we cannot use the usual approach of computing the probability of a formula by finding the proportion of traces that satisfy it. Here frequencies refer to the number of timepoints where formulas hold, and for a set of traces, the frequencies are those in the combined set of timepoints.

For an introduction to the problem of runtime verification, see Leucker and Schallhart (2009).

The satisfaction and probability of PCTL formulas relative to a trace consisting of a sequence of ordered timepoints is as follows. Measurements may be made at every point in time, for some granularity of measurement, or there may be time indices of the measurements such that we can compute the temporal distance between pairs. Each timepoint has a set of propositions true at that timepoint. These may be events that either occur or do not, or whose truth value can otherwise be determined at every timepoint along the trace. As mentioned before, one may only observe positive instances and may have to determine whether not observing a value should be treated as it being false or as an instance where its truth cannot be determined. Each timepoint is initially labeled with the atomic propositions true at that time.[3] From these propositions, one can construct more complex state and path formulas, which describe properties true at a particular instant (a state) or for a sequence of times (a path). In the following, t denotes a time instant in

---

[3] In the event that a structure is given, this procedure is unnecessary and one may proceed with the algorithms of Hansson and Jonsson (1994), using the modified version of leads-to. Note that it is unlikely that we will begin with a structure, and attempting to infer one may introduce errors.

the observed trace. PCTL formulas are defined recursively, so I enumerate the types of formula constructions and how each are satisfied in a trace below.

1. Each atomic proposition is a state formula.

An atomic proposition is true at t if it is in $L(t)$ (the labels of t).

2. If g and h are state formulas, so are $\neg g$, $g \wedge h$, $g \vee h$, and $g \rightarrow h$.

If a timepoint t does not satisfy g, then $\neg g$ is true at t. If both g and h are true at t, then $g \wedge h$ is true at t. If g is true or h is true at t, then $g \vee h$ is true at t, and if $\neg g$ is true at t or h is true at t, then $g \rightarrow h$ is true at t.

3. If f and g are state formulas, and $0 \leq r \leq s \leq \infty$ with $r \neq \infty$, $f U^{\geq r, \leq s} g$ and $f W^{\geq r, \leq s} g$ are path formulas.

The "until" path formula $f U^{\geq r, \leq s} g$ is true for a sequence of times beginning at time t if there is a time i where $r \leq i \leq s$, such that g is true at $t + i$ and $\forall j : 0 \leq j < i$, f is true at $t + j$. The "unless" path formula $f W^{\geq r, \leq s} g$ is true for a sequence of times beginning at time t if either $f U^{\geq r, \leq s} g$ is true beginning at time t, or $\forall j : 0 \leq j \leq s$, f is true at $t + j$.

4. If f and g are state formulas, then $f \leadsto^{\geq r, \leq s} g$, where $0 \leq r \leq s \leq \infty$ and $r \neq \infty$ is a path formula.

Leads-to formulas must now be treated separately in order for their probabilities to be correctly calculated from data. Recall that leads-to was originally defined using $F^{\geq r, \leq s} e$, where the associated probability of the leads-to is that of the F ("finally") part of the formula. Thus, the calculated probability would be that of e occurring within the window $r-s$ after any timepoint, while we actually want the probability of e in the window $r-s$ after c. When checking formulas in a structure, there is no such difficulty, as the probabilities are calculated relative to particular states. However, when checking formulas in traces, we do not know which state a timepoint corresponds to and as a result can only calculate the probability relative to the trace. Thus, the formula $f \leadsto^{\geq r, \leq s} g$ is true for a sequence of times beginning at time t if f is true at t and there is a time i, where $r \leq i \leq s$, such that g is true at $t + i$. When $r = 0$, this reduces to the usual case of leads-to with no lower bound.

5. If f is a path formula and $0 \leq p \leq 1$, $[f]_{\geq p}$ and $[f]_{>p}$ are state formulas.

The probabilities here are in fact conditional probabilities. For $[fU^{\geq r, \leq s}g]_{\geq p}$ the probability p' associated with the data is estimated as the number of timepoints that begin paths satisfying $fU^{\geq r, \leq s}g$ divided by the number of timepoints labeled with $f \vee g$. The formula $[fU^{\geq r, \leq s}g]_{\geq p}$ is satisfied by the trace or set of traces if $p' \geq p$. For a W formula, the probability is estimated the same way as for the preceding case, except that we consider the timepoints beginning paths satisfying $fW^{\geq r, \leq s}g$ (which includes paths where f holds for s time units, without g later holding). For a leads-to formula, $h = f \leadsto^{\geq r, \leq s} g$, the probability is estimated as the number of timepoints that begin sequences of times labeled with h, divided by the number of timepoints labeled with f. Thus, the probability of $f \leadsto^{\geq r, \leq s} g$ is the probability, given that f is true, that g will be true in between r and s units of time.

Let us see that this formulation yields the desired result. Let $p = P(g_{t'}|f_t)$, where $t + r \leq t' \leq t + s$. Dropping the time subscripts for the moment, by definition:

$$P(g|f) = \frac{P(g \wedge f)}{P(f)}.$$

Since the probabilities come from frequencies of occurrence in the data, $P(x)$ for some formula x is the number of timepoints labeled with x divided by the total number of timepoints. Using #x to denote the number of timepoints with some label x, and T to denote the total number of timepoints, we find:

$$P(g|f) = \frac{\#(g \wedge f)/T}{\#f/T}$$

$$= \frac{\#(g \wedge f)}{\#f}.$$

The probability of such a formula is the number of states beginning paths satisfying the leads-to formula, divided by the number of states satisfying f.

Let us summarize the syntax and semantics of PCTL relative to traces using a minimal set of operators (all others can be defined in terms of these). With a set of boolean-valued atomic propositions $a \in A$,

PCTL trace syntax

State formulas:
$$\varphi ::= true \mid a \mid \neg\varphi \mid \varphi_1 \wedge \varphi_2 \mid [\psi]_{\geq p} \mid [\psi]_{>p}$$

Path formulas:
$$\psi ::= \varphi_1 U^{\geq r, \leq s}\varphi_2 \mid \varphi_1 \leadsto^{\geq r, \leq s} \varphi_2$$

where $0 \leq r \leq s \leq \infty, r \neq \infty$, and $0 \leq p \leq 1$. W can be defined in terms of U, and $\vee$ and $\rightarrow$ can also be derived from the operators above.

Now we can recap the semantics of PCTL. There is a labeling function $L(t)$ that maps timepoints to the atomic propositions true at them. We represent the satisfaction of formula f by a timepoint t in trace T as $t \models_T f$. We denote a path (sequence of timepoints) by π, and the subset of π beginning at time i by π^i. A particular time t_i in π is written as $\pi[i]$. Thus, we might have the sequence $\pi = a, ab, b, ac$, where $ab \in L(\pi[1])$. The probability of an until formula $\varphi_1 U^{\geq r, \leq s} \varphi_2$ is:

PCTL trace semantics

$$\frac{|\{t \in T : \pi^t \models_T \varphi_1 U^{\geq r, \leq s} \varphi_2\}|}{|\{t \in T : t \models_T \varphi_1 \vee \varphi_2\}|} \qquad (5.2)$$

and the probability of a leads-to formula $\varphi_1 \leadsto^{\geq r, \leq s} \varphi_2$ is:

$$\frac{|\{t \in T : \pi^t \models_T \varphi_1 \leadsto^{\geq r, \leq s} \varphi_2\}|}{|\{t \in T : t \models_T \varphi_1\}|} \qquad (5.3)$$

This gives the fraction of timepoints beginning paths satisfying the leads-to formula out of all of those satisfying φ_1.

The satisfaction relation $(\models_T)$ is then:[4]

$t \models_T true$	$\forall t \in T$
$t \models_T a$	if $a \in L(t)$
$t \models_T \neg\varphi$	if not $t \models_T \varphi$
$t \models_T \varphi_1 \wedge \varphi_2$	if $t \models_T \varphi_1$ and $t \models_T \varphi_2$
$\pi \models_T \varphi_1 U^{\geq r, \leq s} \varphi_2$	if there exists a $j \in [r, s]$ such that $\pi[j] \models_T \varphi_2$ and $\pi[i] \models_T \varphi_1, \forall i \in [0, j)$
$\pi \models_T \varphi_1 \leadsto^{\geq r, \leq s} \varphi_2$	if $\pi[0] \models_T \varphi_1$ and there exists a $j \in [r, s]$ such that $\pi[j] \models_T \varphi_2$
$T \models_T [\psi]_{\geq p}$	if the probability of ψ in T is $\geq p$
$T \models_T [\psi]_{> p}$	if the probability of ψ in T is $> p$

Prima facie causes are those in the set of hypotheses where the associated probability, calculated from the data using this approach, is greater than the probability of the effect alone (its marginal probability) and where the

---

[4] In some works, such as that of Hansson and Jonsson (1994), the satisfaction relation for paths is distinguished from that of states using a symbol with three horizontal lines rather than two (as in $\vDash$), but this is not universal and the symbol can be difficult to produce.

relationship satisfies our other conditions – that c has a nonzero probability and is prior to e.

5.2. Testing for Causal Significance

The previous chapter introduced ε_{avg}, a new measure for causal significance. This section describes how it can be calculated from data and discusses methods for determining which values are both causally – and statistically – significant. This measure tells us, on average, how much of a difference a cause makes to the probability of an effect holding fixed other possible explanations. It can be nonzero even in the absence of causal relationships, and in fact will be normally distributed in the absence of causal relationships when many hypotheses are tested. One must choose thresholds in all methods (such as with conditional independence tests), but in the interest of making this book self contained, one strategy for doing this in a statistically rigorous way is discussed (though there are multiple methods for doing this).

5.2.1. Computing ε_{avg}

Let us recall the definition for ε_{avg}. With X being the set of prima facie causes of e, we assess the impact of a particular c on a particular e using:

$$\varepsilon_{avg}(c, e) = \frac{\displaystyle\sum_{x \in X \setminus c} \varepsilon_x(c, e)}{|X \setminus c|}, \tag{5.4}$$

where:

$$\varepsilon_x(c, e) = P(e|c \wedge x) - P(e|\neg c \wedge x). \tag{5.5}$$

Here we are interested in c and x, where the relationships are represented by $c \leadsto^{\geq s, \leq t} e$ and $x \leadsto^{\geq s', \leq t'} e$. While the temporal subscripts have been omitted for ease, $c \wedge x$ refers to c and x being true such that e could be caused in the appropriate intervals. $P(e|c \wedge x)$ is defined as $P(e_A|c_B \wedge x_C)$ where this is the probability of e occurring at any such A where the time subscripts are not specific times but rather denote the constraints on their relationship. That is,

$$B + s \leq A \leq B + t, \text{ and}$$
$$C + s' \leq A \leq C + t'.$$

This probability is calculated with respect to a set of data (or, when given, a probabilistic structure) using the satisfaction rules described earlier for determining when c and e are true, and using the same approach for frequency-based probabilities calculated from data. If part of the observed sequence is c at time 0 and x at time 15, where $s = s' = 20$ and $t = t' = 40$, then e must occur in the overlap of these windows, shown in the following in solid gray.

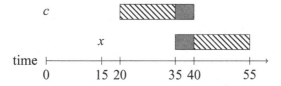

This will be considered an instance of $(c \wedge x) \rightsquigarrow e$ if there is an observation e_A such that: $20 \leq A \leq 40$ and $35 \leq A \leq 55$. If e were true at $A = 10$, then only c would have been true before e, while if e were true at $A = 50$, then c's time window to cause e would be over.

The probability calculation is exactly as described for leads-to formulas in the previous section. Dropping the time subscripts for the moment, we have:

$$P(e|c \wedge x) = \frac{\#(e \wedge c \wedge x)}{\#(c \wedge x)}, \tag{5.6}$$

and

$$P(e|\neg c \wedge x) = \frac{\#(e \wedge \neg c \wedge x)}{\#(\neg c \wedge x)}, \tag{5.7}$$

where these refer to the number of paths where e holds after $c \wedge x$ (or $\neg c \wedge x$) holds, in the appropriate time window, divided by the number of paths where $c \wedge x$ (or $\neg c \wedge x$) holds. These paths are subsequences of the traces (observations), and there may be multiple occurrences of $c \wedge x \wedge e$ in each trace.

There are a variety of methods that can be used to efficiently calculate this causal impact for a set of relationships. The calculation of each individual ε_{avg} is independent from all the other calculations, so this can be easily parallelized. Let us look at one straightforward method for calculating $\varepsilon_x(c, e)$ relative to a trace, T (shown in algorithm 5.1), where c and x have corresponding relationships $c \rightsquigarrow^{\geq r, \leq s} e$ and $x \rightsquigarrow^{\geq r', \leq s'} e$. Assume that all times satisfying c, x, and e are already labeled with these formulas. Then, $c \wedge x$ refers to c and x holding such that either could be a cause of x.

Algorithm 5.1 $\varepsilon_x(c, e)$

1. $c_T = \{t : c \in labels(t)\}$
   $x_T = \{t : x \in labels(t)\}$
   $e_T = \{t : e \in labels(t)\}$
2. $W = W' = \emptyset$
3. $E = E' = 0$
   {Get times satisfying $c \wedge x$}
4. **for all** $t \in c_T$ **do**
5.   **if** $\exists t' \in x_T : [t + r..t + s] \bigcap [t' + r'..t' + s'] \neq \emptyset$ **then**
6. $W = W \bigcup \{(t, t')\}$
7.   **end if**
8. **end for**
   {Get times satisfying $\neg c \wedge x$}
9. **for all** $t' \in x_T$ **do**
10.   **if** $\nexists t \in c_T : [t + r..t + s] \bigcap [t' + r'..t' + s'] \neq \emptyset$ **then**
11. $W' = W' \bigcup \{t'\}$
12.   **end if**
13. **end for**
    {Get times satisfying $c \wedge x \wedge e$}
14. **for all** $(t, t') \in W$ **do**
15.   **if** $\exists t'' \in e_T : t'' \in [t + r..t + s] \bigcap [t' + r'..t' + s']$ **then**
16. $E + +$
17.   **end if**
18. **end for**
    {Get times satisfying $\neg c \wedge x \wedge e$}
19. **for all** $t' \in W'$ **do**
20.   **if** $\exists t'' \in e_T : t'' \in [t' + r'..t' + s']$ **then**
21. $E' + +$
22.   **end if**
23. **end for**
24. **return** $\frac{E}{|W|} - \frac{E'}{|W'|}$

The primary task of the algorithm is to identify instances of $c \wedge x$ that fit these criteria, and then to identify instances of e that fall in the overlap of the time windows from these instances. Similarly, for $\neg c \wedge x$, we find instances of x where there is no overlapping window with an instance of c.

In summary, we begin with a set of prima facie causes (identified by generating or otherwise specifying some set of potential relationships and determining which of these satisfy the conditions for prima facie causality relative to the given data), and then compute the average causal significance for each of these, yielding a set of ε_{avg}'s.

5.2.2. Choice of ε

Once we have calculated the average causal significance for each relationship, we must determine a threshold at which a relationship is causally significant, in a statistically significant way. All methods require a choice of thresholds, such as determining when two variables should be considered conditionally independent (as one cannot expect to find exact independence), or whether including lagged values of one variable significantly improves prediction of another in the case of Granger causality. One could potentially determine appropriate thresholds through simulation (creating data with a structure similar to that of the real data of interest), or by examining the hypotheses manually. However, when testing many hypotheses simultaneously, we can use the properties of ε_{avg} to do this in a more rigorous way. In the absence of causal relationships, these values will be normally distributed, so we can use the large number of tests to our advantage by making one more assumption, that even if there are many genuine causes in the set tested, these are still relatively few compared with the total number of hypotheses tested. Then, we can treat the data as coming from a mixture of two distributions, one of the noncausal relationships (with normally distributed significance scores) and a smaller number of causal relationships with scores distributed according to some other function.

All thresholds have tradeoffs: if ε is too low, too many causes will be called significant (making false discoveries), while if ε is too high we will call too many causes insignificant (leading to false negatives). In this work, I have concentrated on controlling the first case, so that while some causes may be missed, we will be confident in those identified. The priorities of users may vary, though, and some may wish to focus on identifying the full set of causes (at the expense of some of those identified being spurious). Many statistical methods exist for both purposes. This work focuses on controlling the false discovery rate (FDR), which is the number of false discoveries as a proportion of all discoveries. Here the FDR is the fraction of non-causes called significant as a proportion of all causes deemed significant. The key point is that when doing many tests, it is likely that seemingly significant results will be observed by chance alone (just as when flipping a coin many times in a row, some long runs of heads or tails are to be expected). To control for this, we generally compute some statistic (such as a p-value) for each hypothesis, and compare these against the distribution expected under the null hypothesis (here that would be that a relationship is not causal). For a particular value of this statistic, we accept a hypothesis (rejecting the null hypothesis) if this value is significant when compared with the null hypothesis after accounting for the number of tests being conducted. To define the distribution of the null hypothesis, here we would need to know how the ε_{avg}'s would be distributed if there were no genuine causal relationships. One could assume that these would follow a normal distribution with mean zero and standard deviation one (as this is often the case), but as an alternative, methods using empirical nulls allow one to estimate the null directly from the data.

For a more technical introduction to multiple hypothesis testing and false discovery rate control, see appendix A. It is assumed that the reader is familiar with the goals and procedures of these methods, so only the empirical null is discussed in this section.

Calculating the fdr

We assume the results mostly fit a null model when there are no causal relationships (shown experimentally to be the case in chapter 7), with deviations from this distribution indicating true causal relationships. In some cases, the ε_{avg}'s follow a standard normal distribution, with the z-values calculated from these ε_{avg}'s having a mean of zero and a standard deviation of one. These ε_{avg}'s (even with no true causal relationships in the system) are not all equal to zero due to correlations from hidden common causes and other factors influencing the distributions, such as noise. The distribution of ε_{avg} tends toward a normal due to the large number of hypotheses tested.

When there are causal relationships in the system, then there are two classes of ε_{avg}'s: those corresponding to insignificant causes (which may be spurious or too small to detect) and those corresponding to significant causes (which may be genuine or just so causes), with the observed distribution being a mixture of these classes. Since the insignificant class is assumed to be much larger than the significant class, and normally distributed, we can identify significant causes by finding these deviations from the normal distribution. This can be observed for even a seemingly small number of variables, as when testing pairwise relationships between say 20 variables that are only true or false, that means 400 to 1600 hypotheses are being tested. Depending on how the statistical significance is evaluated and which thresholds are chosen, some of these insignificant causes may appear statistically significant. However, it is shown experimentally in chapter 7 that in datasets where there is no embedded causality, none is inferred using the approach developed in this book.

One method for accounting for the large number of tests is by using local false discovery rate (fdr) calculations. Instead of computing p-values for each test and then determining where in the tail the cutoff should be after correcting for the many tests conducted, as is done when controlling the false discovery rate (FDR), this method instead uses z-values and their densities to identify whether, for a particular value of z, the results are statistically significant after taking into account the many tests (Efron, 2004). When using tail-area false discovery rates (the rate when rejecting the null for all hypotheses with z greater than some threshold), the values close to the threshold do not actually have the same likelihood of being false discoveries as do those further out into the tail. Two methodological choices are discussed here: how to calculate the false discovery rate, and how to choose the null hypothesis. The local false discovery rate method can be used with an empirical null (inferred from the data) or standard theoretical null distribution. Similarly the method of finding the null from the data can also be used in conjunction with standard tail-area FDR (Efron, 2007).

When testing N causal relationships, each can be considered as a hypothesis test, where we can accept the null hypothesis, that the relationship is not causal, or can reject it. For each of the ε_{avg} values, we calculate its z-value (also called the standard score), which is the number of standard deviations a result is from the mean. The z-value for a particular ε_{avg} is defined as $z = (\varepsilon_{avg} - \mu)/\sigma$, where μ is the mean and σ the standard deviation of the set of ε_{avg} values. The N results correspond to two classes, those when the null hypothesis is true (there is no causal relationship) and those when it is false (and the relationship is causal). When using this method for determining which relationships are statistically significant, it is assumed that the proportion of non-null cases, which are referred to as significant (or "interesting") is small relative to N. A common assumption is that these are say 10% of N. This value is simply a convention and it is not required that this is the case. Even with a seemingly densely connected set of variables such as a gene network, this still may hold as with approximately 3,000 genes, we would be testing 3000^2 relationships, and ten percent of this is still 90,000 relationships. Then p_0 and p_1 are the prior probabilities of a case (here a causal hypothesis) being in the insignificant and significant classes respectively. These correspond to rejection of the null hypothesis with prior probabilities p_0 and $p_1 = 1 - p_0$. The probabilities are distributed according to density functions $f_0(z)$ and $f_1(z)$. When using the usual theoretical

See Efron (2010) for an in-depth introduction to large-scale testing.

null hypothesis, $f_0(z)$ is the standard $N(0, 1)$ density. We do not need to know $f_1(z)$ and because this class is much smaller than the null class, it will not perturb the observed mixture of the two distributions significantly. The observed z values are defined by the mixture of the null and non-null distributions:

$$f(z) = p_0 f_0(z) + p_1 f_1(z), \qquad (5.8)$$

and the posterior probability of a case being insignificant given its z-value, z, is

$$P(null|z) = p_0 f_0(z)/f(z). \qquad (5.9)$$

The *local false discovery rate* is:

$$fdr(z) \equiv f_0(z)/f(z). \qquad (5.10)$$

In this formulation by Efron (2004), the p_0 factor is not estimated, so this gives an upper bound on $fdr(z)$. Assuming that p_0 is large (close to 1), this simplification does not lead to massive overestimation of $fdr(z)$. One may instead choose to estimate p_0 and thus include it in the FDR calculation, making $fdr(z) = P(null|z)$. To estimate $f_0(z)$, most methods work by locating and fitting to the central peak of the data. Since it is assumed that the underlying distribution is normal, one need only find its mean and standard deviation (which amounts to finding the center of the peak and its width). To find $f(z)$, one may use a spline estimation method, fitting the results. The procedure after testing which relationships meet the criteria for prima facie causality and calculating their ε_{avg} values is then:

1. Calculate z-values from ε_{avg}.
2. Estimate $f(z)$ from the observed z-values.
3. Define the null density $f_0(z)$ from either the data or using the theoretical null.
4. Calculate $fdr(z)$ using equation (5.10).

For each prima facie cause where the z-value associated with its ε_{avg} has $fdr(z)$ less than a small threshold, such as 0.01, we label it as a just so, or significant, cause. With a threshold of 0.01, we expect 1% of such causes to be insignificant, despite their test scores, but now the threshold can be chosen based on how acceptable a false discovery is rather than an arbitrary value at which a relationship is significant.

5.3. Inference with Unknown Times

I have so far discussed how to find whether a relationship is causally significant, but this only involved accepting or rejecting this hypothesis for a relationship between two factors with a particular window of time between them. However, we will not usually know these timings prior to inference and want to ensure both that the correct timings will be found and that an incorrect initial choice will not lead to incorrect inferences. Instead of only accepting or rejecting hypotheses, we want to refine them. What is needed is a framework for automatically finding the timing of relationships as part of the inference process, unconstrained by the initial set of hypotheses tested. We want to potentially begin by searching for relationships between lab values changing 1–2 weeks before congestive heart failure and ultimately make inferences such as "extremely high AST predicts heart failure in 3–10 days." The goal is to make some initial suggestions of the general range of possible times, with the inference procedure taking this as a starting point, inferring the timing of relationships in a way that is not constrained by this initial proposal. The solution is that we can generate a set of candidate windows that cover the whole time series (with multiple observation sequences) or a section of it relating to the times of interest (maybe constrained by some background information on what relationships are possible) and alter these during the inference process to recover the actual windows.[5] We initially proceed as described in the previous section, finding the relationships that are significant within each candidate window. We then iterate over the significant relationships, perturbing the timing associated with each and attempting to maximize the associated significance scores. Iterating over only the significant relationships allows the procedure to remain computationally efficient and enables inference of temporal relationships without background knowledge. We first examine the intuition behind the method along with the primary assumptions made before discussing the algorithm. Its correctness and complexity are discussed in section 5.4.

5.3.1. Intuition and assumptions

Before examining the approach in depth, let us discuss some basic observations about ε_{avg}. If we can identify a significant relationship between

---

[5] With data from ICU patients who are monitored at the timescale of seconds, it is unlikely that one second of data is informative about another second a few weeks later, so it is likely not necessary to generate such hypotheses. One may also use windows that increase in size as temporal distance from the effect increases.

some c and e with a time window that intersects the correct one, this can be used to find the actual time window. There are three main ways a window can intersect the true one: (1) it can contain it, (2) it can be shifted (and contain at least half the window), or (3) it can be contained by the window. If there is a window overlapping less than half the true window, there must be an adjacent window that covers the rest or is fully contained in the true window.

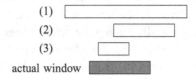

We use changes in ε_{avg} to assess new windows created by modifying the original one. The main operations are contracting, shifting, and expanding the window. Each of these will (barring issues such as missing data, discussed below) increase the ε_{avg} associated with the cases above respectively. Remember that ε_{avg} is defined by:

ε_{avg} is discussed in depth in section 4.2.2 and its calculation from data is discussed in section 5.2.1.

$$P(e|c \wedge x) - P(e|\neg c \wedge x) \qquad (5.11)$$

averaged over all of the x's in X (the set of prima facie causes of e). However, there are time windows associated with the relationships and as noted before, instances of $c \wedge x$ are those where c and x occur such that their windows overlap and either could cause e. Then, $c \wedge x \wedge e$ is when e occurs in that time window. So if we have the following case, where $[r, s]$ is wider than the true window (shown in solid grey):

then we are considering too many cases as being $c \wedge x$. We should only consider instances where c occurs and e follows in the grey window (and this overlaps the window for x), but instead this overly wide window considers more occurrences of c and x (where e is unlikely to occur) as being instances of this relationship. Since e will not occur, this increases the denominator of $P(e|c \wedge x)$, which is defined as $\#(c \wedge x \wedge e)/\#(c \wedge x)$, with no corresponding increase in the numerator, lowering this value and decreasing the difference. If the window's width is correct but its start and end points are shifted, then we exclude the same number of correct times as we include incorrect times. Finally, when the window is too narrow, we make the mistake of characterizing instances of $c \wedge x$ as instances of $\neg c \wedge x$. Both overly small and large windows will reduce the value of ε_{avg} for a significant relationship. This is why the windows do not simply expand without bound. If one instead tried to maximize the conditional probability $P(e|c)$, then the probability would continue to increase as the window size increased and there would be no reason for it to contract. By evaluating the relationships using the average difference in conditional probability, an overly large window reduces the value of this difference by providing more chances for a cause to be spurious.[6]

Now let us look at the assumptions that this rests on.

Assumption 1. A significant relationship with associated time window $w = [ws, we]$ will be found to be significant in at least one time window that intersects w.

We assume that relationships will be identified during the initial testing across many windows. This depends primarily on the windows being at a similar timescale as the true relationships (not orders of magnitude wider) and the observations of the system being representative of the true distribution (not systematically missing). Note that it is not necessary for a cause to raise the probability of its effect uniformly through the time window though.[7] In some cases the probability may be raised uniformly throughout the window, while in other cases the distribution may look Gaussian, with the probability being significantly increased near a central peak, and less so by the ends of the time period. This is not an impediment to inference, assuming we sample frequently enough from the peak. If the windows are orders of magnitude wider though, the relationship will be so diluted that we cannot expect to identify it. If the observations are systematically missing

---

[6] A similar method could also be applied to discretization of continuous-valued variables such as lab measurements, by allowing us to propose an initial range based on standardly used normal values and refine this after inference. For example, we may have some initial idea of how to partition values of glucose based on prior knowledge about usual low/normal/high ranges, but we may not know that for a particular result a value ≥ 140 is required, even though in general a value above 120 is considered high. Relationships would be represented using a logic that allows expression of constraints on continuous-valued variables (Kleinberg, 2011). Instead of discretizing the variables prior to inference, constraints on their values would be included as part of the logical formulas representing relationships. For example, we may have:

$$[(c \geq v) \wedge (c \leq w)] \rightsquigarrow^{\geq r, \leq s} e. \qquad (5.12)$$

Then, v and w would be altered in each step instead of r and s.

[7] For example, a cause c may raise the probability of an effect e at every time in 8–14 days (i.e., at each time in this window $P(e|c) > P(e)$). However, if the cause perhaps acts through two different mechanisms, there could be peaks around 10 and 12 days so that $P(e|c_{10}) > P(e|c_9) > P(e)$, for example. The probability is raised at each time, but the increase is larger at particular times.

or nonuniform, and the probability is non-uniform, we may also be unable to identify the true relationships.

While this approach may seem similar to that of dynamic Bayesian networks (DBNs), there are some fundamental differences. With DBNs a user proposes a range of times to search over, and then relationships are found between pairs of variables at each of the lags in that set of times. This assumes that if one searches over the range $[2, 20]$ and one of the relationships is a causes b in 3–8 time lags, we will find edges between a at time t and b at times $t + 3, t + 4, \ldots, t + 8$. This is unlikely given the noisiness and sparseness of actual data and computational issues (since the full set of graphs is not explored) and one may only infer that a leads to b in 3, 6, and 7 time units. The key distinction is that DBNs assume that an edge between a and b will be inferred for every time in the actual window, while we assume only that we will find a relationship between a and b in at least one time range intersecting the true window (and from that time range can find the true window).

We make one more assumption that pertains primarily to cases of large-scale testing, when a significant number of hypotheses are explored. If the overall set is not so large, this is not needed.

Assumption 2. The significant relationships are a small proportion of the overall set tested.

This assumption is for the sake of computational feasibility. Since we are only refining the relationships found to be ε-significant, the procedure is done on a much smaller group of relationships than the full set tested, which we assume is quite large. If we can identify significant relationships in at least one window that intersects their true timing, and this set of significant relationships is not enormous, then we can limit the number of hypotheses that need to be refined. If instead we conducted the iterative procedure on the full set of hypotheses tested (significant and insignificant) it would be quite computationally intensive.

5.3.2. Algorithms

Let us now look at the details of the algorithms for inferring the timing of relationships without prior knowledge. For each significant relationship, we iteratively reevaluate its ε_{avg} with a new set of windows created by expanding, shrinking, and shifting the current window. At each step, the maximum value of ε_{avg} is compared against the previous value. If the score improves, the highest scoring window is the new starting point and iteration continues. Otherwise, if there is no improvement in the score or no further steps are possible (the window's lower bound must be no less than one, and the upper bound cannot be greater than the length of the time series), the current window is returned.

Where $1 \leq ws \leq we \leq T$, $we_i = ws_{i+1}$, and T is the length of the time series, the procedure is as follows.

1. $W \leftarrow [[ws_1, we_1], [ws_2, we_2] \ldots [ws_n, we_n]]$.
    $A \leftarrow$ set of atomic propositions or formulas.
2. Generate hypotheses $c \leadsto^{\geq ws, \leq we} e$ for each pair $c, e \in A$ and $[ws, we] \in W$.
3. For each $[ws, we] \in W$, test associated hypotheses finding those that are ε-significant.
4. For each ε-significant relationship, $c \leadsto^{\geq ws, \leq we} e$.

$$(c, e, ws, we) \leftarrow \text{refine-}\varepsilon(c, e, ws, we).$$

5. Where S_w is the set of all ε-significant relationships in $w \in W$, and $S = S_{w1} \bigcup S_{w2} \bigcup \ldots \bigcup S_{wn}$, recompute ε_{avg} for all hypotheses with $X = X \bigcup S$.
6. Reassess statistical significance of all hypotheses using the newly calculated ε_{avg}.

Steps 1–3 are as described before, with the only difference being that this is repeated for a set of adjacent windows and the significance of relationships within each window is evaluated separately.

In step 4, we iterate over the candidate windows ($w \in W$) and the relationships found to be significant. We perturb and refine the window associated with each relationship using the refine-ε procedure of algorithm 5.2 until no alterations improve the associated ε_{avg} for the relationship. Note that the significant relationships are assumed to be a small fraction (usually around 1%) of the set tested, so this is done on a much smaller set of relationships than for the initial testing. For each relationship, using algorithm 5.2 we repeatedly recompute the significance the cause makes to its effect as we explore new potential timings (expanding, shrinking, or shifting the initially proposed window). This algorithm expands each window by half (evenly on each side), splits evenly down the middle, and shifts by one time unit left and right. This is a heuristic and many others may be investigated for efficiently exploring the search space. With sufficient computing power one may choose to expand/contract by one time unit on each end of

---

Algorithm 5.2 refine-$\varepsilon(c, e, ws, we)$

---

1. $\varepsilon_{new} \leftarrow \varepsilon_{avg}(c, e, ws, we)$
2. **repeat**
3. $t \leftarrow we - ws$
4. $\varepsilon_{max} \leftarrow \varepsilon_{new}$
5. $\varepsilon_{new} =$

$$max \begin{cases} \varepsilon_{avg}(c, e, (ws - \lfloor t/4 \rfloor), (we + \lceil t/4 \rceil)) \\ \varepsilon_{avg}(c, e, ws, (ws + \lfloor t/2 \rfloor)) \\ \varepsilon_{avg}(c, e, (ws + \lfloor t/2 \rfloor), we) \\ \varepsilon_{avg}(c, e, (ws - 1), (we - 1)) \\ \varepsilon_{avg}(c, e, (ws + 1), (we + 1)) \end{cases}$$

6.   Update ws, we with values from new max
7. **until** $\varepsilon_{new} \leq \varepsilon_{max}$
8. **return** (c, e, ws, we)

---

the candidate window (in separate steps). This is still not intractable if one caches results intelligently. While in theory this procedure has the same worst case behavior as the heuristic proposed, in practice the heuristic will converge more quickly, though it may only approach the fixpoint. However, in many cases variables are not sampled at every time unit or at a scale representative of the true timing, and measurements may be sparse. Thus, an approach that makes smaller steps can get stuck in local maxima in these cases and the heuristic is more suitable.

Finally, in step 5, the significance scores are recalculated in light of the inferred relationships. Remember that the significance is the average difference a cause makes to its effect holding fixed (pairwise) all other causes of the effect. This final step was not necessary before since the background was unchanged – some things compared against may turn out to be spurious, but a single set of relationships would be tested and thus each cause would have been compared against each other thing that could have made it spurious. Now we test relationships separately, so that if A causes B and B causes C (both in 20–40 time units), and we use windows 20–40 and 40–60, A may seem to cause C when looking at the later window alone since the relationship between B and C is not fully taken into account. Thus, we now ensure that B will be included in the background when assessing A's significance during the final recalculation of ε_{avg}. This step also allows us to identify repeated observations of cycles as such.

5.4. Correctness and Complexity

This section shows that the procedures for verifying formulas over traces and inferring the timing of relationships are correct and analyzes their computational complexity.

5.4.1. Correctness

The correctness of methods for labeling timepoints with non-probabilistic state formulas is trivial, so this section focuses on path formulas, state formulas formed by adding probability constraints to path formulas, and methods for inferring the timing of relationships.

Correctness of procedure for checking until formulas in traces

Theorem 5.4.1. *The satisfaction by a path beginning at timepoint t of the until formula $fU^{\geq r, \leq s}g$, where $0 \leq r \leq s < \infty$ is given by:*

$$
sat_U(t, r, s) = \begin{cases} true & \text{if } (g \in labels(t)) \\ & \land (r \leq 0), \\ false & \text{if } (f \notin labels(t)) \\ & \lor (t = |T|) \\ & \lor (s = 0), \\ sat_U(t+1, r-1, s-1) & \text{otherwise.} \end{cases} \tag{5.13}
$$

Proof. Assume trace T, where times $t \in T$ satisfying f and satisfying g have been labeled. Then, it can be shown by induction that any time t will be correctly labeled by equation 5.13. By definition, a timepoint t begins a sequence of times satisfying $fU^{\geq r, \leq s}g$ if there is some $r \leq i \leq s$ such that g is true at $t + i$ and $\forall j : 0 \leq j < i$, f is true at $t + j$.

Base cases:

$$
sat_U(t, r, 0) = \begin{cases} true & \text{if } g \in labels(t), \\ false & \text{otherwise.} \end{cases} \tag{5.14}
$$

$$
sat_U(|T|, r, s) = \begin{cases} true & \text{if } (g \in labels(|T|)) \land (r \leq 0), \\ false & \text{otherwise.} \end{cases} \tag{5.15}
$$

In the first base case, since we have already stipulated that $r \leq s$, we know that if $s = 0, r \leq 0$. However, in the second base case we must add the condition on r, to ensure it is less than or equal to zero. If $s = 0$, the only way the formula can be satisfied is if t is labeled with g. Similarly, if $t = |T|$, then this is the last timepoint in the trace and t can only satisfy the formula if it is labeled with g.

Inductive step: Assume we have $sat_U(n, r, s)$. Then, for $s > 0$ and $n + 1 \neq |T|$:

$$sat_U(n - 1, r + 1, s + 1) = \begin{cases} true & \text{if } (g \in labels(n - 1)) \\ & \quad \wedge (r \leq 0), \\ false & \text{if } f \notin labels(n - 1), \\ sat_U(n, r, s) & \text{otherwise.} \end{cases}$$

$$(5.16)$$

Timepoint $n - 1$ satisfies the formula if it satisfies g or if it satisfies f and the next timepoint, n, satisfies the formula. However, we assumed that we can correctly label timepoints with f and g as well as $sat(n, r, s)$. □

Corollary. *The satisfaction by a sequence of times beginning at timepoint t of the until formula $f U^{\geq r, \leq \infty} g$ where $r \neq \infty$ is given by $sat_U(t, r, |T|)$.*

Corollary. *The probability of the formula $f U^{\geq r, \leq s} g$, in a trace of times T, where $0 \leq r \leq s \leq \infty$ and $r \neq \infty$ is given by:*

$$\frac{|\{t \in T : sat_U(t, r, s)\}|}{|\{t' \in T : (f \vee g) \in labels(t')\}|}. \qquad (5.17)$$

Correctness of procedure for checking unless formulas in traces

Claim. *The satisfaction by a timepoint t of the unless formula $f W^{\geq r, \leq s} g$, where $0 \leq r \leq s < \infty$ is given by:*

$$sat_W(t, r, s) = \begin{cases} true & \text{if } (g \in labels(t) \wedge r \leq 0) \\ & \quad \vee (f \in labels(t) \wedge s = 0), \\ false & \text{if } (f \notin labels(t)) \\ & \quad \vee (t = |T|) \\ & \quad \vee (s = 0), \\ sat_W(t + 1, r - 1, s - 1) & \text{otherwise.} \end{cases}$$

$$(5.18)$$

Proof. Assume trace T, where times $t \in T$ satisfying f and satisfying g have been labeled. Then, we will show by induction that any time t will be correctly labeled by equation (5.18). By definition, a timepoint t begins a path satisfying $f W^{\geq r, \leq s} g$ if there is some $r \leq i \leq s$ such that g is true at $t + i$ and $\forall j : 0 \leq j < i$, f is true at $t + j$, or if $\forall j : 0 \leq j \leq s$, f is true at $t + j$.

Base case:

$$sat_W(t, r, 0) = \begin{cases} true & \text{if } (g \in labels(t)) \\ & \vee (f \in labels(t)), \\ false & \text{otherwise.} \end{cases} \quad (5.19)$$

$$sat_W(|T|, r, s) = \begin{cases} true & \text{if } (g \in labels(|T|) \wedge r \leq 0) \\ & \vee (f \in labels(|T|) \wedge s = 0), \\ false & \text{otherwise.} \end{cases} \quad (5.20)$$

If $s = 0$, the only way the formula can be satisfied is if t is labeled with either f or g. Similarly, if $t = |T|$, then this is the last timepoint in the trace and t can only satisfy the formula if it is labeled with f or g in the appropriate time window.

Inductive step: Assume we have $sat_W(n, r, s)$. Then, for $s > 0$ and $n + 1 \neq |T|$:

$$sat_W(n - 1, r + 1, s + 1) = \begin{cases} true & \text{if } (g \in labels(n - 1)) \\ & \wedge (r \leq 0), \\ false & \text{if } f \notin labels(n - 1), \\ sat_W(n, r, s) & \text{otherwise.} \end{cases} \quad (5.21)$$

Timepoint $n - 1$ satisfies the formula if it satisfies g or if it satisfies f and the next timepoint, n, satisfies the formula. Note that we assume $s > 0$ and thus the formula cannot be satisfied by only f being true. However, we assumed that we can correctly label timepoints with f and g as well as $sat(n, r, s)$. □

Corollary. *The satisfaction by a path beginning at timepoint t of the unless formula $f W^{\geq r, \leq \infty} g$ where $r \neq \infty$ is given by $sat_W(t, r, |T|)$.*

Corollary. *The probability of the formula $f W^{\geq r, \leq s} g$, in a trace of times T, where $0 \leq r \leq s \leq \infty$ and $r \neq \infty$ is given by:*

$$\frac{|\{t \in T : sat_W(t, r, s)\}|}{|\{t' \in T : (f \vee g) \in labels(t')\}|}. \tag{5.22}$$

Correctness of procedure for checking leads-to formulas in traces

Claim. *The satisfaction by a path beginning at timepoint t of the leads-to formula $f \leadsto^{\geq r, \leq s} g$ is given by:*

$$sat_L(t, r, s) = \begin{cases} true & \text{if } f \in labels(t) \\ & \quad \wedge (trueU^{\geq t+r, \leq t+s} g) \in labels(t), \\ false & \text{otherwise.} \end{cases} \tag{5.23}$$

Proof. Assume that there is a trace T, where times $t \in T$ satisfying f and satisfying g have been labeled. We have already shown that we can correctly label times that begin sequences where until formula are true, and thus we can correctly label whether a state t satisfies $trueU^{\geq t+r, \leq t+s} g$. We have also assumed that states satisfying f are already correctly labeled with f and that we can label timepoints with conjunctions, so we can label states with the conjunction of these formulas. By definition of leads-to – that g holds in the window $[r, s]$ after f – we can correctly label times with such formulas. □

Corollary. *The satisfaction by a path beginning at timepoint t of the leads-to formula $f \leadsto^{\geq r, \leq \infty} g$ or $f \leadsto^{\geq r, <\infty} g$, where $r \neq \infty$ is given by $sat_L(t, r, |T|)$.*

Corollary. *The probability of the formula $f \leadsto^{\geq r, \leq s} g$, in a trace of times T, where $0 \leq r \leq s \leq \infty$, where $r \neq \infty$ is given by:*

$$\frac{|\{t \in T : sat_L(t, r, s)\}|}{|\{t' \in T : f \in labels(t')\}|}. \tag{5.24}$$

This case is similar to the until and unless case, with the exception that the denominator consists of the set of states satisfying f, instead of $f \vee g$, since the probability is interpreted as being the conditional probability of g in the window r–s after f.

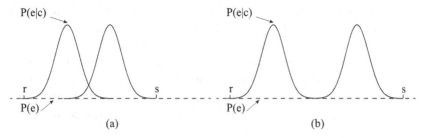

Figure 5.2. Varying distributions of the probability of an effect, *e*, given a cause, *c*.

Correctness of procedure for inferring time windows

I now discuss why the procedure for inferring the time windows associated with relationships will converge toward the true times. Note that the false discoveries are unchanged from the case when the timings are known, since these are primarily due to chance, or unmeasured common causes, so we focus on showing that the algorithm converges toward the actual timing. Assumption 1 states that a significant relationship will be found to be significant in at least one window intersecting the true window. Implicit is the assumption that if cause leads to effect at two disjoint timescales the window does not overlap both. Note, however, that this is an unlikely case and that a case where the probability of the effect is increased in a bimodal manner after the cause (where there are two peaks and a dip in between that is still greater than the marginal probability of the effect) can be handled by the approach without issue. The approach will not fit to only one peak, as doing so would significantly decrease the value of ε_{avg} (as there would be many seeming cases of $\neg c \wedge x$ leading to *e*). The only difficult case is where there are two disconnected time windows, where at some point in between the probability is less than or equal to the marginal probability of the effect. These two cases can be illustrated as shown in figure 5.2. When the testing uses small windows we may be able to find each window individually while a large initial window may lump both time periods together. However, it is unlikely that such a case can occur without there being another factor that determines the timing (for example a cause may operate through different mechanisms). Some scenarios such as repeated observations of a cycle may appear to have this structure, though they do not and can be correctly handled by the approach. Finally, this method converges to the most causally significant timing given the data, that is the timing with the most evidence in the data. Due to the granularity of measurement and the nature of the relationship, some cases may have a sharp transition between when it holds and when it does not (such as the efficacy of an emergency contraceptive). In other more challenging cases, we are still able to find the relative timescale of the relationship but the window boundaries may be less exact. While smoking may have the capacity to be carcinogenic immediately, the usual timing is likely much longer and we will be able to infer this from the data, determining the significance of various possible timings. This information is important when planning interventions and developing methods for verifying hypotheses experimentally. The next chapter discusses how to use these relationships to explain particular (token) occurrences, and does so in a way that allows uncertainty about timing information. This is partly because inferring a particular timing does not imply that it is impossible for the relationship to occur outside of this.

We now show that if assumption 1 is met, we can find the true timing of the relationship. As noted, the algorithm described earlier in this chapter is a heuristic that approaches the exhaustive procedure. We show the correctness of that method and then show experimentally in chapter 7 that the heuristic described here behaves similarly (though this is one of many possible approaches and future work should involve investigating other strategies).

Claim. *Where refine-ε defines ε_{new} as in (5.25), the true relationship is $c \rightsquigarrow^{\geq ws, \leq we} e$, and $[r, s] \cap [ws, we] \neq \emptyset$, the function refine-$\varepsilon(c, e, r, s)$, converges to (c, e, ws, we).*

$$
\varepsilon_{new} = max \begin{cases} \varepsilon_{avg}(c, e, (r+1), s) \\ \varepsilon_{avg}(c, e, (r-1), s) \\ \varepsilon_{avg}(c, e, r, (s+1)) \\ \varepsilon_{avg}(c, e, r, (s-1)) \end{cases}
\tag{5.25}
$$

Proof. We begin by showing that $[ws, we]$ is a fixpoint of the algorithm. Once the function reaches the window $[ws, we]$, no changes can increase ε_{avg} and thus refine-$\varepsilon(c, e, ws, we) = (c, e, ws, we)$. Implicit is the assumption that the relationships are stationary (in that their timing does not change during the observation period) and that the time series is ergodic.

At each timepoint ε_{avg} is recalculated with each of $r \pm 1$ and $s \pm 1$. If $r = ws$, lowering it adds incorrect instances of c when calculating $P(e|c \wedge x)$, lowering this value (which is defined as $\#(c \wedge x \wedge e)/\#(c \wedge x)$). This is because it is assumed that more instances of c will lead to e, but being outside the timing that will not happen, increasing the denominator with no corresponding increase in the numerator. Further, this removes cases of $\neg c$ that would not have led to e from the right side of the difference, increasing that value (and further reducing the difference). Similarly, increasing r shifts instances of $c \wedge x$ that result in e to being cases of $\neg c \wedge x$, decreasing the probability difference. The case is exactly the same for the endpoint $s = ws$. Thus, since iterations only continue while perturbing the windows results in an increase in ε_{avg} and no modifications can increase this value for $[r, s] = [ws, we]$, refine-$\varepsilon(c, e, ws, we) = (c, e, ws, we)$, and it is a fixpoint of this function.

Next, it is necessary to show that this is in fact the only fixpoint for (c, e, r, s). Assume that there are two fixpoints, (c, e, ws, we) and (c, e, ws', we'), where $[ws, we] \neq [ws', we']$. As previously assumed, there is a significant relationship between c and e and both windows intersect $[ws, we]$. If $[ws', we']$ is a fixpoint, it means the associated ε_{avg} can no longer be improved. However, if $ws > ws'$ then we can increase ε_{avg} by increasing ws', since ws is the actual time and if $ws > ws'$ instances of $\neg c \wedge x$ are misclassified as $c \wedge x$. If $ws' > ws$ then ε_{avg} can be increased by decreasing ws', since we are missing positive instances of c, which instead look like cases of e occurring with $\neg c$. The argument where we differs from we' is identical. Thus, since the ε_{avg} associated with (c, e, ws', we') can be improved, the algorithm will continue to iterate and this is not a fixpoint. Then the only fixpoint for (c, e, r, s) is (c, e, ws, we). □

5.4.2. Complexity

We now analyze the time complexity for each of the algorithms and procedures discussed. Note that each procedure (aside from the model checking ones) assumes that all timepoints have already been labeled with the formulas of interest. The complexity of that task is not included in that of the other procedures since it is assumed that this is performed once, with the results saved for use in the later tasks.

Complexity of model checking over traces

The complexity of labeling times along a trace, T, with a proposition is proportional to the length of the time series, which is also denoted by T, making this $O(T)$. Assuming states are labeled with f and g, labeling the sequence with each of $\neg f$, $f \vee g$, $f \wedge g$, and $f \rightarrow g$ is also of time complexity $O(T)$.

Next, we have until, unless, and leads-to path formulas, and finally the calculation of the probabilities of these formulas. For an until or unless formula, such as $fU^{\geq r, \leq s}g$, the worst case for a single timepoint is when $r = 0$ and involves checking the subsequent s timepoints. For $s \neq \infty$, the worst case complexity for the entire sequence is $O(Ts)$, while for $s = \infty$, it is $O(T^2)$. However, these formulas naively assume all timepoints are labeled with f and thus all $t \in T$ are candidates for starting such a path. Instead of T, the formulas should use T', the number of states labeled with f (which may be significantly fewer than the total number of timepoints). For a leads-to formula, $f \leadsto^{\geq r, \leq s} g$, the complexity for labeling a single timepoint is $O(|s - r|)$, where $s \neq \infty$. Where $s = \infty$, this is $O(T)$. As for the until/unless case, assuming all timepoints are labeled with f, then the complexity for a trace is $O(T \times |s - r|)$ or $O(T^2)$, though in practice most times will not be labeled with f and thus these will be significantly reduced.

Once states have been labeled as the start of path formulas or with the appropriate state formulas, calculating the probability of a state formula is $O(T)$.

For any formula f, the worst case complexity of testing f in a trace T, assuming that the subformulas of f have not already been tested, is thus $O(|f| \times T^2)$, where $|f|$ is the length of the formula and T is the length of the trace.

Complexity of testing prima facie causality

For a single relationship, $f \leadsto^{\geq r \leq s} g$, again assuming times satisfying f and g are labeled as such, we simply calculate the probability of this formula along the trace ($O(T)$) and compare this with the probability of $F^{\leq \infty}g$ (also $O(T)$). Thus, for M relationships the complexity is $O(MT)$. With N possible causes of N effects, this is $O(N^2 T)$.

Complexity of computing ε_{avg}

Assuming timepoints are already labeled with c, e, and x, the computation of $\varepsilon_x(c, e)$ has complexity $O(T)$. Thus, in the worst case, computation of one $\varepsilon_{avg}(c, e)$ is $O(NT)$, where there are N causes and all N causes are prima facie causes of an effect e. To compute the significance for each cause of e this is repeated N times so the complexity is $O(N^2 T)$. Finally, repeating this for all M effects, the complexity is $O(MN^2 T)$. In the case where the causes and effects are the same (say when testing relationships between pairs of genes), then $N = M$ and the worst case complexity is $O(N^3 T)$.

Complexity of inferring time windows

Calculating ε_{avg} for a single cause of an effect e with a single associated time window is $O(NT)$ where T is the length of the time series and N, the number of variables, is an upper bound on the number of potential causes of e. At each iteration, we recompute ε_{avg} a fixed number of times, and there are at most T iterations. In each of the W windows there are at most N effects with M significant causes of each. The worst case for the whole procedure is $O(WMN^2T^2)$. Note that M is assumed to be a small fraction of N ($\sim 1\%$) and W is generally much smaller than N, so the main component is N^2T^2. One factor of T is an upper bound on the number of iterations, so in practice this is significantly lower (as shown in the experimental section). Recall that the complexity of the initial testing procedure where windows are known is $O(N^3T)$, so the refinement procedure is comparable and usually much faster. This is shown experimentally in chapter 7.

6

Token Causality

Why did Alice develop heart disease in her fifties? What led to the volatility in the U.S. stock market in August 2011? Who shot John F. Kennedy? The inference method described so far aims to find causal relationships that hold in general, while these questions seek causal explanations for one-time events. We do not want to know what causes heart disease, stock market crashes, or death by shooting in general but rather aim to determine why each of these particular events happened. This is a challenging problem, as we need to make such determinations with incomplete and often conflicting information. Few algorithmic methods have been developed to automate this process, yet this may have wide applications to situations with continuous monitoring, such as in intensive care units. Physicians there are overwhelmed with information and need to distinguish between factors causing a particular patient's current symptoms and side effects of their underlying illness to determine the best course of treatment.

This chapter begins in section 6.1 with a discussion of the distinction between type and token causality, and review of methods for token-level reasoning. In section 6.2, I introduce a new approach that links the type-level theory developed in earlier chapters with token-level observation sequences and develops methods for ranking explanations with incomplete and uncertain information. Finally, this is illustrated through worked out examples in section 6.3 and analysis of test cases that have proven difficult for prior approaches in section 6.4.

6.1. Introduction to Token Causality

6.1.1. What is token causality?

So far I have discussed a method for inferring type-level (general) causal relationships, but in many cases we aim to find the cause not of a kind of event, but of a particular event occurring at a specific point in time and space.[1] When we are assigning credit or blame (such as determining who contributed to a company's profits or caused a car accident), the goal is to explain an occurrence by enumerating its causes (and potentially also their relative contributions). The connection between these two types of relationships is not fully understood, but type-level relationships relate to general, statistical, properties that may be learned from repeated observations of a system. Such relationships allow us to make future predictions of the occurrence of the effect after the cause has occurred. Token-level causes instead relate to single events and help to explain the occurrence of something that has already happened. This is the difference between finding that mass protests lead to political regime change, and finding that the political protests in Libya in 2011 led to the Libyan uprising and regime change. In short, token-level causality relates to the question of "why" on a particular occasion and type-level causality relates to the question of "why" in general.

Here we aim to explain an event's occurrence, but one may also explain the connection between processes (elucidating how they are connected).

6.1.2. Why do we need a notion of token causality?

One may wonder whether we need a second notion of causality to solve these sorts of problems. When we want to find out who caused a car accident, why a house caught on fire, or what made a person ill, knowing the type-level causes of accidents, fires, and illnesses may give us some hypotheses, but these relationships alone are not enough to determine the token-level causes. At first glance, it may seem that a type-level cause can explain these observances, but while a type-level cause can indicate that a token-level case is likely to have a particular cause, it does not necessitate this. Further, a token-level case may correspond to multiple type-level relationships. Bob's death may be a token of "death," "death caused by cancer," "death caused by prostate cancer," "death of a 77-year-old man," and so on.

Using diagnosis as an example, if a doctor suspects that a patient has a particular illness, she may try to show how the patient's history and symptoms fit with the known course of the suspected illness and would come up with this potential diagnosis in the first place by observing the similarity of a patient's case to the known disease. When a patient arrives

---

[1] The definition of an "event" is ambiguous as it is unclear at what point something goes from being a single event to being a sequence of events. For the moment we will stick to extreme cases, where the distinction is clear. However, it is not assumed that an event is instantaneous in time. While an effect could be instantaneous, I consider the token-level event to include the actual occurrence of both the cause and the effect. Thus, since a cause here precedes its effect in time, the entire event must have a non-trivial duration.

with a cough, his doctor's initial hypothesis may be that he has the common cold. However, more information can be gleaned through medical tests and a review of his prior medical history. Thus, after finding out that the patient also has fever, shortness of breath, and chest pain, the doctor may update her original hypothesis and order a chest x-ray to confirm the diagnosis of pneumonia. While the type-level relationships provide initial hypotheses, they are confirmed or rejected based on the token-level information.

Conflating this correlation between type and token levels with the necessity of a token relationship following from a type-level one is akin to conflating causation and correlation. An extreme example of this is choosing a treatment based entirely on the population-level causes of a patient's symptoms. Type-level relationships would give causes of say, headaches and fatigue, and treatment for these would be based on what has proven effective over the entire population. Each individual's treatment would be based not on their actual disease (which may be a subtype that requires a different treatment), but on what worked in the population. A patient with chronic fatigue syndrome may then be treated for depression as this is likely a more common explanation for the same symptoms. The difference between this and making a best guess based on treatments that are frequently effective in the population is whether other information is being ignored. We may have hypotheses based on known type-level relationships but we must be willing to abandon these in the face of evidence against them. Thus, what is needed is a way of reasoning about single cases that takes this into account, allowing us to use knowledge gleaned from type-level relationships while allowing that the sequence of events may be entirely different in token cases.

Discrepancies between inferred type-level causes and token cases arise in two primary scenarios. First, if the sample from which the type-level relationships are inferred differs from that of the token case, the cause in that single case may also differ. Without background knowledge or the ability to experiment on the system, we may not be able to identify such a discrepancy. Say we learn that smoking causes lung cancer within 10 to 20 years, and then have a patient who smoked and developed lung cancer in 13 years. However, the patient also happens to have a genetic mutation such that smoking lowers his risk of lung cancer and, in fact, it was his exposure to radon during his career as an experimental physicist that caused his lung cancer.[2] In this case, without further knowledge of the connection between lung cancer and radon exposure, the likely token-level explanation

---

[2] This is also an example of the mechanism connecting cause and effect failing. Here smoking was prevented from causing cancer by the genetic mutation. Another case could be a gun that is fired, but which was unloaded before firing.

(that smoking caused his lung cancer) would be incorrect. To know that smoking can be prevented from causing cancer, we must either have background knowledge of this mechanism (that can be used to guide the exploration of new relationships) or must have previous type-level data where this occurs (such as data on groups of people with and without the mutation and for people exposed to radon). When type-level relationships are used for token-level explanations, this means that these are limited to the current state of knowledge and we cannot infer new general relationships during the explanation process.

A second case where type and token may differ is when a type-level cause that is less significant, or even insignificant (referring to the magnitude of the ε_{avg} causal significance scores), is a cause at the token level. Note that this can happen even when we have relationships at exactly the right level of granularity, since individuals can differ in their particular responses to a cause, even though on the whole many responses are similar enough that we can find the causal relationships in the first place (e.g., not everyone who smokes will develop lung cancer, and some smokers may develop lung cancer as a result of their asbestos exposure). Even without background knowledge this case is amenable to automated inference. Problems may arise though when multiple causes occur such that type-level significant and insignificant causes both occur, or knowledge of a scenario is highly incomplete. Consider chickenpox, where close contact with an infected person is a highly significant cause. Another less likely cause is the chickenpox vaccine, which usually prevents the illness but causes it in a small percentage of people vaccinated. Now, say we know a person received the vaccine and then developed chickenpox, but do not know if she was exposed to anyone with the illness. Depending on the probability that she came in contact with an infected person, given that she now has the illness, both potential causes (exposure and the vaccine) may be equally significant at the token level.

6.1.3. How can we reason about token causality?

Most of the prior work in this area has addressed either the metaphysics of token causality (what it is), or how people make causal judgments, but what is needed are practical methods for automating causal explanation.[3] These types of explanations can have enormous practical significance in medicine, as clinicians want to know not only what is happening, but

---

[3] In this chapter, "causal explanation" refers to explaining the occurrence of a particular event (as opposed to explaining the relationship between general factors).

why it is happening, to inform treatment decisions. For instance, a brain injury caused by a patient's initial stroke will be treated differently than one caused by seizure activity (as treatment of seizures has risks, and may not be administered if they are not causing immediate damage). Many of these determinations must be made quickly, but a critical care patient may have dozens of variables monitored each second over a period of weeks, along with decades of previous lab values and findings. It is nearly impossible for humans to sift through this deluge of data to find sometimes subtle and complex patterns, and in fact this problem of information overload has been found to lead to medical errors (Jennings et al., 1982; Morris and Gardner, 1992). A clinician's diagnosis from continuous monitoring can also be orders of magnitude slower than that of an automated system (McIntosh, 2002). Instead, if this type of explanation can be done computationally, clinicians can be alerted to a patient's status by a bedside monitor continuously processing their data. The need for this type of automation is not limited to biomedicine, but may be found in other areas, such as finding the causes of sudden changes in stock market volatility and software failures.

While there is a need for automated algorithms, the majority of work on token causality has been in philosophy and has addressed the nature of the relationship between type and token causality. However, there is no consensus on this: we may learn type-level claims first and then use these to determine token-level cases (Woodward, 2005); the type-level relationships may follow as generalizations of token-level relationships (Hausman, 2005); or they may be treated as entirely different sorts of causation (Eells, 1991). One approach to token causality that is closer to practice is Sober's connecting principle, which says that when there is a type-level relationship between two events, and they token occur, the support for the hypothesis that the cause token-caused the effect is proportional to the strength of the type-level relationship (Sober and Papineau, 1986). Thus, the support for the hypothesis that extensive radiation exposure caused Marie Curie's death would be proportional to the strength of the corresponding type-level relationship (that extensive radiation exposure causes death with a high probability).

Eells's view is also described in section 2.3.3 of chapter 2.

Lewis's counterfactual approach primarily applies to token-level cases.

Definition 6.1.1 (Connecting Principle). If C is a causal factor for producing E in population P of magnitude m, then the support for the hypothesis that C at time t_1 caused E at time t_2 given that they both token occur in P at these times is m.[4]

---

[4] Sober and Papineau 1986, 101.

C and E are types of events and there are corresponding token events that occur at particular places and times (denoted by t_i). Sober uses Eells's average degree of causal significance (ADCS) for m, which can range from -1 to $+1$.

See section 2.3.3 for a discussion of the ADCS.

$$m = \sum_i [P(E|C \wedge K_i) - P(E|\neg C \wedge K_i)] \times P(K_i) \qquad (6.1)$$

This denotes the impact of cause C on effect E in population P. Each K_i is a background context and these are formed by holding fixed all factors in all possible ways. According to Sober, the relevant population is the most specific one using all details about the case. With illness, if a person's age and weight are known, the population is comprised of individuals with those properties. If less is known, perhaps only that the patient is male, then the population is simply all men. Truly using all of the available information though results in a population of size one – the single case being studied. Even relaxing this requirement somewhat, we rarely have arbitrarily specific type-level relationships that allow us to take advantage of all knowledge. Thus, this is not exactly practical, but can be used as a starting point for developing an automated approach. The main idea is that a known type-level relationship between some c and e is good evidence for c token causing e if we see that both have occurred. A type-level cause is precisely such due to its frequency of observation in the population, so that if we find 80% of people who are poisoned and not given an antidote die shortly after, then we have reason to believe that when we see a person who is poisoned, not given an antidote, and subsequently dies, this is another instance of poisoning being fatal. Clearly, the type-level relationship alone is not enough as we would not suggest poisoning as a cause of death if the person was known to not have been poisoned. As will be discussed shortly, we do not always have this information and may need to assess the probability of a cause relative to an incomplete set of observations.

Another approach might be to look to fields such as psychology to see how people handle this type of task in practice. Experimental work on how people actually make causal judgments in individual cases could be a starting point for algorithms, but it has been inconclusive. It has been argued that children learn of and then reason about causality using a similar approach as scientists do, namely through the observation of statistical regularities and interventions on their environment (Gopnik, 2004). However, more recent results have found that judgments of causality are in many cases inextricable from questions of morality, and while it is thought that causal judgments influence moral judgments (Sloman et al., 2009), other work has shown that moral judgments may also influence causal ones (Alicke, 1992). Work in legal reasoning may also provide some clues, but one of the primary problems in that area is determining not just why things happened but exactly what happened (Lagnado, 2011). However, this is a separate problem from that studied here, as we are not analyzing cases where there may be deception, but rather assume that the observations represent the true events or perhaps a censored or noisy version of them.

While type-level relationships are likely candidates as initial token-level hypotheses, there are still many practical matters to address before this process can be translated into an algorithm. To determine whether the cause and effect actually occurred, they need to be represented in a testable form. Researchers in computer science have addressed the problem of automating this type of reasoning to solve problems like fault diagnosis, finding the reasons for a system's malfunctions based on its visible errors (Lunze and Schiller, 1999; Reiter, 1980). While cause and effect are in a structured form and there are many algorithms for evaluating them, these methods developed generally require one to begin with a model of the system, and treat causality similarly to regularity theories, where one variable being true always precedes another being true in some amount of time (Halpern and Shoham, 1991; Shoham, 1988).

Most of the computational theories fail to capture causality in the way that the philosophical theories do. One of the few computational methods for analyzing token causality is the work by Pearl and collaborators on linking type-level structural models with counterfactuals (Halpern and Pearl, 2005; Hopkins and Pearl, 2007; Pearl, 2000). This work uses inferred type-level models and the truth value of variables at the token level to evaluate counterfactuals to determine how these actual values of the variables contributed to the occurrence of the effect. This approach faces difficulties in practical application due to its handling of time, subjective nature, and link between type and token-level information. The most critical barrier to applying this work to real-world cases is the omission of time from the discussion of token causality, preventing use of these works to actually automate the process. If we learned that smoking caused lung cancer and then observed that a patient who smoked was diagnosed with lung cancer, we would first have to decide if this should be considered an instance of the type-level relationship. Without timing information, smoking Wednesday and developing lung cancer Thursday would fit that pattern, even though we would likely find that relationship implausible. That disbelief is an implicit judgment about the temporality of the relationship, yet this critical aspect appears nowhere in the type-level knowledge or token-level observations.

For this process to be amenable to automation, these conditions need to be explicit and cannot require human judgment about each case. Furthermore, allowing that would lead to inconsistent and subjective determinations, so that a factor may be a cause to one person and not to another.

The subjective nature of the structural model-based approach has been recognized by its developers, but is in conflict with philosophical theories of causality and intuitions.[5] Halpern and Hitchcock (2010) have argued that this subjectivity is in keeping with psychological work on causal judgments, but that work has shown that it is difficult to design experiments that do not muddle causal and moral judgments, and that in some cases moral considerations are a fundamental part of a person's reasoning process (Knobe, 2009). Halpern and Hitchcock discuss the example of a traffic accident, where an engineer might fault the road design and a sociologist may blame the pub that served the driver alcohol, while a psychologist could say that it happened due to the driver's recent breakup and so on. However, these are not pointing to different causes for the accident but rather different levels of granularity and abstraction. Whether or not the engineer cares about the driver's blood alcohol level has no bearing on whether it contributed to the accident. Thus, while the engineer may wish to assess the relative impact of different features of the road, it is only her queries that are subjective, and not the answers. The driver's drinking will have the same contribution to the accident regardless of whether the engineer considers it.

Further, Pearl's approach lacks the flexibility needed to deal with challenging real-world data. There may be gaps in seemingly continuous measurements due to factors such as equipment malfunctions (a medical device may be accidentally shut off or move from its original location). In other cases (such as in electronic health records), events may be documented after their occurrence, leading to inaccuracies in the reported timings (Hripcsak et al., 2009). Thus, even if there is an exact match between type and token, it may not appear that way from the data and the relationship may not be inferred. Instead, since we have discussed how to infer the timing of causal relationships, we begin with this information and can make use of it for token cases, while allowing that the token-level timing may differ somewhat from that at the type level.

While many of the philosophical theories of token causality are impractical if translated directly, we can take inspiration from them, adapting them to suit the needs of methodology. Instead of attempting to determine

---

[5] This applies only when judging the fact of causality rather than adding on issues such as blame and moral responsibility, which are surely subjective.

whether a type or token-level claim is necessary for (or can be reduced to) the other, we will use the type-level inferences as evidence for the token-level claims to develop a methodology for analyzing token cases in an automated way.[6] In some cases, the result will be that the most significant type-level cause is indeed the most significant token-level cause, but getting to that answer requires relating a series of observations to previously inferred type-level causes. Since the inferred relationships are represented using logical formulas with time constraints between cause and effect, we need to determine whether the observations constitute an instance of each known relationship (and make allowances for timings falling slightly outside the known ones). If we do not have the truth value for all propositions at all times, then we need to calculate the probability, given the observations, of the token case satisfying the logical formulas associated with each causal relationship. Then, with a set of possible type-level relationships that could explain the token case, we rank their significance for it. This does not aim to find the true cause of every effect in an error free manner but rather to find the most probable causes given the type-level inferences and token-level observations.

6.2. From Types to Tokens

We now turn our attention to the formulation of a new approach to token causal explanation. The goal is to take previously inferred type-level relationships (found using the methods from chapters 4 and 5) and a sequence of token-level observations (a series of times and propositions true at those times), and use these to find a causal explanation for an event that is part of the observation sequence.

Before we can determine the significance of an explanation, we must first determine which factors will be considered as possible token-level causes. Since there may be multiple causes that are significant at the type level, along with multitudes of insignificant causes, we need a way of systematically exploring these that allows for differences between the type and token levels while remaining computationally feasible. Section 6.2.1 discusses how we can begin by examining significant type-level causes, since the measure of token-level significance to be defined will be largest for actually occurring genuine and just so causes. If none of these occur or their truth values cannot be determined, their probabilities of occurrence

---

[6] This work is in the spirit of the connecting principle and is in keeping with other reformulations of it such as that described by Russo (2009).

will be calculated relative to the observations and insignificant type-level causes will also be evaluated. This will assess the relative significance for a set of hypotheses, which are type-level relationships of the form $c \rightsquigarrow_{\geq p}^{\geq r, \leq s} e$. Remembering that c and e are logical formulas, a token-level hypothesis is that an instance of c at time t_1 token caused an instance of e at time t_2, where these are satisfied based on the observation sequence.

Taking inspiration from Sober's work (Sober and Papineau, 1986), section 6.2.2 introduces a measure of token-level significance that allows for automation of this process even with incomplete and uncertain information. In cases such as diagnosis, we cannot do all possible medical tests and patient histories contain many omissions, so this approach allows for the possibility that we may only have evidence pointing to the occurrence of a cause. Further, the observed timing may differ from the known timing so instead of discounting a factor that occurs just outside a known window, an approach for weighting these deviations will be introduced. The result is a ranking of possible explanations using a measure of their type-level significance (ε_{avg}) weighted by their probabilities of occurrence and a factor that weights how closely these events adhere to the type-level timings. Thus, each factor is not deemed causal or noncausal, but rather its token-level causal significance is assessed quantitatively, with factors having the highest value of the measure being likelier explanations for the effect's occurrence. When c and e are known to occur consistently with the type-level timings, the significance of the token-level hypothesis is exactly equal to the type-level significance of the relationship, $\varepsilon_{avg}(c_{r-s}, e)$. *The measure ε_{avg} was developed in chapter 4.*

Finally, in section 6.2.3, I bring all of these pieces of the puzzle together and discuss a procedure for taking type-level relationships and token-level observations, and determining the significance of potential token causes. This means finding the truth value of hypotheses relative to the observation sequence, calculating the probability of token causes occurring (when they are not known to be satisfied), and assessing how the actual timings compare to those inferred.

6.2.1. What can be a token cause?

If one sees that a person was in a car accident and later died, their initial hypothesis for cause of death would likely be that it was due to being in an accident. After learning that the passenger was wearing a seatbelt, it would likely be said that the death was despite the seatbelt, as seatbelt usage prevents death. However, there can be cases where a seatbelt does in fact cause death, such as through neck or chest injury. Thus, while it would likely be inferred that seatbelts lower the probability of death during a car accident at the type level, they can still be causes at the token level. This disconnect between relationships that hold in general and the possibility that individual cases may differ substantially from these is one reason that philosophical theories have suggested that the general properties should actually come from causes found in individual cases (so that seeing seatbelts cause death in specific instances leads us to infer that there is a relationship between seatbelts and death), or that these two problems must be treated separately. However, the only feasible approach for automated inference is to build on type-level information. This does not mean assuming that a type-level cause is automatically a token cause, but rather using this information to guide the search for explanations.

Instead of attempting to enumerate every imaginable cause of an effect, we can begin by evaluating those that are significant at the type level and then, if those are not found to occur, move to insignificant type-level causes. Since the measure to be described is proportional to the calculated type-level causal significance scores, the hypotheses with the highest levels of this value (ε_{avg}) are just so and genuine causes. If two potential token causes occurred in a particular instance and one is a type-level genuine cause while the other is type-level insignificant, the more likely explanation for the effect is that it was token caused by the type-level genuine cause. Thus, once we know that a just so cause of the effect took place, if we aim to find the causes with the highest level of significance, we do not need to look any further as only other genuine or just so causes could have higher values.

Say that a student, Alice, achieved a perfect score on the final exam in her calculus class. Alice says that this was because she remembered to wear her lucky sweater. Bob disagrees and tells Chris that Alice must have studied a lot (or has an innate aptitude for calculus). If Alice then confirms that she did spend a lot of time studying, what should Chris believe? We may safely assume that studying is a genuine cause for success on an exam, and that any possible role played by sweaters is negligible. Putting aside individual prior beliefs Chris might have about the impact of sweaters and luck on exam success, he would not continue to ask about increasingly unlikely factors once he knows that Alice has studied for the exam (i.e., a type-level genuine cause has token occurred). However, if Alice instead said that she had not studied, then Chris may be more willing to accept the sweater hypothesis, or may attempt to find out more about Alice's mathematical abilities. This case would be somewhat trickier if instead Alice said that she fared well on the exam because she had a cup of coffee beforehand. It may be that in general coffee has a minor impact on exam performance, but that for Alice it helps her concentrate and thus improves her performance (or may have a placebo effect since she believes it works). Without information about Alice's past history and what affects her grades, this situation can only be assessed using the type-level relationships and thus we cannot account for varying information or beliefs between individuals. The approach in this book could potentially be extended to include beliefs, using these to weight the significance of a hypothesis for each individual. However, it is not clear whether the significance of a causal explanation should be allowed to vary between individuals. It would not change the fact of what actually caused the effect, but could be important in cases where type-level information is not necessarily public and is scattered across individuals.

Epistemic logic deals with formalizing knowledge and beliefs. See Fagin et al. (1995) and Hintikka (1962) for introductions to this area.

Instead, Sober's original approach (which linked token-level significance directly to type-level significance) and the approach taken here (which begins by evaluating type-level causes but uses a measure such that token-level significance may be lower than type-level significance) use type-level relationships as a starting point for token-level explanations. In contrast to Pearl's work, it aims to make objective assessments of causality, and when individual judgments are needed, requires these to be specified in a formal way to make them explicit. While an insignificant cause can be a token-level cause, we begin by assessing the just so and genuine causes. We are considering the most plausible hypotheses first, and may miss atypical cases where there is an unusual explanation for the effect, and both it and a genuine cause token occur. However, if these more plausible causes are found not to have caused the effect, then we go back to the set of all possible causes, using the facts we have about the situation to narrow these to a smaller set of those that are satisfied by the data and then assess the significance for each of these.[7]

Beginning with the most significant causes is primarily a methodological choice, so the set of hypotheses may be constrained in other ways.

6.2.2. Significance of token causes

Since the goal here is not to find a single explanatory factor, but rather to assess the relative import of each explanation given what is observed, we need to develop a measure for token-level significance. This measure links token and type-level significance, and must do so in a way that allows for incomplete information and uncertainty about the timing of events. Finding

---

[7] One could potentially use this as an iterative process to find new type-level causes. If there are many token-level cases where the only possible cause is one that was previously deemed insignificant, then this must be reevaluated.

that *a* causes *b* in 10 to 20 days means only that these were the most significant timings relative to a set of data, not that *a* does not have the capability to cause *b* outside of these, say in 9 or 23 days. This discrepancy may also be due to bias or errors in the original data. Without further information, we would not want to immediately exclude a case that differs slightly from the type-level inferences, yet one that differs significantly should be treated differently. We may also have incomplete knowledge of an event, such as when there may be a cause of a particular illness with symptoms and a medical history for a patient that make that diagnosis seem likely, but we will not know for sure whether it is true or false. This is quite common in biomedical inference, where we rarely see the thing itself, but instead see indicators or evidence for it. When making inferences from electronic health records (EHRs), we do not observe a patient's actual heart failure, but instead see the manifestations of this heart failure in symptoms, medications to treat the symptoms, and so on. This is true in many cases involving measurement or observation. A classic example of spurious causality is that of a falling barometer seeming to cause rainfall since it happens earlier than and raises the probability of it. We know that decreasing air pressure causes both the barometer to fall and the rain to occur, yet our knowledge of the decreasing air pressure is only via the barometer (which is likely not perfect and can introduce noise into the observations). This is one of the challenges of causal inference and why some domain knowledge is required to interpret results – as we would need to understand that the event of a falling barometer corresponds to decreasing air pressure (and that other ways of manipulating a barometer will not have the same results).

Thus, unlike previous approaches such as Sober's and Pearl's, my measure of token-level significance incorporates deviations from the type-level timing and the probability of a cause's occurrence given the observation sequence. When a cause is known to occur in the same way as inferred at the type level, the significance will be the same as that at the type level. Using only type-level knowledge and an incomplete set of relationships (we do not know all possible factors that bring about the effect, posing difficulties for counterfactuals), we cannot distinguish between how a factor impacts an effect in general and how it does so on a specific occasion. Thus, the maximum value for the token-level significance will be the ε_{avg} of the associated type-level relationship.

Before formalizing this, let us discuss the notation for token-level cases. While this approach could be used with type-level relationships represented in other ways, I assume that they may be complex and that there is a window between cause and effect. These are represented as PCTL formulas of the form:

$$c \rightsquigarrow_{\geq p}^{\geq r, \leq s} e \tag{6.2}$$

where c and e are state formulas, $1 \leq r \leq s \leq \infty$, $r \neq \infty$, and p is a probability.[8] Where X is the set of prima facie causes of e, the type-level significance of c for e is defined as:

$$\varepsilon_{avg}(c_{-s}, e) = \frac{\displaystyle\sum_{x \in X \backslash c} \varepsilon_x(c, e)}{|X \backslash c|} \tag{6.3}$$

with:

$$\varepsilon_x(c_{-s}, e) = P(e|c \wedge x) - P(e|\neg c \wedge x). \tag{6.4}$$

This measure is introduced in chapter 4, with more detail on its calculation given in section 5.2.1.

Note that there are still time windows associated with the relationships between c and e and between x and e (as they are of the form shown in equation (6.2)), and that when calculating the probabilities these windows constrain the instances of each formula that will be considered.

Then, a token case (also referred to as an event) is defined by a sequence of times and propositions true at those times. When referring to an effect having "token occurred," this means that the PCTL state formula that represents the effect is satisfied at some actual time (t), and is denoted by e_t. The corresponding token-level causal hypothesis is that c at time t', caused e_t. We assume that if the type-level relationship is relative to a particular population, then c and e must token occur in that same population. However, given the ambiguity of the definition of a population, it is likelier that one will define the properties related to the population by additional propositions as part of the cause c. Token-level causal relationships are written as:

$$c_{t'} \rightsquigarrow e_t. \tag{6.5}$$

While the leads-to operator is used, this is not a PCTL leads-to formula, but rather means that c at time t' "led-to" e at time t. These are actual times so that we can distinguish between the significance of c occurring 10 days before e versus 17 days. For example, a person may be exposed to two individuals with a contagious illness such as the flu one week apart. We do not want to know only that being exposed to someone with the flu caused their

---

[8] The probabilities here do not relate directly to Eells's probability trajectories (discussed earlier in this chapter and in chapter 2). While in theory one could calculate the probability of a relationship being satisfied at each time instant given the observations up to that time, these would not produce the same results as Eells's analysis as they would still be based on the type-level distributions.

illness but rather want to determine which exposure was the likely culprit (as this could be important for tracing an outbreak back to its original source).

Definition 6.2.1 (Significance of a token cause). With a type-level relationship of the form $c \rightsquigarrow_{\geq p}^{\geq r, \leq s} e$, with $\varepsilon_{avg}(c_{r-s}, e)$, the significance of c occurring at time t' as a token cause of e at time t relative to a set of observations $\mathcal{V}$ is:

$$S(c_{t'}, e_t) = \varepsilon_{avg}(c_{r-s}, e) \times P(c_{t'}|\mathcal{V}) \times f(c_{t'}, e_t, r, s). \qquad (6.6)$$

The intuition is that something has high type-level significance precisely because it is a more common cause of an effect. That is, lung cancer being caused by smoking is more likely than it being caused by exposure to pollutants if (all else being equal) smoking has a higher value of ε_{avg}. On the other hand, if somehow pollutants were capable of causing lung cancer much more quickly than smoking and an instance of lung cancer was observed shortly after both exposures, then it should have higher significance. When cause and effect occur consistently with the type-level information, the significance is equal to the type-level significance. When the timing differs, the score is weighted by this difference and finally when it is not known whether the cause occurred, this score is weighted by the probability of its occurrence.

The probability of an event is calculated relative to the set of observations, a sequence of times with the propositions true at each time (denoted by $\mathcal{V}$). The probability $P(c_{t'}|\mathcal{V})$ is that of c occurring at time t' given the observation sequence, $\mathcal{V}$. This set of observations may be large and contain many irrelevant facts, so a likely heuristic is to limit the set to causes and effects of c when calculating its probability. When explaining a death, the day of the week on which the person died is unlikely to have any bearing on the cause of death, though there may be other insignificant causes that together form a significant cause. However, that conjunction would be a significant cause and thus included. We cannot yet disentangle the probability of an event's occurrence from the probability that it is known to have occurred. Thus, an event that actually occurred could have a probability other than one if it is not known and entailed by the other knowledge.

Next, the function f weights how much the observed timings differ from the window $[r, s]$, so that if $t - s \leq t' \leq t - r$, then $f(c_{t'}, e_t, r, s) = 1$. Otherwise, $f(c_{t'}, e_t, r, s) \in [0, 1]$ and the function is monotonically decreasing on either side of the window $[t - s, t - r]$. This function, f, is specific to each relationship. It may simply be a stepwise function that is 1 in this window and 0 outside of it, when it is known that c can only cause e precisely within this window. In other cases, this function may be linear or may decay exponentially. The key purpose for this weighting is to allow that the cause may still be capable of producing the effect outside of the known time window, but perhaps these timings are less frequently observed. This means a known instance of a cause with a low value for f (as its timing is significantly outside the known window) could have a lower token-level significance than an instance where c's occurrence is not known (but is supported by the other observations), such as a case with a probability of 1 and somewhat low f, and another with a lower probability and f of 1. This is not a counterexample, but rather means that as we gain more information, the set of possibilities narrows. Once we know that c occurs at time t', we are assessing that particular occurrence rather than the hypothetical one of c at some other time. To determine the function $f(c_{t'}, e_t, r, s)$, one can use the original data used to infer the relationship between c and e, and calculate how the conditional probability of e given c changes when moving further away from the inferred window. In other cases, when this initial dataset may not be representative of all or even most instances of the relationship, one can use other knowledge such as that of how the cause produces the effect to determine whether it is possible for it to happen outside the window and to determine how steeply f should decline.

Thus, when c is known to occur according to the known timings, P and f are one and the significance is exactly that of the type-level relationships (the same case discussed by Sober and Papineau (1986), where the probability of the evidence was assumed to always be one). For instance, the significance of c at time 4 for e at time 14 where there is a causal relationship $c \rightsquigarrow^{\geq 10, \leq 12} e$, is exactly equal to the type-level significance $\varepsilon_{avg}(c_{10-12}, e)$. If instead c occurred at time 0, the significance would be weighted by $f(0, 14, 10, 12)$, which has a value between zero and one. In this way, we can account for the timing of relationships, such as the incubation period of the flu, allowing one to determine not only which exposure caused an illness but the relative importance of each in the case of multiple exposures.

6.2.3. Algorithm for calculating significance of token causes

With sets of type-level genuine, just so, and insignificant causes of a particular, actually occurring, event, we now aim to determine the significance of instances of each relationship for this event. To do this, we must first use the facts about the situation to determine which of these indeed occurred – and when. When there is not enough information to determine if a cause occurred, its probability will be calculated relative to the observation sequence. Since the significance of each hypothesis is the associated type-level ε_{avg} weighted by the probability of the cause occurring at a particular time given the observations (and potentially also weighted by a function of the difference between this timing and the known timing), the largest possible value for the token-level significance is ε_{avg} (as the probability and temporal weights can be at most one). If any genuine or just so type-level causes have occurred consistently with the type-level timings, they will have the highest values of this significance. As the goal is to find the causes with the highest level of significance, we can begin by taking these sets and testing whether any of their members are true on the particular occasion. Where $\mathcal{V}_i$ indicates the set of propositions true at time i and e_t is the occurrence of event e at actual time t, the procedure for finding relationships with the highest levels of significance is as follows.

1. $X \leftarrow$ type-level genuine and just so causes of e
   $\mathcal{V} \leftarrow [\mathcal{V}_0, \mathcal{V}_1, \ldots, \mathcal{V}_t]$
   $EX \leftarrow \emptyset$.
2. For each $x \in X$, where $x = y \rightsquigarrow^{\geq r, \leq s} e$, for $i \in [t - s, t - r]$ if $\mathcal{V}_i \models y$ the significance of y_i for e_t is $\varepsilon_{avg}(y_{r-s}, e)$ and $EX = EX \bigcup \{x\}$.
3. For each $x \in X \setminus EX$, where $x = y \rightsquigarrow^{\geq r, \leq s} e$, and

$$i = \underset{j \in [0, t)}{\operatorname{argmax}}(P(y_j | \mathcal{V}) \times f(j, t, r, s)),$$

the significance of y_i for e_t is

$$S(y_i, e_t) = \varepsilon_{avg}(y_{r-s}, e) \times P(y_i | \mathcal{V}) \times f(i, t, r, s).$$

We begin by finding occurrences that exactly match the type-level relationships as these have the maximum significance value for that type-level relationship (as both P and f are equal to one, so $S = \varepsilon_{avg}$). For relationships without exact matches, the times with the highest significance after weighting by f and P are identified using that the instance of a cause with the maximum value of S is that with the largest value of $P(c_{t'}, \mathcal{V}) \times f(t', t)$. This finds occurrences at times in $[0, t)$ since e occurs at time t and c must be earlier than that.

The probability of a particular cause (c) token occurring at a particular time t', conditioned on the observation sequence, can be calculated using the original data from which the type-level relationships are inferred (calculating the frequency of sequences where the evidence holds) or can be done using a probabilistic model. The procedure for testing in both data (traces) and a probabilistic Kripke structure is straightforward, and uses the methods described in chapter 5 for testing prima facie causality. Since $\mathcal{V}$ is a set of time indexed propositions, the conditional probability $P(c_{t'}|\mathcal{V})$ is:

$$\frac{P(c_{t'} \wedge \mathcal{V})}{P(\mathcal{V})} = \frac{P(c_{t'} \wedge \mathcal{V}_0 \wedge \mathcal{V}_1 \ldots \wedge \mathcal{V}_t)}{P(\mathcal{V}_0 \wedge \mathcal{V}_1 \ldots \wedge \mathcal{V}_t)}. \tag{6.7}$$

The observation sequence begins with the first observation at time 0 and continues through the occurrence of the effect at time t.[9] When there are no observations at $\mathcal{V}_i$, $\mathcal{V}_i = true$. This conjunction can be represented and tested using "until" formulas.[10]

To determine if a cause is satisfied by the observation sequence or if its probability needs to be calculated, we must define the satisfaction relation. First, recall the syntax of PCTL formulas using a minimal set of operators. With a set of boolean-valued atomic propositions $a \in A$, where $0 \le r \le s \le \infty, r \ne \infty$, and $0 \le p \le 1$:

State formulas:
$$\varphi ::= true \mid a \mid \neg\varphi \mid \varphi_1 \wedge \varphi_2 \mid [\psi]_{\ge p} \mid [\psi]_{>p}$$

Path formulas:
$$\psi ::= \varphi_1 U^{\ge r, \le s} \varphi_2 \mid \varphi_1 \leadsto^{\ge r, \le s} \varphi_2$$

The semantics are as follows. With observation sequence $\mathcal{V}$ (a single trace), the satisfaction of a formula f by a timepoint $\mathcal{V}_i$ in $\mathcal{V}$ is denoted by $\mathcal{V}_i \models_V f$. A sequence of times is denoted by $\pi = \mathcal{V}_0, \mathcal{V}_1, \ldots, \mathcal{V}_t$ and the subset of π beginning at time i is represented by π^i. A particular time $\mathcal{V}_i$ in π is written as $\pi[i]$.

$$\mathcal{V}_i \models_V true \qquad \forall \mathcal{V}_i \in \mathcal{V}$$
$$\mathcal{V}_i \models_V a \qquad \text{if } a \in \mathcal{V}_i$$

All times satisfy the formula *true*, and a timepoint satisfies a proposition if it actually occurs at that time (and thus is in its set of labels).

$$\mathcal{V}_i \models_V \neg\varphi \qquad \text{if not } \mathcal{V}_i \models_V \varphi$$
$$\mathcal{V}_i \models_V \varphi_i \wedge \varphi_2 \qquad \text{if } \mathcal{V}_i \models_V \varphi_1 \text{ and } \mathcal{V}_i \models_V \varphi_2$$

---

[9] The observation sequence need not end at t and may continue past it in cases where this information is available. This may be important in cases where c is not directly observed and has multiple effects (including e). If another effect occurs more regularly than e but takes longer, knowledge of its occurrence after e makes the occurrence of c seem more probable.

[10] For example, if $\mathcal{V}_0 = \{a\}$ and $\mathcal{V}_1 = \{b, c\}$, then $\mathcal{V}_0 \wedge \mathcal{V}_1 = a \wedge (true U_{\ge 1}^{\ge 1, \le 1} b \wedge c)$.

State formulas are built from propositions and connectives as described. A time satisfies the negation of a formula if it does not satisfy the formula, and it satisfies the conjunction of two formulas if it satisfies each individually.

$$\pi^i \models_V \varphi_1 U^{\geq r, \leq s} \varphi_2 \qquad \text{if } \exists j \in [r, s] \text{ such that } \pi[i + j] \models_V \varphi_2 \text{ and}$$

$$\forall k \in [0, j) \, \pi[i + k] \models_V \varphi_1$$

This says that the until formula is true for the path beginning at time i if there is a time j in the window where φ_2 holds, and at every time before that (beginning with time i), φ_1 holds.

$$\pi^i \models_V \varphi_1 \rightsquigarrow^{\geq r, \leq s} \varphi_2 \qquad \text{if } \pi[i] \models_V \varphi_1 \text{ and } \exists j \in [r, s] \text{ such that}$$

$$\pi[i + j] \models_V \varphi_2$$

Like until, a leads-to formula is satisfied for the path beginning at time i if i satisfies φ_1 and there is a time between r and s units after i that satisfies φ_2.

$$\mathcal{V}_i \models_V [\psi]_{\geq p} \qquad \text{if } \pi^i \models_V \psi$$

$$\mathcal{V}_i \models_V [\psi]_{> p} \qquad \text{if } \pi^i \models_V \psi$$

Finally, in the token case, probabilistic state formulas are true at a time i if there is a sequence of times beginning at i that satisfy the path formula ψ.

Using these semantics, one can identify if any cause is true in the token case and occurs consistently with the type-level timings. When a type-level relationship is not found to be instantiated in that way, we find the occurrence with the highest significance value. One cannot assume that if the probability of a genuine or just so cause is nonzero, then the support for the corresponding token hypothesis will be greater than for any insignificant causes. Due to the functions P and f, the significance may be lowered enough that a type-level insignificant cause (perhaps one with probability 1) has higher token-level significance. When there are many insignificant causes, testing whether each occurred may be computationally intensive, but it is possible to define a threshold so that if the significance of a hypothesis is below it, insignificant and other causes are examined. In any case, we begin with the significance values for token-level occurrences of genuine and just so causes. When these values are very low or zero, we must examine other possible explanations such as the previously discarded insignificant causes (and perhaps those that are not even prima facie causes). Further, it is possible for a negative cause (one that prevents an effect) to be a token cause. After examining all of these, the result is a set of possible explanations ranked by their support, with those having the highest values being the likeliest explanations for the effect.

6.3. Whodunit? (Examples of Token Causality)

In this section, I discuss a few examples of how the procedure described can be used in various scenarios, beginning with a high level overview and then examining cases involving both data and structures, and finally a challenging example that is dealt with abstractly. Here the focus is on how exactly to go about reasoning about these cases. In the next section, I discuss potential counterexamples and how the answers arrived at relate to those from other theories.

6.3.1. The return of Bob and Susie (and the adverse event)

We begin with Bob and Susie, each armed with a rock that they may throw at a glass bottle. This is a classic example with a simple structure that can nevertheless be found in real-world examples. After discussing the usual scenario, I will show how it relates to a more practical problem: finding which dose of a drug caused an adverse event.

Each child stands the same distance from the bottle in this version of the rock throwing example. Assume that we know of one type-level genuine cause (with all other causes being insignificant) of such a bottle breaking in this system, represented by:

$$T \rightsquigarrow_{\geq p_1}^{\geq 1, \leq 2} G. \tag{6.8}$$

Throwing a rock (T) from a certain distance causes the glass to break (G) in greater than or equal to one and less than or equal to two time units, with at least probability p_1. Since this is a type-level cause, we have the associated causal significance value, $\varepsilon_{avg}(T_{1-2}, G)$. In this system, it is only possible for T to cause G in precisely this time window, so the function $f(c_{t'}, e_t, 1, 2)$ is one if $t - t' \in [1, 2]$ and zero otherwise.

We have the following facts about a particular instance:

1. Bob threw his rock at time 3.
2. Susie threw her rock at time 4.
3. The glass broke at time 4.
4. The only genuine cause of a broken glass is that in formula (6.8).

As a timeline:

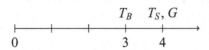

$$T_B \quad T_S, G$$

Later examples in this chapter use only the timeline as a shorthand for such a set of facts. Each proposition's time of occurrence is marked, where T_B denotes T being true due to Bob's throw and T_S due to Susie's. According to the type-level relationship in (6.8), for T to cause G, it would have to occur between times 2 and 3. T_B satisfies T and is consistent with this known timing. Remember, only exact timings are allowed in this example. Thus, T_B is a possible token cause of T and has significance $\varepsilon_{avg}(T_{1-2}, G)$. The instance of T at time 4, however, does not satisfy this relationship as it could only cause G at $t = 5$ or $t = 6$, but we aim to explain the instance of G at time 4. Thus, in this case, the only significant token cause is the instance of T due to Bob's throw. While in this system T_B must have caused G, its significance is still not one. If T had an ε_{avg} of one, meaning that it is the only type-level cause of the effect and no other factors make any difference to it, then in that case the significance would be one.

While children throwing rocks at a bottle may not seem to have many similarities to practical problems, there are important cases with a very similar structure. Instead of two instances of rock throwing, consider two instances of a particular drug being given. In most cases the drug is very effective at curing illness, but in some people it may cause a severe adverse event. If the adverse event happens, it almost always appears within a day or two of the drug being administered, and it is not physiologically possible for the drug to cause the event more than a week after initially being given. If a patient has two doses of the drug, two weeks apart, and then develops an adverse event 2 days after the second dose, can we determine which one caused her complications? This sequence of events is depicted in the following:

$$d \qquad\qquad\qquad\qquad\qquad d \quad a$$

where

$$d \rightsquigarrow_{\geq p}^{\geq 1, \leq 2} a. \tag{6.9}$$

The function f that weights significance as a function of how much the window differs from the known one is:

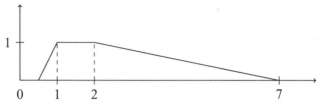

We are not concerned with the exact value of f, but only its properties. It takes a value of 1 during the known window, falls quickly to zero beforehand (it hits zero when d is 0.5 time units prior to a) and falls slowly to zero after the window until there is a week between cause and effect. After a week, it is no longer possible for an instance of d to cause the instance of a. Now we can repeat the same process for explaining the glass breaking. When temporal information is included, it is trivial to determine the cause of the adverse event, but it would be quite difficult without this. As before, we begin by iterating over the known window, seeing if there are times that satisfy d in $[16 - 2, 16 - 1] = [14, 15]$. This is the case at $t = 14$, as d occurs at that time (corresponding to the known window 1–2 time units before a). This instance will have the highest level of significance for a_{16}, $\varepsilon_{avg}(d_{1-2}, a)$. Say we still want to see how significant the instance of d_0 is for a_{16}. This would be $\varepsilon_{avg}(d_{1-2}, a) \times P(d_0|V) \times f(0, 16, 1, 2)$. While $P(d_0|V) = 1$, $f(0, 16, 1, 2) = 0$, as it is not possible for d_0 to cause a_{16}. This result would be difficult to achieve with other methods, where the absence of timing information may make it seem overdetermined and one could not distinguish between the two instances (one with the capacity to cause the effect at the time it occurred, and the other without this capability). If we instead knew only that the drug can cause an adverse event, there would be nothing in that relationship to tell us which of the doses was more likely to be responsible, since in some cases it takes a significant amount of time for side effects to appear (making it likelier that the first dose was the culprit). If instead of d_0 the first instance was closer to a_{16}, within the one-week window but outside the 1–2 day one, we would find that it is possible for it to have caused the event, but it would have much lower significance for it than the second dose does. This distinction is important if one later wishes to assign blame, so even when it is not possible to determine a single explanation, narrowing down a set of possible causes and assigning relative significance values to different explanations can be useful. The case here was not overdetermined but would seem so in the absence of time. Conversely, other cases may fail to seem overdetermined when they actually are when not allowing for flexibility in timings as we do here.

6.3.2. *An abstract example*

Let us now look at an abstract but somewhat more complicated scenario. Say we aim to explain the occurrence of an event, e, at time 7, relative to the following sequence of observations (denoted by $\mathcal{V}$):

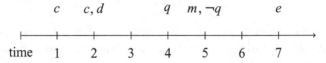

At the type level, we have previously inferred the following causes of e (with this set denoted by X):

1. $c \wedge d \leadsto^{\geq 3, \leq 5} e$
2. $m \leadsto^{\geq 1, \leq 1} e$

For each relationship in X, we have the associated values of ε_{avg}. The first step is to ascertain which of the relationships are satisfied by the observations, since the maximum significance is when a type-level relationship is consistent with the sequence of observations. Using the known window of 3–5 time units between $c \wedge d$, we examine the timepoints in $[7 - 5, 7 - 3]$ to determine if any satisfy $c \wedge d$. Time 2 is the first (and only) time that satisfies $c \wedge d$, as both c and d are observed then. Since this relationship occurs in a manner consistent with the type-level information, the maximum significance of $c \wedge d$ as a cause of e at time 7 is $S(c_2 \wedge d_2, e_7) = \varepsilon_{avg}(c \wedge d_{3-5}, e)$.

Next, we repeat this process for m. However, there is no instance of m in the window $[7 - 1, 7 - 1]$ (i.e., at time 6). Thus, the goal is now to find the time with the maximum value of $P \times f$. Observe that m actually occurs at time 5, although this is outside the known timing of exactly one time unit between m and e. Since $P(m_5|\mathcal{V}) = 1$, the significance of m_5 for e_7 is $\varepsilon_{avg}(m_1, e) \times f(5, 7, 1, 1)$. Depending on how f is defined, this may be significantly lower than the significance for $c \wedge d$ and may even be zero (in the case where the window forms a strong constraint). Since f is monotonically decreasing, the only occurrence of m that could have a higher significance for e is one at time 6, since this would be in the known window and f would be equal to one. Now, m is not known to occur at this time, but it may be possible that it did, given what was observed. We assumed that the absence of an observation means negation, so not observing m at a particular timepoint implies $\neg m$ at that timepoint, but this may simply be due to a lack of measurements at that time. We can still assess the significance of m_6 for e_7, which will be $\varepsilon_{avg}(m_1, e) \times P(m_6|\mathcal{V})$, as $f(6, 7, 1, 1) = 1$. Depending on the probability, which could be very high given the occurrence of m_5 if m usually persists, and the value of $f(5, 7, 1, 1)$, the instance of m_6 may have higher significance for e_7 than the observed instance of m_5.

6.3.3. Probability of death from choking

During the play Macbeth, the audience sees a battle between Macbeth and Macduff, but never sees Macbeth's actual death. Instead, they must infer from Macduff returning alone holding Macbeth's head that Macbeth is dead, that Macduff killed him, and that the manner of death was beheading. If we wanted to analyze this case more formally, and determine whether beheading was indeed Macbeth's cause of death, we would have to calculate the probability that this occurred given the evidence presented.

As another example, consider a person, Susan, who chokes on a piece of food and later dies. A stranger, Ted, happened to be in the same room as her at the time. People often choke without dying, and rarely do if the Heimlich maneuver is correctly administered. Thus, a significant cause of death (D) may be choking (C) and failure to administer the Heimlich maneuver ($\neg H$). There were no other witnesses in this case and Ted will not say what happened. However, we can use the facts we do have along with a previously inferred type-level model to determine the likelihood that he failed to act and the significance of $C \wedge \neg H$ for death.

We begin with C_1 and D_2, and one type-level relationship: $(C \wedge \neg H) \leadsto^{\geq 1, \leq 1} D$. The times have been simplified from more realistic ones so we may focus on the probabilities. We have a type-level model of the relationships between these variables, shown in figure 6.1. Using this model, we can calculate the probability of any time satisfying $\neg H$ given the observations C_1 and D_2. From the structure, we know that if $C \wedge \neg H$ does occur, it can only happen at the timepoint immediately before D. Thus, we aim to determine $P(\neg H_1 | C_1 \wedge D_2)$.

$$P(\neg H_1 | C_1 \wedge D_2) = \frac{P(\neg H_1 \wedge C_1 \wedge D_2)}{P(C_1 \wedge D_2)} \tag{6.10}$$

$$= \frac{0.01 \times 0.5 \times 0.25}{(0.01 \times 0.5 \times 0.25) + (0.01 \times 0.5 \times 0.01)} \tag{6.11}$$

$$= \frac{0.25}{0.26} \approx 0.96 \tag{6.12}$$

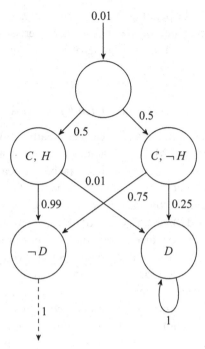

Figure 6.1. Example of a choking incident, where a person may choke (C), may or may not receive the Heimlich maneuver (H), and will either die (D) or survive ($\neg D$).

The probability of each conjunction is the probability of the set of paths satisfying it. The only time when $\neg H \wedge C$ can occur is one that satisfies the related type-level relationship, so $f = 1$. Thus, the significance, $S(C_1 \wedge \neg H_1, D) = \varepsilon_{avg}(C \wedge H_1, D) \times \frac{0.25}{0.26}$, and will thus be close to the maximum value for this relationship. As a result, we can infer that Ted most likely did not perform the Heimlich maneuver.

6.3.4. The case of Ronald Opus

Before moving to a set of common counterexamples, let us look at one complex case where it is not entirely clear what the "correct" answer should be. The purpose of this is to show first that token causality can be quite challenging, but that even in such a convoluted scenario it is possible to make some inferences. Further, this example shows how the question of responsibility and blame is separate from what can be accomplished with automated explanation methods, and will require other types of reasoning to be integrated. It will also show what happens when no significant causes occur and we must examine alternative hypotheses.

Take the following example, a paraphrased and condensed version of one presented by Don Harper Mills (Wikipedia, 2008):

A medical examiner viewed the body of Ronald Opus and determined that he died due to a gunshot wound to the head. It was found that he had jumped from a high building, intending to commit suicide, as was revealed in the note he had left. However, a few feet into his jump he was shot and instantly killed. There was a net erected for window washers just two floors down from the roof, and it is assumed that this net would have prevented the completion of the suicide. It was also assumed that neither the jumper nor the shooter was aware of the net. Accordingly, the medical examiner ruled this a homicide, as Ronald would not have died had he not been shot.

It turns out that directly across the street from where Ronald was shot, an old couple had been arguing. The husband had threatened his wife with a shotgun, but due to his anger he could not hold the gun straight. Thus when he pulled the trigger he shot the jumper across the street. The man and his wife insisted that they did not know that the gun was loaded and that he was merely threatening the woman, as he frequently did, with an unloaded shotgun. Since he had no intention of killing anyone, it seemed that the shooting of the jumper was an accident (as the gun had been accidentally loaded).

However, there was a witness who had seen the couple's son load the shotgun a few weeks prior. Their son, upset that his mother had cut him off financially, and knowing that his father threatens his mother with an unloaded gun when he is upset, had loaded the gun with the expectation that his father would shoot her. Thus it now seems the son is responsible for Ronald's death.

Upon further investigation it was revealed that their son, the same Ronald Opus, had become quite distraught about his situation, and his failure to get his mother murdered. In fact he was so upset that he jumped off the building across the street, but was killed on his way down by a shotgun blast through the window. The case was ruled a suicide.

The goal now is to use the facts about this case to determine Ronald's cause of death. Unlike the previous examples, where the answers were intuitively clear, it is not immediately obvious how to reason about this case. It is even more difficult to try to understand it using an automated method, where there is no room for intuition and background knowledge. This brings us to the first obstacle: throughout the example are references to what the father knew and what Ronald knew. However, the approach developed here gives no way to represent the knowledge of different people, only the facts of the case. We will not attempt to reason about the manner of death – whether it is a homicide, suicide, or accident – as we cannot represent people's intentions or states of knowledge (so it would be possible for someone to commit murder by shooting a person with a gun that they did not know was loaded). We attempt to dissect this example and determine the relative significance of various possible hypotheses to show that we can make some advances even in such difficult cases.

Let us begin by summarizing what is known. At some time a few weeks before the man and his wife had the fatal argument, Ronald was seen loading his father's gun. During the course of the argument, a suicidal Ronald jumped off a building across the street. Shortly after, his father pulled the trigger, firing the fatal shot through the window. As a timeline, this is:

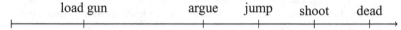

Note that these facts about the case have been taken for granted. We have not questioned who the witness was who saw Ronald load the gun, nor their possible motives. The witness could have been the husband or wife or a third party who wanted to protect the husband. We have accepted that the husband was once again threatening his wife, with no intention of killing her on this particular occasion, despite his pulling the trigger. Further, we have believed that both are being truthful when they say they did not know that the gun was loaded or that Ronald was outside the window. We have assumed that neither Ronald nor his father knew about the net outside. These facts will be accepted to simplify a difficult task, but the reader should keep in mind what has been assumed and how the scenario would change if these assumptions did not hold. I also omit time indices and avoid exact calculations as the case is already quite complex, but remember that the events and causal relationships have associated time windows. It is assumed that the occurrences fit within the known time windows for any relevant type-level relationships.

When calculating the significance of a token cause, this value is based on the type-level significance combined with cause and effect actually occurring. It is assumed that if the relationships are found relative to defined populations, this occurrence is in the same population. Otherwise if these features are part of the relationship, their satisfaction is simply part of the satisfaction of the relationship. The first task is to identify the type-level causes of death.[11] Before we can do this, we must identify the relevant populations. Assume the mother's actions (being the subject of threats)

---

[11] In this example, I assume that despite being somewhat simplistic these relationships were originally inferred from data. Of course, other approaches for explaining such scenarios may appeal to work in criminology much as work on understanding drug side effects incorporates medical and chemical knowledge.

did not contribute to her son's death, and that we have relationships and populations at the desired level of granularity. Ronald's father frequently threatens his wife with an unloaded gun and is part of a population of people who frequently wield unloaded guns and for whom shooting a gun has a very low probability of death. In fact, in that population (F), shooting is not a positive type-level cause of death and there may even be no instances of a gun being loaded within it.

Ronald, on the other hand, is part of a population of people who are homicidal (H), as he was plotting the murder of his mother, and later suicidal as well $(S \wedge H)$, as he was distressed about the failure of his plans. One would think that someone with either of these features shooting a gun is a type-level cause of death, but unfortunately the shooter here was not part of these populations. If the relevant type-level causes are:

$$(jump \wedge no\ net) \rightsquigarrow death\ (\text{in } S) \qquad (6.13)$$

$$loaded\ gunU(shoot \wedge loaded\ gun) \rightsquigarrow death\ (\text{in } S \wedge H) \qquad (6.14)$$

then none actually occurred. What we can do then is assess the strength of other, possibly insignificant, causal relationships, such as loading a gun in H (perhaps one that is later shot by someone else), jumping from a building with a net in S and shooting a gun in F. These are:

$$load\ gun \rightsquigarrow death\ (\text{in } H) \qquad (6.15)$$

$$jump \wedge net \rightsquigarrow death\ (\text{in } S \wedge H) \qquad (6.16)$$

$$shoot \rightsquigarrow death\ (\text{in } F) \qquad (6.17)$$

As before, we begin by testing which of these actually occurred, and then use the associated ε_{avg} values to determine the significance for each. All three relationships are satisfied by the observation sequence. Then, it seems likely that jumping with a net rarely results in death and that the ε_{avg} for the relationship in (6.15) is likely quite high, and certainly much higher than that associated with (6.17). Remember, this is not just loading or shooting a gun, but a gun loaded by someone homicidal (6.15) versus a gun shot by someone who never loads their gun (6.17) (and it seems unlikely that shooting unloaded guns should cause death). While the details may change based on the length of time between the loading and shooting (accounting for the fact that a gun may become unloaded by someone other than the initial loader), the ranking of these potential causes should persist, with loading a gun being more significant than shooting a presumably unloaded gun and jumping out of a window onto a net.

The intuition behind including the population information is that each man had different intentions (and sets of knowledge) so that the same action by both can correspond to different causal relationships with different significance values.[12] Ronald knew that his father would hold and possibly pretend to shoot the gun, and loaded it with the intent to kill his mother. Ronald had full knowledge of the scenario surrounding the gun and this is somewhat taken into account by using relationships from population H. His father instead assumed that the gun was in the same state where he left it, and would behave as it had in the past (that is, it would not be loaded). Reasoning about the father with relationships from F captures this in a crude way, as he continued to act as part of F.

Ronald loading the gun has the highest level of significance for his death, but determining whether this corresponds to a suicide, homicide, or accident goes beyond the type of reasoning we can do here. In the original telling of the story, the focus was on the manner of death, so it was ruled a suicide, but it was not said whether it was due to Ronald loading the gun or jumping off the building.

6.4. Difficult Cases

We now look at a few test cases, including classic scenarios that have been posed as counterexamples to other theories of causality. Since the examples are usually abstract and the main goal is to examine how this approach can reason about them and what result is arrived at, details such as the time subscripts of events are omitted in cases where the problem is clear without them (unlike in the previous section where we aimed to go through the process in detail to understand how it proceeds).

6.4.1. Redundant causation

Symmetric case

During Act V of Hamlet, Claudius is both stabbed with a poisoned foil and forced to drink poison. Was it Hamlet stabbing him, the poison on the end of the sword, or the poison he drank that caused Claudius's death? This is a case of symmetric redundant causation (called overdetermination), where multiple known type-level causes of an effect occur in the token case such

---

[12] This could instead have been an added proposition in the relationships, so that we have *load* $\land$ H or *shoot* $\land$ F.

that any could have caused the effect. In the case of Claudius, even if his cause of death was narrowed down to poisoning, we would likely not be able to determine which source of poison contributed most to his death.

One frequently used example of overdetermination is that of Bob and Susie throwing rocks at a bottle, where their rocks hit such that either could have caused the bottle to break. Going back to this example one last time, recall that Bob and Susie are each armed with a rock that they may throw at a glass bottle. Now Bob is standing closer to the bottle than Susie is, so that she aims and throws her rock earlier than Bob throws his, but their rocks hit simultaneously, breaking the glass shortly after impact. This scenario may correspond to the following type-level relationships:

$$T_B \rightsquigarrow^{\geq 1, \leq 2}_{\geq p_1} G \tag{6.18}$$

$$T_S \rightsquigarrow^{\geq 3, \leq 4}_{\geq p_2} G \tag{6.19}$$

where T_B corresponds to a rock being thrown by someone standing at Bob's distance, and T_S Susie's distance. The observations are as follows:

As a timeline:

T_S T_B G

├──┼────┼─┼──→

0   1   3   4

1. Susie threw her rock at $t = 1$.
2. Bob threw his rock at $t = 3$.
3. The glass broke at $t = 4$.
4. The only significant causes of a broken glass are those in formulas (6.18) and (6.19).

To determine the significance of the causes for G, we first determine if any of the type-level relationships are satisfied by the observations. The occurrence of T_S at time 1 is consistent with the known window, since G is at time 4 and the known window is 3 to 4 time units. Similarly, T_B also occurs within the known window as 3 is in [2,3]. Thus, we know that the maximum value of the significance for each relationship is the associated ε_{avg} value. If these are equal, then the support for either as a token cause of the glass breaking will be the same. However, if people standing closer to the bottle generally fare better, then the significance of T_B may be higher. In that case, we would not say T_S is not a cause, but rather that T_B just has higher significance. While this is a simple case, it has proven difficult for other approaches, such as those based on counterfactuals (which ask if the cause had not happened, would the effect have happened), as with overdetermined cases there is always a backup cause so that if one does not occur or fails, the other would have led to the effect. As a result, the effect depends on neither. There are also many pathological examples where one slower causal process begins before another faster one (such as a rock being thrown from a shorter distance so both hit at the same instant), so if we instead looked for the earliest cause that could have led to the effect, we would overlook the possible contribution from the later one.

This example illustrates a particular problem structure in a straightforward way. Such cases can also be found in medical examples where instead of children throwing rocks, we may have possible culprits for a patient's heart failure or carriers of an infectious illness. In these cases, it is desirable to be able to identify multiple potential causes with their associated weights. In the previous section, I discussed the case of two doses of a drug and a resulting adverse event, where this case could have seemed overdetermined without timing information. Now let us examine another scenario that may seem like it has a single cause if we do not allow for temporal uncertainty, but is in fact overdetermined, though with one explanation having higher significance than the other.

p_a
p_b c_a c_b p_c
0 1 5 14

Arthur and Betty separately contract chickenpox on a Saturday (p_a, p_b). Sunday, Charles and Arthur go to brunch, where they linger for a while, working on the crossword (c_a). On Wednesday, Charles and Betty go to a matinee together (c_b). Exactly two weeks after Arthur and Betty initially became ill, Charles develops chickenpox (p_c). He did not come into contact with any other infected people and wants to know who to blame for ruining his weekend. In this case there is only one relevant type-level cause:

$$c \rightsquigarrow^{\geq 10, \leq 21}_{\geq 0.70} p. \tag{6.20}$$

Contact with a person who has chickenpox (c) leads to developing chickenpox (p) in 10–21 days with a probability over 70%. Once again, we begin by finding times that are within the known time window. This means identifying if there are times in the window [0,4] where p is satisfied, since observations begin at time zero, the known window is 10–21 time units, and we aim to explain p_{14}. The instance c_{a4} satisfies this, and has the associated significance $\varepsilon_{avg}(c_{10-21}, p)$. The second contact (with Betty) is only one day outside of this time window. While 10–21 days may be the most likely incubation period, it does not mean that it could not potentially be somewhat shorter or longer (leading to a function f as shown in the margin). Thus, if Charles still wanted to know what the significance of his contact with Betty was for his developing chickenpox, he can calculate this with:

1
10   21

$$S(c_{b5}, p_{c14}) = \varepsilon_{avg}(c_{10-21}, p) \times f(5, 14, 10, 21). \tag{6.21}$$

The value of $f(5, 14, 10, 21)$ will be less than one, but perhaps not significantly lower. While the significance of Charles's contact with Arthur for his chickenpox will be greater than that for his contact with Betty, this will be nonzero. The key point is that without allowing for some flexibility in the timings through the weighting function f, we would only have found that contact with Arthur caused Charles's chickenpox, even though contact with Betty was only a short time outside the known window and still significant.

Asymmetric case

In the previous (symmetric) case, either rock being thrown and either exposure to an infected person could have caused broken glass and illness. In the asymmetric case, multiple causes actually occur, but only one in fact produces the effect. We can perturb the rock throwing scenario slightly to make it asymmetric, and an example of preemption. Now Bob throws his rock a bit earlier than Susie throws hers, so that his rock hits and breaks the glass before hers does and the glass is already broken when Susie's rock hits it. Thus, we should deem Bob's throw the cause of the glass breaking. However, if T_S occurs at such a time that it could cause G according to the inferred rules, we have no way to account for the fact that the bottle is already broken and Susie's throw no longer has the capacity to cause G. We do not have a way of augmenting the type-level relationships with the observations to add further constraints. However, since there is a small window of time in which a rock hitting a bottle can cause it to break, modeling the events more finely can allow us to correctly handle this case. In particular, we can add variables such as H to denote a rock hitting the bottle. In practice, if one routinely finds incorrect token causes, this would be an indication that the type-level relationships are too coarsely grained to capture the details of the system so one must go back and infer relationships that are more detailed and at a finer timescale. As with the overdetermined case, this type of scenario has been difficult to handle using counterfactual methods (since either would have caused it, even if only one actually did) and those that seek the earliest cause that accounts for an effect (since Susie could stand even further away so that she throws first but her rock still hits second).

The key difficulty with preemption is when the relationships are not modeled finely enough or the timings are inaccurate. Had we not observed the rocks hitting the bottle, the idea that either could have caused it to break would be acceptable. The contradiction is that we cannot augment the type-level relationships with this further information. Instead, we would have to infer new relationships such as that throwing the rock causes it to hit the bottle, and hitting the bottle causes it to break; or specifying that the rock hits an unbroken bottle. A more realistic example is that of multiple factors affecting troponin levels. These are often used as markers for cardiac injury, as troponin is released into the bloodstream during cardiac damage and is thus raised in the hours after a heart attack. Troponin levels are also raised after high intensity or endurance exercise. Say Ben runs a marathon on Sunday, experiences a silent heart attack (one without obvious symptoms such as chest pain) on Tuesday, and is found to have elevated troponin levels at his doctor's visit on Thursday. Without knowledge of the timing between exercise and troponin levels (and in the absence of classic heart attack symptoms) a doctor may believe that Ben having run a marathon caused his high troponin levels. Instead, by making use of the knowledge that troponin levels raised through exercise are back to normal after a day, while those as a result of heart attacks remain elevated for multiple days, his doctor can conclude that Ben indeed had a heart attack (as his exercise could not account for the elevated troponin at the time it is observed) and treat him appropriately.

6.4.2. Transitivity and causal chains

Romeo seeing Juliet's apparently dead body leads him to drink poison, which in turn causes his death. In some methods, causality is considered to be transitive, so that if a causes b and b causes c, a is also said to cause c. Philosophical work has discussed whether the most temporally direct factor should be considered a cause or whether it is the first event that starts the chain that brings about the effect (Broadbent, 2012; Eells and Sober, 1983). This book does not attempt to resolve such questions, but rather discusses how we can reason about these types of chains even with incomplete information. Say we did not know whether Romeo in fact poisoned himself, and wanted to determine his cause of death.

First, assume that:

$$S \rightsquigarrow^{\geq 1, \leq 2} P \tag{6.22}$$

$$P \rightsquigarrow^{\geq 1, \leq 1} D \tag{6.23}$$

where this says that seeing a dead lover (S) leads to poisoning oneself (P) in 1–2 hours, and poisoning brings about death (D) in exactly one hour. Then say we observe only S_2 and D_5. We do not know whether P or $\neg P$ is true, as in this example no one saw Romeo buy or administer the poison and no one asked him about it. How can we explain D_5? We first test whether any type-level causes of it are true in the known time window.

This fails as we have no observed instances of P. We would not instead find S as a cause of D, as we have only inferred relationships between S and P, and P and D.[13] We would then attempt to find the maximum value of $P(P_i|S_2 \wedge D_5) \times f(i, 5, 1, 1)$. Given the narrow time window and the type-level relationship between S and P (where P is most likely to follow in 1–2 time units), the highest value of this measure is likely to be for P_4, leading to:

$$S(P_4, D_5) = \varepsilon_{avg}(P_1, D) \times P(P_4|S_2 \wedge D_5) \qquad (6.24)$$

since this is consistent with the known time window and $f = 1$. The key point here is that by allowing for incomplete information, we can still correctly evaluate the closest link in a causal chain – even if it was not actually observed.

Causal chains are ubiquitous. When giving explanations for an event we often trace the series of events that led up to its occurrence. For instance, a patient with congestive heart failure is generally prescribed a blood pressure medication called an ACE inhibitor. ACE inhibitors can have side effects though and may lead to elevated potassium levels. A particular patient's medical record may be incomplete, but using this method it will still be possible to determine how likely it is that their elevated potassium is being caused by the ACE inhibitor prescribed for their heart failure – even without direct observation of the medication being prescribed or taken.

6.4.3. The hard way

Finally, we look at a set of examples that have a shared structure, but can lead to different intuitions about their token causes. The general feature of these problems is that a cause that usually prevents an effect ends up bringing it about in the particular case. Thus, the effect occurs but is said to have happened "the hard way," with most odds stacked against it. While there are many examples of this type, I discuss three of the most widely used and introduce one of my own. The initial examples of this case may seem far-fetched, but the structure is not uncommon and is best illustrated through a few slightly different versions of the problem. In some places, I point out real-world equivalents of the problems discussed.

---

[13] The initial inferences could have been between S and D, had P not been measured or known at the type level.

Sherlock Holmes and the boulder

We begin with an example by Good (1961a), with some modifications by Hitchcock (1995). Sherlock Holmes takes a walk below a cliff where his nemesis, Moriarty, is waiting for him. Moriarty has set a boulder on the edge of the cliff so that when he sees Holmes walk past, he will push the boulder off the edge, giving him a 90% chance of killing Holmes. Holmes's friend Watson, however, sees what Moriarty is plotting and decides to push the boulder out of Moriarty's hands. Just as Holmes walks below them and Moriarty is about to push the boulder, Watson runs over and pushes it first, trying to aim it in another direction. This random push, since Watson is unable to see Holmes and be sure that the boulder is aimed away from him, has a 10% chance of killing Holmes. In an unfortunate turn of events, the boulder falls directly on and kills Holmes.

Ignoring the timing of events, the relevant type-level relationships are that a boulder pushed by an enemy (E) is a type-level cause of death by boulder (D), with probability 0.9

$$E \rightsquigarrow_{\geq 0.9} D,$$

while a boulder pushed by a friend (F) is likely not a type-level cause of death, but this depends on the probability of death by boulder. That is,

$$F \rightsquigarrow_{\geq 0.1} D,$$

but we do not know $P(D)$, so we are not sure whether the probability of death is raised (let alone significantly so). Say the marginal probability of death by boulder (this includes boulders pushed and those falling from above) is lower than 0.1. Then, F is a prima facie cause of D. It may still be an insignificant cause of D but the value of ε_{avg} is quite likely to be positive. Now, one type-level cause of death has occurred – F. The significance of F as a token cause of death is positive, but probably small (since F actually occurred consistently with whatever the actual timings are, the significance is precisely the earlier computed ε_{avg}). Nevertheless, no other causes occurred, so we are left with F as the only possibility for explaining D. While this is accurate, in that it was a boulder being pushed by his friend that caused his death, some may reject this answer since Watson's intention was to save Holmes and despite the boulder actually killing him, his push had a much lower probability of killing Holmes than Moriarty's would have. If we believe that Moriarty's pushing the boulder was inevitable, Watson lowered Holmes's probability of death (this is discussed in detail by Hitchcock (1995)). Instead, the usual analysis is relative to no boulders being pushed, in which case Watson's pushing the boulder did in fact raise Holmes's probability of imminent death.

The second possibility is that $P(D)$ is somewhere in between that conditioned on F and E, say 0.5 (perhaps there are frequently falling boulders). In that case, there is only one significant cause of death at the type level, but it did not occur since Moriarty was prevented from pushing the boulder. Thus, we must examine other possible causes, testing relationships comprised of the facts about the scenario. The primary possibility is that F led to D. However, at the type level, F lowers the probability of death (it generally prevents it, causing $\neg D$). As a result, $\varepsilon_{avg}(F, D)$ will be negative, and the significance of a boulder pushed by Watson as the token-cause of Holmes's death is negative. What does it mean for the actual cause to have negative significance? Remember, we are implicitly, through the ε_{avg}, comparing one possible cause to others. When a preventative is the token cause of death, it may potentially be given the interpretation that the effect occurred "despite" the cause, as it usually has the opposite outcome. In the case where the cause is only insignificant, it is not clear if one may use the same interpretation, but rather may only assume that the effect was unlikely to have occurred even though it did. In this example, we could attempt to find a richer set of relationships, so that perhaps witnessing a foe attempting to push a boulder onto someone is a cause of a friend rushing in and pushing it instead (since pushes by foes are more deadly than those by friends, a friend is likely to attempt to save the person in this manner). That would not change the outcome here, as we do not include transitivity in the explanations (so that a causing b, which in turn causes c, makes a a cause of c). Thus, we would only say that witnessing Moriarty about to push the boulder caused Watson to push it, and Watson's pushing it caused Holmes's death.

The plant and the defoliant

Another example, due to Nancy Cartwright (1979), has the same structure as the case of Sherlock Holmes and the boulder, but may result in a different interpretation. Here Nancy wants to get rid of some poison oak in her garden, so she sprays it with a defoliant that will cause the plant to die with probability 0.9. However, even after a few months, the plant is still alive. Assume that the probability of plant death in the absence of a defoliant is only 0.1. We will reframe this in terms of survival though so this case better parallels that of Holmes. Thus, spraying the plant with the defoliant leads to survival with probability 0.1, while the probability if no action is taken is 0.9. In the example with Holmes, the probability of death from Moriarty's push was 0.1, whereas the probability of death if no action was taken by Moriarty was 0.9.

In this case though it is unlikely that we would even ask what caused survival, as the plant was alive both before and after the spraying. When reasoning about death or other events with a clear onset time, the system is in a different state and we aim to determine what caused that change. As we do not usually ask what caused a state to persist, this is likely responsible for our intuition that the spraying did not cause survival, while it can at least be argued that Watson caused Holmes's death, regardless of $P(D)$.[14] Despite this, we can still assess the significance of spraying with a defoliant (D) for survival (S). Since $P(S|D) < P(S)$, D is not a prima facie cause of survival and is in fact a negative cause of survival (as it lowers its probability). As in the first part of the Holmes example, ε_{avg} is negative, so the significance of D as a token cause of S is also negative. One can again interpret this as that the plant survived *despite* the spraying of the defoliant (a type-level preventative). This is consistent with the intuition that the defoliant should have caused death as it normally does and the plant was in the lucky 10% that are not affected by defoliants. Recall though that this hypothesis is only tested because of our knowledge of the problem. It is unlikely that we would normally wonder what caused survival and, if we did, there would be genuine causes (sunlight, water, etc.) that did occur and would be found responsible for this, so we would not examine insignificant causes like the defoliant (never mind that we would not usually attempt to explain survival at a particular time). Yet we can still test this hypothesis and arrive at an answer that is consistent with intuition.

The golfer and the squirrel

Another classic example of this type is the golfer and the squirrel. This was introduced by Rosen (1978), but this telling contains modifications by Salmon (1980b), Hitchcock (1995), and me.

> Alvin, a slightly above average golfer, tries to make a birdie on a particular hole. He hits the ball and it looks like he might just make the shot. However, a mischievous squirrel comes by and kicks the ball. Usually when such squirrels

---

[14] Another way of explaining this is that the situation would correspond better to the Holmes case if there was a 99% effective defoliant, so using the weaker one relative to the stronger version can be argued to have caused the survival of the plant (Hitchcock, 1995). Alternatively, this case can be understood in terms of capacities. While the push of a boulder is capable of causing death, the spray of a defoliant does not seem to have the needed capability to cause survival, and would not be an effective strategy for promoting survival (Cartwright, 1979).

kick golf balls they lower the probability of making birdies. In this case, though, the squirrel kicked the ball right toward the hole and Alvin made the shot.

Now the question is: what caused the birdie? The squirrel's kick (K) lowered the probability of a birdie (B), but it seems to have caused it. This is similar to the case of Holmes, where Moriarty pushing the boulder should normally have lowered Holmes's probability of death, but instead raised it. In both cases, the token-level probability of the effect after the cause differs significantly from that at the type-level. As discussed in section 2.3.3, Eells developed an approach to account for this using probability trajectories, which examine the probability of the actual effect before and after the cause and up to the time the effect actually occurred. In that way one could distinguish between the general properties of squirrels and golf balls, and how this particular squirrel affected the probability of this particular golf ball going into the hole. However, it is unlikely that without extensive background knowledge we would ever be able to know this trajectory (the probability of a birdie at each moment in time from Alvin's shot to the actually occurring birdie).

Let us analyze this case as before. First, we must determine the type-level causes of birdies. For the sake of simplicity, the times of cause and effect are omitted, but we assume that there is some known window of time after the ball is hit in which a birdie may be made (so that hitting the ball on Tuesday cannot cause a birdie on Friday). Assume that an above average golfer hitting the ball (A) raises the probability of a birdie (B), so that:[15]

$$P(B|A) > P(B)$$

and in fact

$$A \leadsto B. \tag{6.25}$$

However, kicks by squirrels (K) lower the probability of birdies:

$$P(B|K) < P(B),$$

so K is not a prima facie cause of B and is likely a negative cause of B.

This case differs somewhat from the others in that both the type-level positive and negative causes occur and interact. In the case of Holmes, Moriarty does not actually push the boulder. Since a significant type-level cause occurs, and it is the only one, we will find that Alvin's hitting the ball has the highest significance for the birdie (with the value being that

---

[15] If Alvin was a terrible golfer, the analysis would be unchanged, with the exception that the hypothesis with the most support (Alvin or the squirrel causing the birdie) could change depending on just how bad a golfer Alvin is.

of the type-level ε_{avg}). If we assess the significance of the squirrel for the birdie, we will find as before that squirrels have negative significance for birdies and thus have negative significance for the token case. We cannot capture that this particular squirrel happened to kick this particular ball in just such a way that we know it was actually responsible for the birdie. Here we diverge from the results of Eells, who used the probability trajectory (showing that the probability of the birdie became higher after the kick and remained high until the actual birdie occurred) to find that the squirrel kicking the ball caused the birdie. The probability trajectory allows Eells to distinguish between the general properties of squirrels and golf balls, and how this particular squirrel affected the probability of this particular golf ball going into the hole in a way that was different from squirrels in general.

Since we do not know and cannot represent this change in probability, we will only find that the birdie occurred perhaps despite the squirrel (something that has negative significance for it), and will not be able to find the squirrel's true contribution to the birdie. While this result may be problematic, it is also important to consider how often – and in what cases – we would actually be able to know of such a trajectory and get results that are inconsistent with our knowledge of the situation. A possible real world equivalent is: Alvin has a genetic mutation that gives him an above average probability of developing lung cancer. Once he finds out about this, he stops smoking to protect his lungs. Two years later, he is diagnosed with lung cancer. In general, we would say that smoking cessation lowered Alvin's probability of lung cancer. Thus, stopping smoking would have negative significance for lung cancer. However, later research shows that, oddly enough, people with Alvin's mutation are more likely to develop lung cancer once they stop smoking. We can use this added information to find that stopping smoking is a positive cause of developing lung cancer for these people. The first assessment was correct as far as knowledge at the time, but once we learn more about the underlying relationships, we can better explain Alvin's condition. With the squirrel, perhaps this particular squirrel was of a type that kicks golf balls into holes. If we later obtain this information, we could find that its kick was a significant token cause of the birdie

A car accident and seatbelt use

We now return to the earlier example of a car accident in which a seatbelt causes death, which turns out to be another example of things happening "the hard way," where a factor that usually prevents an effect brings it about in a particular situation.

> On Monday morning Paul drove his car to work, wearing a seatbelt as he always does. Unfortunately, on this particular drive he was in a bit of a rush and collided head on with an ice cream truck making one of its stops. The collision resulted in injury to Paul's carotid artery. He later died, apparently due to this injury.

Let us make this example a bit more difficult than the others by assuming we do not have arbitrarily specific relationships, but instead only have a general type-level one between seatbelts and death (that is, not one involving carotid artery injury specifically). This relationship accounts for the myriad ways (including through carotid artery injury) that a seatbelt can cause death. However, since seatbelts generally prevent death, the associated probability will be quite low. Let us further assume that a seatbelt can only cause death in the context of a car accident. Then we have the following relationships between death (D), car accidents (C), and wearing a seatbelt (S):

$$P(D|C \wedge \neg S) > P(D|C \wedge S) > P(D), \tag{6.26}$$

and a general relationship between car accidents and death:

$$P(D|C) > P(D). \tag{6.27}$$

We can also assume that $P(D|C \wedge \neg S) > P(D|C) > P(D|C \wedge S)$. For ease, the time subscripts have been omitted and it is assumed that the token events are within the known type-level time frames, but there are type-level relationships such as $\neg S \wedge C \rightsquigarrow D$ with some time window and probability. While it may be that being in a car accident and not wearing a seatbelt is a significant type-level cause of death, the same event while wearing a seatbelt likely results in a much lower probability of death, but still higher than not being in a car accident at all. Thus, it is still at least a prima facie cause of death.

Given the relationship $C \rightsquigarrow D$ (say that this is all a single population, not separate populations of seatbelt users and non-users or good drivers and bad drivers), where C is a significant type-level cause of death, we find that it occurred in the token case and it has a value of support equal to the associated ε_{avg}. This means that unless $C \wedge S$ is a significant type-level cause, the algorithm discussed would not automatically evaluate its significance for the effect. Thus, regardless of whether the specific injury was caused by the seatbelt, it would still be the car accident that is significant for death. While this explanation is not as precise as we may desire, note that the seatbelt injury only occurs within the context of a car accident, so this could be viewed as death by car accident, with the mechanism being carotid artery injury due to the seatbelt. There is a general relationship between car accidents and death, and this may be fulfilled by a variety of means (such as through seatbelt or airbag injury).

As before, one may still want to evaluate the significance of a type-level insignificant (or negative) cause for a particular effect. Just as we tested other unlikely hypotheses outside the general algorithm in the previous sections, we can determine the significance of $C \wedge S$ for death. This did occur and the significance will be exactly equal to that of $\varepsilon_{avg}(C \wedge S, D)$, which will be less than that of $\varepsilon_{avg}(C, D)$. Thus what we may know to be the "true cause" will be less significant than a more general cause. This case has a slightly different structure than the previous ones, since we included the general car accident-death relationship. If we omitted this and only had $C \wedge \neg S$ as a type-level genuine cause, with $C \wedge S$ as an insignificant or negative cause of death, we would have the same case as the example of Holmes, Watson, and Moriarty. Similarly, we could have previously examined the probability of death when hit by a boulder (regardless of who pushed it) and found that to be the cause of death. In the modified seatbelt case, where the relationship $C \rightsquigarrow D$ is omitted, there are no occurring significant type-level causes. Following the approach outlined, we would then examine insignificant and other causes. In that case, $C \wedge S$ would be found as a potential cause and would again have low significance. As before, this would be an unlikely occurrence but the seeming cause of death.

7

Case Studies

Thus far, I have evaluated the approach developed here conceptually, but the goal is to apply the methods to actual data. Before applying a new approach to a new domain, though, it must first be evaluated on datasets where the true relationships are known. This chapter discusses two types of applications: validation on simulated neuronal and financial time series (to determine how well the algorithms can recover known causes) and experimentation on financial time series (to discover novel relationships).

7.1. Simulated Neural Spike Trains

We begin our study of applications with synthetically generated neural spike trains. The underlying relationships here are simple (one neuron causing another to fire in some predefined window of time), but the data allow validation of the algorithms for inferring relationships and their timing, and comparison against other methods. There has been much recent work on determining the connectivity between neurons by applying causal inference methods to spike train measurements (Brown et al., 2004; Hesse et al., 2003; Kamiński et al., 2001) but timing information is a central part of the causal relationships, so it will be useful to compare the approach to others that include this information to varying extents. I begin with a comparison where all algorithms are provided with the known times before examining how well the approach can recover these timings without such prior knowledge.

7.1.1. Synthetic MEA data

The data were created to mimic multi-neuronal electrode array (MEA) experiments, in which neuron firings may be tracked over a period of time.[1]

---

[1] The data were provided as part of the 4th KDD workshop on Temporal Data Mining. It is publicly available at: http://people.cs.vt.edu/~ramakris/kddtdm06/.

183

Data was generated for five different structures, with neurons denoted by the 26 characters of the English alphabet. Each dataset contained 100,000 firings generated using one of the five structures plus a degree of noise (this is a parameter that was varied). A total of 20 datasets were generated, with two runs output for each structure and each of two noise levels. The five structures include a binary tree of four levels (figure 7.2a), a chain of neurons, and so called "scatter gather" relationships in various configurations (figure 7.1).

At each timepoint, a neuron may fire randomly (with the probability of this happening being dependent on the noise level selected, with a higher noise level meaning a higher probability) or may be triggered to fire by one of its causes. Additionally, there is a 20 time unit refractory period after a neuron fires (when it cannot fire or cause another neuron to fire) and then a 20 time unit window after this when it may trigger another to fire. When making use of this background information, the algorithm need only search for relationships where one neuron causes another to fire during a window of 20–40 time units after the causal neuron fires. Thus when testing for prima facie causality, the relationships tested are of the form $c \rightsquigarrow_{\geq p}^{\geq 20, \leq 40} e$, where c and e represent the firing of individual neurons.

7.1.2. Comparison with BNs, DBNs, and bivariate Granger causality

We compare the results to those found with the TETRAD IV (Glymour et al., 2004) implementation of the PC algorithm of SGS (Spirtes et al., 2000) for inferring BNs, the Banjo package for DBN inference (Hartemink, 2008), and the `granger.test` function in the MSBVAR R (Brandt, 2009) package for testing bivariate Granger causality. All algorithms tested for simple pairwise relationships between neurons, but the use of timing information varied. When possible, the default settings for each software package were used.

The implementation of the algorithm developed here, called `AITIA`, tested for relationships where one neuron causes another in 20–40 time units. The empirical null was calculated from the set of ε_{avg} values using the method and R code made available by Jin and Cai (2007).

TETRAD IV was given the full time series data and for each input it produced a graph with both directed and undirected edges (with the undirected edges indicating a relationship where the algorithm was unable to determine whether the nodes cause each other or have a common cause). Undirected edges were not considered to be true or false positives, they

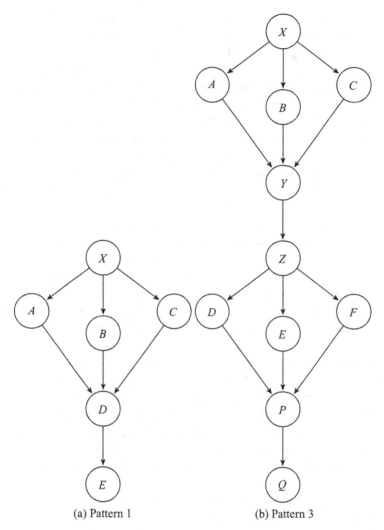

(a) Pattern 1   (b) Pattern 3

Figure 7.1. Two of five neuronal patterns. A third is comprised of pattern 3 with no connection between Y and Z. Pattern 4 is shown in figure 7.2a, and the fifth is a simple chain of twelve nodes.

were ignored in these calculations to provide better comparison with other algorithms.

The Banjo package was used with simulated annealing, testing for links between neurons in 20–40 time units (note that this is not a window, but rather determines whether A causes B in 20 time units, 21 time units, and so on with one arrow in the graph for each of these temporal links). Based on information in the documentation and the size of the problem, the algorithm was allowed to run for 30 minutes on each input file. The algorithm output the graph with the highest score, indicating edges between each of the neurons for each of the timepoints. The algorithm never identified relationships between a pair of neurons for the entire time window (i.e., an edge between them for each value in [20,40]), so all inferences were collapsed to be between two neurons. If there was an edge between two neurons for any value in [20,40] that was called a positive. If ten edges were found between two neurons, that still corresponded to one relationship. There was no penalization for a failure to discover all 20 lags between pairs of variables.

The `granger.test` function used a lag of 20 time units, as it is not possible to specify a range of time using this implementation.[2] The algorithm output F-scores and p-values for each possible pairwise relationship. To determine the threshold at which a relationship was considered a positive result, we used the same false discovery control approach as was used with our own algorithm. Note that the function used here is a bivariate Granger causality test. The multivariate test was investigated, but is extremely computationally complex, as it scales linearly with both the number of variables and number of lags included and is polynomial in the number of variables (unlike the approach in this book, which does not have the added factor of lag length). While the logic-based approach (implemented in `AITIA`) took approximately 2.5 hours to test relationships between all pairs of variables on one of the datasets and minimal RAM, the GCCA Matlab toolbox implementation of the multivariate test used all 8GB of RAM on the same PC and was finally stopped when it had run for 48 hours and had not yet finished.

The results for all algorithms over all datasets (five patterns with two runs each for a low and high noise level) are shown in table 7.1. While I have primarily focused on controlling the FDR, statistics for the FNR (fraction of false negatives out of all negatives – these occur when we fail to identify a causal relationship) are also included as there is generally a tradeoff between controlling the FDR and FNR. Here we see that in fact we have the lowest values for both the FDR and the FNR, with an FDR of less than 1% (two orders of magnitude lower than the competing

---

[2] If we had used 40, then in scenarios such as A causes B and B causes C, the algorithm would be likely to find A causes C.

Table 7.1. *Comparison of results for four algorithms on synthetic MEA data. The software implementation of the approach developed here is called* AITIA

Method	FDR	FNR	Intersection
AITIA	0.0093	0.0005	0.9583
Granger	0.5079	0.0026	0.7530
DBN	0.8000	0.0040	0.4010
PC	0.9608	0.0159	0.0671

approaches). Note that for all methods, the FNR is fairly low. This is due to the small number of true positives compared with the large number of hypotheses tested. Finally, since there were two runs for each embedded pattern at each noise level, we tested the robustness of the findings by calculating the size of the intersection between those runs (the number of significant causal relationships found in both runs, as a fraction of the size of the union of both runs). AITIA was the most consistent according to this measure.

Looking at the results for each algorithm, the false discovery rate for the PC algorithm is not unexpected, as the method tests for relationships between neurons, without testing the timing of that relationship. However, it is interesting to note that DBNs fared worse than bivariate Granger causality by all measures, even though these methods often find causal relationships between common effects of a cause. One possible reason for this is that since the graphical model methods score the entire graph, in theory they must search exhaustively over all graphs, but this is not feasible, and thus heuristics must be used. While greedy algorithms may get stuck in local maxima, simulated annealing algorithms must be stopped before they overfit the data. This overfitting is likely what happened, and why DBN methods perform better when the consensus of a set of graphs is taken (Zou and Feng, 2009). On the other hand, both Granger causality and the logic-based approach of this book evaluate relationships individually and do not require these heuristics, so they consistently return the same results for the same input.

Let us look at one of the five structures recovered in more detail. Figure 7.2a shows the true embedded structure, which is one of the most difficult to infer, as neurons such as D and E are both highly correlated with H and I. The results for the approach developed in this book are shown in figure 7.3, with a histogram of the computed z-values for the

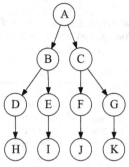

(a) Inferred by AITIA

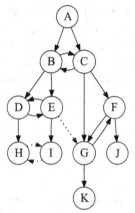

(b) Inferred by bivariate Granger test

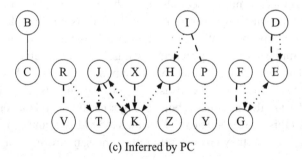

(c) Inferred by PC

Figure 7.2. Graphs representing inference results, with arrows denoting that the neuron at the tail causes the neuron at the head to fire: 7.2a Arrows denote relationships where the cause leads to the effect in 20–40 time units, 7.2b Arrows denote that a neuron causes another to fire in 20 time units, 7.2c Arrows denote conditional dependence relationships and have the usual BN interpretation. Dashed and dotted arrows refer to relationships that were found in one of the two runs for this parameter setting, with solid lines denoting relationships found in both runs. The DBN results appear separately in figure 7.5, as the graph is quite large.

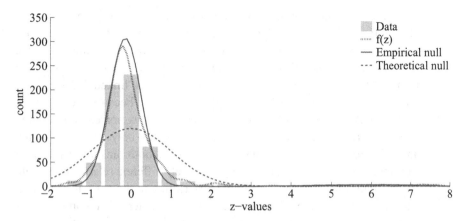

Figure 7.3. Neural spike train example. We tested pairwise causal relationships, taking into account the known temporal constraints on the system.

641 prima facie causal hypotheses. The empirical null in this case is given by $N(-0.14, 0.39)$, so it is shifted slightly to the left of the theoretical null, and is significantly narrower. It is visually apparent that while the null is normally distributed, it is not fit well by the theoretical null and the empirical null provides a better fit to the distribution. The tail of the distribution extends quite far to the right, continuing up to 8 standard deviations away from the mean (almost 20 times the empirical standard deviation). A close-up of this area is shown in figure 7.4. The results obtained here are consistent with the known causal structures that were used to create the simulated data.

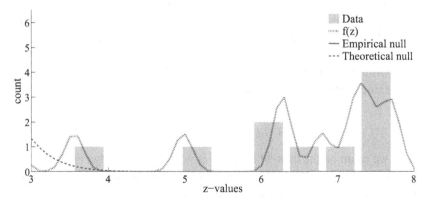

Figure 7.4. Close-up of the tail area of figure 7.3. The relationships in this area are exactly those of figure 7.2a.

Figure 7.2 compares the results on this structure with those from other algorithms, to better visualize the false discoveries and non-discoveries made by each. Looking at the output from the bivariate Granger test, we see that in this case all of the true relationships were identified, but that neurons with a common cause were also found to be linked. For example, there is no causal relationship between B and C, but because they are both caused by A, the bivariate Granger test found a strong correlation between them. The results from the PC algorithm show that only one relationship, an undirected one between B and C, was found in both runs for this dataset. That means that depending on the input, entirely different relationships were found, suggesting that the algorithm is overfitting to the particular dataset, while also missing the true relationships since the temporal component is excluded. Note that this is one of the cases where the assumptions made by the PC algorithm hold, as all common causes are measured and in the dataset, and since there are no inhibitory relationships, none could be "canceled out" by an unlucky distribution. However, that approach is also very dependent on the variables being correctly specified, so we would have to know that there are temporal relationships and know their timing to create indicator variables for these. Finally, the DBN results for this dataset, shown in figure 7.5, show that while the correct relationships were identified (again remembering that an edge between A and B means A causes B at some specific time within 20–40 time units, but for ease of representation we are not showing the edge for each temporal relationship), there are many erroneous edges. Unlike the results of the Granger algorithm, these edges are totally unrelated to the embedded pattern (i.e., they are not misinterpreting a correlation as a causal connection). In large part these relationships are found in only one run, suggesting that the software is overfitting the particular distribution given. This is why some methods fare well when taking the consensus of results from multiple runs, but that is not always feasible as in some cases there is insufficient data to split it this way while in others no such split is possible (for example, there is one run of the stock market in a given year).

7.1.3. *Inference of time windows*

Now we examine the case where there is no prior knowledge of the timing of relationships and we attempt to infer both the existence and timing of the causal relationships from the data. In this case, we aim to evaluate how sensitive the procedure is to the initial windows generated, how closely

Figure 7.5. Graph representing results from DBN algorithm on pattern 4 of the synthetic MEA data. Arrows denote relationships whether the neuron at the head causes the neuron at the tail to fire at some specific time within the range [20,40]. Dashed and dotted arrows refer to relationships that were found in one of the two runs for this parameter setting, with solid lines denoting relationships found in both runs.

the inferred timings correspond to the actual timings, and how the false positive and negative rates compare to the previous case when timings were given. Due to the computational complexity of the experiments (testing many possible windowings), we focused on three of the five patterns that provide insight into different types of relationships: scatter-gather graph,

Table 7.2. *The set of windowings tested and the
start and end times for each*

Name	Window boundaries
W7	1-8, 8-15, 15-22, 22-29, 29-36, 36-43
W13	1-14, 14-27, 27-40, 40-53
W27	1-27, 27-55
PWR2	1-2, 2-4, 4-8, 8-16, 16-32, 32-64, 64-128
PWR4	1-4, 4-16, 16-64

binary tree, and a chain of neurons (omitting the two scatter-gather graphs
and connected scatter-gather graphs).

Method

The testing procedure is as follows. For the set of window boundaries (pairs
of start and end times) $W = \{[w_1, w_2], [w_2, w_3], \ldots, [w_{n-1}, w_n]\}$ and set
of propositions being $AP = \{A, B, \ldots, Z\}$, we generate hypotheses for
all pairs $(a_1, a_2) \in AP$ and $(ws, we) \in W$ of the form: $a_1 \leadsto^{\geq ws, \leq we} a_2$.
Since the true relationships have $ws = 20$ and $we = 40$, in all windowing
schemes $w_n > 40$ and one case went well beyond this to identify potential
weaknesses in the approach. Two main windowing methods were tested:
one where all windows have the same width, and one where the windows
increase exponentially in size. To determine the effect of window size,
windows of width 7, 13, and 27 (corresponding roughly to 1/3, 2/3, and 4/3
of the true width) with the boundaries shown in table 7.2 (W7, W13, and
W27 respectively), and windows formed using powers of 2 and 4 (PWR2
and PWR4) were tested.

Hypotheses for each window were tested using the method described in
section 5.3, where we begin by finding the significant relationships in each
window, and then iteratively refining these. All hypotheses in a windowing
were then reevaluated (recomputation of the ε_{avg} values) in light of the newly
refined hypotheses. Finally, the union of all relationships found significant
within each subwindow of a windowing is taken, using the convention
of taking the higher scoring timing where multiple relationships with the
same variables are inferred. Note that this somewhat understates positive
discoveries, since a true relationship found in multiple windows will only
be counted once, while propagating errors, as an error made in only one
window will be included in the final set. However, this is a better measure

Table 7.3. *Results across all tested datasets*

Windowing	FDR	FNR	avg. # of iterations
W7	0.046	0.003	6.31
W13	0.045	0.002	6.65
W27	0.151	0.006	5.76
PWR2	0.226	0.002	4.66
PWR4	0.462	0.011	3.59

than taking the intersection of multiple inferences, which can obscure cases of overfitting.

Results

We begin by analyzing how well the relationships in the dataset are inferred and whether the algorithm converges as expected. A true positive is defined as a relationship between variables where such a relationship exists in the dataset (with any timing) and a false positive as an identified relationship between variables where no such relationship exists. A false negative is the failure to identify a positive relationship. The false discovery rate (FDR) is the ratio of false discoveries out of all discoveries, and the false negative rate (FNR) is defined similarly. The inferred timings are evaluated separately. FDR and FNR results are shown in table 7.3, with the average number of iterations for a refined hypothesis. The number of iterations is significantly less than the worst case (T, which is 100,000 here) and even less than $log(T)$. Also, as expected, insignificant relationships go through few (if any) iterations. For comparison, the initial testing procedure (finding significant causes to then refine) took around 2.5 hours per window, per dataset, on a desktop PC, while the refinement procedure took around 40 minutes per window, per dataset, on the same PC.

When making use of the known time windows, the FDR and FNR were approximately 0.009 and 0.0005 (as discussed in section 7.1.2), so when using smaller windows, the FDR is close to the case when we have prior knowledge about timings, while the FNR is increased somewhat. Evenly spaced windows fared better than exponentially generated ones, and (in terms of false discoveries), windows that are smaller than the true timing are preferable to those that are larger. Note that the last windowing, which includes a window bounded by 16–64, fares the worst. This is a case where the assumption that a cause will be significant in at least one window

Table 7.4. *Timings inferred for true positive relationships. These are also shown in figure 7.6*

Windowing	start			end		
	mean	med	std	mean	med	std
W7	18.31	20	3.08	39.35	37	4.66
W13	17.70	19	3.29	40.90	40	4.75
W27	16.76	19	4.88	40.38	40	5.81
PWR2	17.15	19	4.09	38.75	36	5.38
PWR4	13.21	15	4.61	49.21	43.5	10.48

intersecting the true window does not hold. This is due to the window being much larger than that of the actual relationship, so there are extremely few true positives, and thus while a similar number of false discoveries are made, they represent a larger proportion here. The total number of false positives in W7 was 3, while in PWR4 it was 12, and W27 was 8. Note that in all cases, the FDR and FNR were still lower than those of the other algorithms compared against using background knowledge.

Next, we evaluate the inferred timings for the true positives. Table 7.4 shows the mean, median, and standard deviation for the window start and end points, which are quite close to the actual value of [20,40]. Figure 7.6 depicts the average start and end points found in each window along with bars showing a standard deviation at each end, and N (the number of relationships being averaged). Note that the inferences made are comparable across windows, except for those made with the powers of 4 windowing.

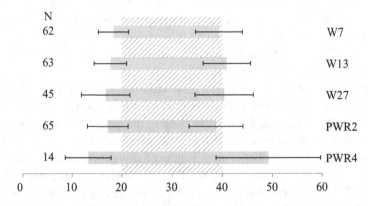

Figure 7.6. Inferred timings for each windowing. Bars show one standard deviation in each direction from the average start/end values. N is the number of significant relationships whose timings were inferred.

This is unsurprising, since the large window violates assumption one, leading to far fewer true positives than other windows (only 14), making the results susceptible to outlying values and resulting in a large standard deviation. A larger initial window also mixes direct/indirect relationships and may only reach a local maxima (due to large expansions/contractions).

7.2. Finance

7.2.1. Simulated financial time series

Data

Before applying the proposed approach to actual financial market data, we must first evaluate it on datasets where the true relationships are known and the method can be compared to others to determine how well these can be recovered in data with this type of structure. Prior work in collaboration with researchers in mathematical finance used a factor model (Kleinberg et al., 2010) to generate simulated returns for portfolios (groups of stocks that share particular characteristics). In that work, causal relationships were embedded in two ways, first by shifting the times when individual factors affect individual portfolios (so that some respond earlier than others and the earlier responders would be seen as causes of the later ones), and second through direct dependence between portfolios. However, since the factors are not independent of the portfolios, determining what should be considered a cause in these datasets can be somewhat challenging. In this book I have simplified how causality is embedded, but use this to incorporate a larger number of more complex relationships (whereas the prior work simulated sets of shifted factors, but only three direct portfolio-portfolio relationships).

The data simulated here were created using a factor model (Fama and French, 1992) to generate data for 25 portfolios over two different 4,000 day time periods.[3] Aside from one dataset where no causal relationships were embedded (included as a check to insure that no causes in means no causes out), each of the others included dependencies between individual portfolios at varying time lags. At each timepoint t, a portfolio's return depends on the values of the three factors at time t plus a portfolio specific

---

[3] The method for simulating data here is based on an approach developed by Petter Kolm (Kleinberg et al., 2010), but differs in how causality is incorporated and the types of causal structures that are simulated.

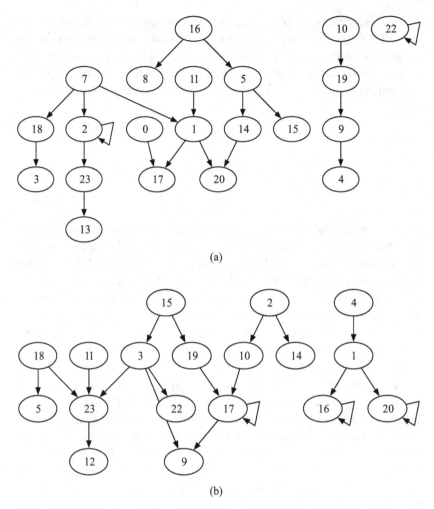

Figure 7.7. Graphs representing embedded causal relationships in simulated financial time series. These are two of the structures involving 20 randomly generated relationships with influence at the timescale of one day.

error term. The ten datasets contain one with no causal relationships, six with sets of randomly generated relationships that have the same lag, two with a set of randomly generated relationships having random lags in the range [0,3], and finally one dataset with many causes for two portfolios. To summarize, the datasets are:

1. No dependency between portfolios.
2–6. 20 randomly generated relationships at a lag of 1 time unit (samples shown in figure 7.7).

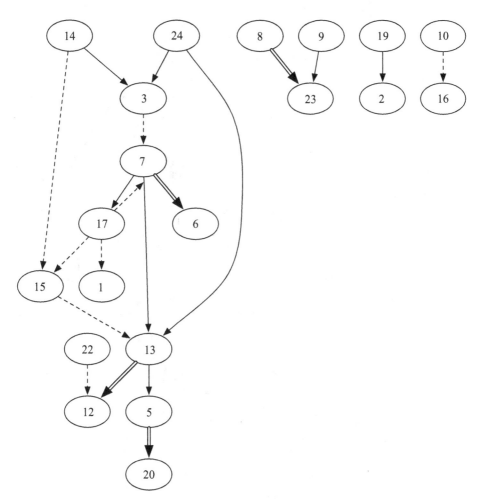

Figure 7.8. Graph representing embedded causal relationships in simulated financial time series. This structure contains 20 randomly generated relationships with influence at timescales from 1 to 3 days. Solid edges indicate a timescale of one day, double edges indicate two days, and dashed edges indicate three days.

7. 40 randomly generated relationships at a lag of 1 time unit.
8. 20 randomly generated relationships with random lags between 1 and 3 time units (figure 7.8).
9. 40 randomly generated relationships with random lags between 1 and 3 time units (figure 7.9).
10. Many-to-one relationships at a lag of 1 time unit (figure 7.10).

Then, each of these structures were embedded in data for two time periods.

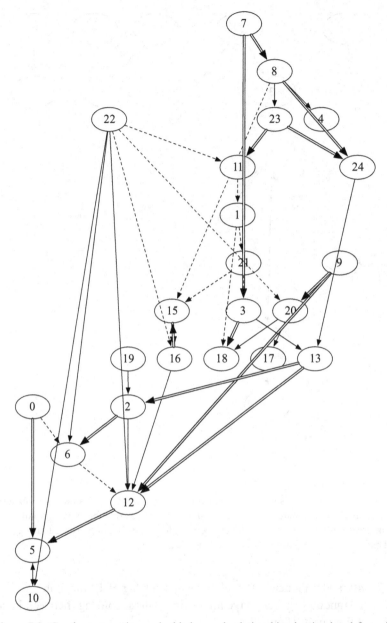

Figure 7.9. Graph representing embedded causal relationships in simulated financial time series. This structure contains 40 randomly generated relationships with influence at timescales from 1 to 3 days. Solid edges indicate a timescale of one day, double edges indicate two days, and dashed edges indicate three days.

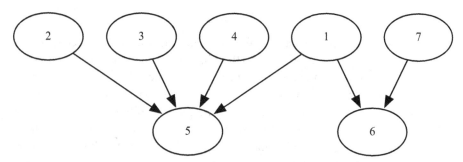

Figure 7.10. Graph representing embedded causal relationships in simulated financial time series. The portfolios here depend on one another at exactly one day.

The return of a portfolio i at time t is given by:

$$r_{i,t} = \sum_j \beta_{ij} f_{j,t'} + \varepsilon_{i,t}. \tag{7.1}$$

In data generated with causal relationships, $\varepsilon_{i,t}$ is the sum of the randomly generated idiosyncratic (also called error) terms and all $\varepsilon_{k,t-l}$ where portfolio k is a cause of portfolio i's returns at a lag of l time units. To construct these series, the Fama-French daily factors (Fama and French, 1993) from July 1963 through July 2011 were used along with the 5×5 size/book-to-market portfolios, also generated by French and Fama (2011). For each structure, two 4,000 day datasets were constructed, using daily returns from July 2, 1975 through April 30, 1991, and April 12, 1995 through March 2, 2011 (timepoints 3,000 to 7,000 and 8,000 to 12,000). Specifically, the 25 size/book-to-market portfolios were regressed onto the market, HML (high minus low), and SMB (small minus big) factors (see Fama and French (1993) for the definition of these factors) and the empirical distribution of the regression coefficients β_{ij} and correlations of the resulting residuals of the portfolios were estimated by bootstrapping over different time periods. The simulated return series data was then generated by randomly drawing betas and residual correlations from these empirical distributions, and then applying (7.1) for the two non-intersecting time periods of 4,000 daily observations of the market, HML, and SMB factors. The random relationships were generated by repeatedly drawing pairs of portfolios and possible lags from the set of variables until the desired number of unique relationships was achieved. Self-cycles and feedback loops were allowed, as there were no constraints on the types of relationships that could be generated. The data are also publicly available and can be downloaded from http://www.cs.stevens.edu/~skleinbe/causality_book/.

Tests & results

As in the previous example, the bivariate Granger test implemented in the MSBVAR `granger.test` (Brandt, 2009) function in R was used as this is a standard method used in analyzing such data and a standardly used implementation of the method. Prior work (Kleinberg et al., 2010) comparing these two approaches investigated results on the return time series (sequences of $r_{i,t}$), the error returns used to generated the returns (sequences of $\varepsilon_{i,t}$), and combinations of these with the known factors. However, it was found that due to the dependency of the factors on the portfolios, one cannot assume that factors would be found as a common cause of all lagged portfolios. This book focuses on the return time series, as attempting to isolate the residuals through regression can introduce errors. Both algorithms tested pairwise relationships between portfolios at lags of 1, 2, and 3 days. For the algorithm developed here, the data was discretized so this meant testing whether a positive/negative return for one variable caused a positive/negative return in another. It is anticipated that this may lead to a somewhat larger proportion of false negatives. Earlier work (Kleinberg, 2011) developed a temporal logic for continuous and discrete variables and reformulated ε_{avg} using expected values instead of conditional probabilities. That method achieved a somewhat lower FDR and FNR when the continuous-valued data was used in that form rather than discretized.[4]

The procedure was to define the set of hypotheses to be tested (relationships between pairs of variables at lags of 1, 2, or 3 time units), then use each algorithm to find the significance of each relationship in this set. This resulted in a set of ε_{avg} values for the approach here and F-statistics with associate p-values for the Granger test. Results from the Granger test on many datasets had significant numbers of relationships with p-values of zero. As these were not sufficiently discriminative, the F-statistics were used instead.[5] For each algorithm, relationships with an fdr < 0.01 were called statistically significant. In general, choosing a threshold for the Granger test is challenging, as in many cases there were large numbers of relationships with large values of the F-statistic, and the true positives and

---

[4] Note that this was found in financial time series, but may not be true in other applications, where data may be noisy and error prone and discretization can be beneficial.

[5] For example, in one dataset where no causes should be inferred, over 150 relationships at each lag had p-values of exactly zero (with many others having extremely low but nonzero values). Using F-statistics instead led to 54 false discoveries on this dataset, allowing more spurious causes to be weeded out.

Table 7.5. *Comparison of results for two algorithms on synthetic financial data. The implementation of the algorithm developed here is* AITIA

Method	FDR	FNR	Intersection
AITIA	0.0241	0.0082	0.4714
bivariate Granger	0.7226	0.0077	0.1501

false positives were interleaved (so that one must either choose a very high value and accept many false negatives to reduce the false positives, or vice versa). This tradeoff can be seen in the ROC curves shown in figure 7.11. The theoretical null hypothesis fit the ε_{avg} values well, while the fdrtool package (Strimmer, 2008) provided better results for granger.test. In both cases the methods were used to automatically determine which relationships were below this fdr threshold. For calculating the false discovery rate (FDR) and false negative rate (FNR), a true positive is inferring a relationship between portfolios when one is embedded, with the timing being that of the actual lags.

Table 7.5 shows the FDR, FNR, and intersection rates for the generated returns. These values are totals using all datasets (i.e., summing false discoveries and all discoveries and calculating the FDR at the end). As was done with the simulated neuronal data, the two datasets generated for each structure were used to calculate the consistency of results from each algorithm. The intersection rate is defined as the fraction of relationships in the intersection of results from both time ranges for a given structure out of the number of relationships in the union of results.

Recall first that one of the types of datasets generated had no causes embedded, and can thus be used to verify that when there is no causality in a dataset, no causality is found. This was the case for AITIA (the software implementation of the method developed in this book), which made zero discoveries in the noncausal datasets during both time spans (this was true as well for the earlier tests (Kleinberg et al., 2010)). While this is a simple test, it is an important check. Note that the bivariate Granger method failed this test, as many relationships were found in both timespans in these datasets that had no causal relationships.

AITIA once again achieved a significantly lower FDR than the Granger test. Here the intersection for both algorithms is lower than for the simulated neuronal data, though. Both approaches also had a somewhat higher rate of false positives and negatives than with the neuronal time series (for

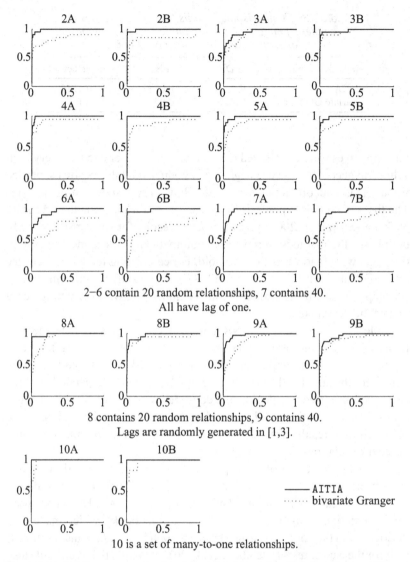

2–6 contain 20 random relationships, 7 contains 40.
All have lag of one.

8 contains 20 random relationships, 9 contains 40.
Lags are randomly generated in [1,3].

10 is a set of many-to-one relationships.

Figure 7.11. ROC curves on simulated financial time series. Numbers denote different structures while *A* and *B* refer to the two time periods. Structure 1 contains no causes.

AITIA, FDR of 0.0241 versus 0.0093). This is not unexpected, as the way the continuous-valued time series are generated makes inferences far more challenging than with the neuronal data where discrete events simply do or do not occur. Here, influences can interact and potentially cancel out

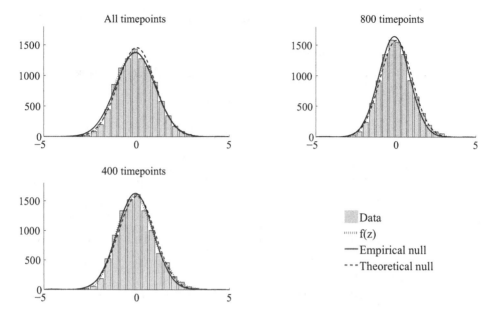

Figure 7.12. Test results for inference on various sized subsets of the actual market data.

in some instances. Thus the reduced intersection, particularly with AITIA, is because the FNR is increased, so that while there are still many true positives (the FDR is also increased, but not as much), different positives may be found in each dataset.

7.2.2. Actual financial data

After validating the method on simulated data, we now aim to apply it to actual financial time series. The algorithm was tested on daily stock returns using the CRSP database, downloaded through WRDS.[6] To somewhat reduce the large number of variables in the dataset and ensure that there was data for each stock at each timepoint, testing began with all stocks that were in the S&P 500 for the entirety of January 1, 2000 through December 31, 2007, and which remained in the S&P 500 through September 2009. Since this yielded over 2,000 trading days and hundreds of stocks, random subsets of 100 stocks in this set were first tested.

---

[6] Wharton Research Data Services (WRDS) was used in preparing the analysis of actual market returns. This service and the data available thereon constitute valuable intellectual property and trade secrets of WRDS and/or its third-party suppliers.

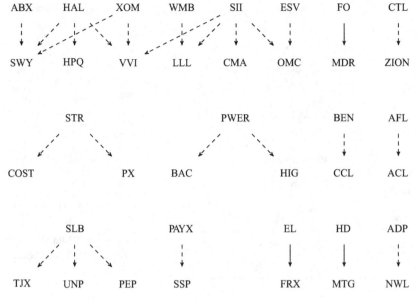

Figure 7.13. Relationships found in one year of actual market data.

Over the entire time course, no significant relationships (with fdr < 0.01) were found when testing for pairwise relationships between stocks at a timescale of one day. During the last 800 timepoints a single significant relationship was identified, though there were again zero for the last 400 timepoints. Figure 7.12 shows the histograms for the test results, which illustrate that in all cases they conform closely to the null normal distribution. No significant relationships were found at longer timescales (i.e., multiple days). One explanation for the few discoveries made is that at the timescale of one day and over long periods of time, relationships between companies do not persist (and are overshadowed by market-wide factors).

Finally, hypothesizing that there may be shorter term relationships between stocks, the time series was restricted to one year of trading using the last 252 timepoints from the series. Due to the shorter time series, it was feasible to examine a larger set of stocks: all of those in the S&P 500 during the 2000–2007 time period. There were 386 such stocks, and 27 significant relationships. The significant relationships are shown in figure 7.13 and are primarily of the form "a price increase in x causes a price decrease in y in exactly 1 day" (denoted by a dashed line in the figure), with a few of the form "a price increase in x causes a price increase in y in exactly 1 day" (denoted by a solid line in the figure). Many of the causes in this set are companies involved in oil, gas, and energy, while financial companies appear to be influenced by results from the technology sector.

8

Conclusion

At the core of many disciplines – including biomedicine, finance, and the social sciences – is the search for causes. To predict future events, understand the connection between phenomena, explain why things happen, and intervene to alter outcomes, researchers must determine the causal relationships governing the behavior of the systems they study. Automating this process has been a difficult pursuit for many reasons, from insufficient data and computing power to the more fundamental question of what causality is and how it can be inferred from observational data alone.

However, many of the previous barriers to inferring complex causal relationships are falling. Through technological advances enabling interrogation of the activities of single cells, the increasing adoption of electronic health records, and the prevalence of sites like Twitter that broadcast the thoughts and actions of millions of users, we now face a flood of data. As predicted by Moore's law, computers have also become faster and cheaper, making it possible to analyze this newly generated information. These datasets are too large for manual analysis, making automated inference not just a possibility, but a necessity. Medical doctors now have patients who log their own vital statistics and symptoms between visits and must integrate this data (that captures critical moments between appointments and admissions) with the patient's history and their own background knowledge. Stock traders are confronted with worldwide financial, political, and other events (reported at a rate far faster than one could read), and must extract the pertinent information and reconcile it with what is known about how markets behave in response to news. Causal relationships are not the end goal here, but rather are needed to inform actions (such as assessing a patient's course of treatment or determining if a stock portfolio is overexposed to a particular type of risk). Before discontinuing a treatment, a doctor must be sure that her particular patient's symptom is a drug side effect and not due to the underlying illness being treated. Traders must be able to predict when their models will stop working, but models based on correlations can lead to black boxes whose reasons for success and failure are unknown. Instead, accurate prediction, explanation, and intervention requires causal knowledge.

More fundamentally, though, we need to know when to act. One of the central points of this work is that a theory of causality with no reference to (or a simplified treatment of) time is a fundamentally limited way of understanding time series data and impedes decision making. Without time we cannot adequately assess risk (as far future events may be less concerning than near term ones), explain the occurrence of events (as timing information is needed to automate explanation), or intervene (as one must know when a cause is effective). Causes and effects are not simply variables that are true or false at discrete time instants, but have durations, histories, and windows of efficacy. Inference is then a problem of understanding the relationships between sequences of events over time, where these events may be comprised of many interacting parts. This requires a new notion of causality that goes beyond pairwise relationships and is built around the temporal and probabilistic relationship between cause and effect.

Motivated by the need for a solution and encouraged by the increasing presence of two pieces of the puzzle (data and computing power), this book has reexamined the theory and process of causal inference and developed a powerful new approach to inference and explanation of complex temporal relationships.

Taking inspiration from the philosophical literature, this book has developed new measures of the impact of a cause on an effect at both the type and token-level. Representing causal relationships and the conditions for probabilistic causality in terms of probabilistic computation tree logic (PCTL) enabled us to move beyond the prior paradigm of simple pairwise events separated by a discrete (or, in many cases, unspecified) amount of time. Here causal relationships are represented more expressively than with statements like "a causes b," and this structured description allows arbitrarily complex relationships to be efficiently tested. As the rules for constructing statements are given by the syntax of the logic, this enabled straightforward methods to be developed for evaluating them in observational data (without first inferring a model). Incorporating temporal information also allows the inference of cycles and feedback loops. This book augmented PCTL to reason about the truth value of formulas involving windows of time and developed algorithms for verification in traces, to determine when formulas are satisfied (and with what probability) without requiring knowledge of the underlying structure.

Many potential (prima facie) causes, those that precede and raise the probability of their effects, may arise by chance or due to common causes, so the majority of work for probabilistic inference methods is in weeding out these spurious causes. Focused on computational feasibility and practical applications, this book introduced a new method for evaluating the significance of causes by calculating the average impact a cause has on the probability of its effect given (pairwise) each of the other possible causes of the same effect. Once this causal significance is calculated, we must determine which values of it are statistically significant. When many hypotheses are tested at once, the resulting significance scores (ε_{avg} values) for non-causal relationships follow a normal distribution. Since the set of significant relationships is also much smaller, methods for false discovery rate control could be applied to choose an appropriate threshold for these values. Using an empirical null allowed this to be done without knowledge of the null distribution in some cases by fitting this empirically to the results (providing a better fit than the theoretical null for simulated neuronal time series).

Finally, all prior work for inferring temporal relationships required users to specify a particular time lag or set of lags to be searched over. However, an incorrect initial choice could lead to inferring a subset of the true timings or even making no inferences. This was a major limitation, since if we do not know that there is a causal relationship between two variables we likely do not know its timing. With limited domain knowledge (perhaps of putative mechanisms) though, we may have an idea of the relative timescale (such as whether a relationship occurs on the order of days or months). Thus, I used the properties of the causal significance measure introduced to develop methods for inferring the timing of relationships without prior knowledge by iteratively perturbing the window for each relationship (shifting, expanding, and contracting it) while attempting to maximize the associated ε_{avg}. This can be done because probabilities such as $P(e|c \wedge x)$ refer to instances of e occurring within the related time windows such that either c or x could have caused it. Thus, when a window is overly wide, for example, $P(e|c \wedge x) - P(e|\neg c \wedge x)$ is reduced since too many instances that should be $\neg c \wedge x$ are considered as $c \wedge x$ with no corresponding increase in occurrences of e so as the window shrinks, instances are moved back to their correct category. By further assuming that a significant relationship will be found significant in at least one window overlapping its true timing, we can refine only the relationships initially found to be significant (a small fraction of the initial large set of hypotheses tested). This approach converges to the actual timings and was shown not to be sensitive to the exact boundaries of the initial candidate windows generated (though vastly oversized windows may lead to many false negatives). Future work will involve exploring other heuristic algorithms for searching the space of possible time windows with significantly (and systematically) missing data. In general, the approaches in this book enable one to infer significant causal relationships relative to a set of data. These nearly always need to be confirmed through other methods (using background knowledge or conducting experimental studies), since we rarely have the background knowledge needed to know that they are truly genuine. However, this approach gives experimentalists a set of highly significant targets (with their full complexity and timing) to be investigated further.

In addition to finding general causes, such as those of a particular disease, we also aim to find explanations for individual occurrences, such as ranking possible explanations for a particular patient's cancer given her medical history and symptoms. Here we aim to understand the relative significance of causes for a token-level event. This is a significant practical problem in many areas but one of the most interesting and important is found in medicine, where different causes of an event can have a large impact on treatment decisions. Further, this type of reasoning must be not only formalized but automated for many applications such as analyzing critical care data streams, where early detection of complications is critical and the data are too complex and voluminous for humans to quickly make sense of. Despite the need for computational methods, token causality has been addressed mainly by the philosophical literature, where researchers aim to define what it is and how it relates to type-level causality. To solve practical problems, though, we need algorithms that can find the relative significance of potential explanations and do this with incomplete and uncertain information. For diagnosis of patients, there will often be missing tests (we cannot retroactively order glucose tests 6 months ago) whose truth value needs to be determined from the other available information. Type-level timings may also deviate from those at the token level due to uncertainty about the timing of token-level events and the type-level timings not strongly constraining the relationship. The known timing of an event may be inexact, such as when a patient says that he had a headache "about a week ago," where there is some region around 7 days where this likely occurred. Similarly, finding that one factor causes another in say 100–150 time units does not necessarily mean that it is not possible for this to occur in 96 or 152 time units. While some time windows may correspond to exact windows of efficacy, others may be more fluid. I developed a method that uses the significance of the general (type-level) relationships to assess the significance of potential token causes in a way that allows for incomplete information and accounts for the (potentially uncertain) timing of occurrences. We can then take an event to be explained, and a sequence of time-indexed token observations, and use these to determine the significance of the type-level causes for this instance of the effect. This does not require complete knowledge of the scenario (i.e., the truth value for all propositions in the system), and outputs a significance score for each possible token cause (rather than simply caused/did not cause). This approach was shown to handle many of the common tests cases and counterexamples found in the philosophical literature, including redundant causation and transitivity. In particular, the inclusion of temporal information and allowance for multiple causes of varying significance means that some previously overdetermined cases can now be correctly found to have a single significant cause while others that should have seemed overdetermined but did not, due to overly strict enforcement of the type-level timings, now do. Further, we can also use this method for predictive purposes (prognosis), where the effect has not yet occurred and we want to determine its likelihood.

In chapter 7, the methods developed were applied to simulated data (to allow evaluation of findings against some ground truth) and real data (to discover novel relationships). First, one set of data was generated by other researchers to mimic the structure of neurons firing over time. The embedded timing information and variety of data structures allowed comparison against other approaches (BNs, DBNs, and Granger causality) and evaluation of the methods developed for inferring the timing of relationships. When making use of the known timing information, the approach developed here achieved an FDR of less than 1% (two orders of magnitude lower than the other methods) while also achieving the lowest FNR. Further, the inferences were highly robust, with over 95% of inferences made in both datasets for a particular structure and noise level. When the timing of relationships was also inferred, this approach still had the lowest FDR (regardless of how candidate windows were generated) and the timings themselves converged quickly and closely to the actual timings. Analysis of financial data is a second primary area of application, so simulated stock portfolio time series were generated before application to actual stock price data. The continuous financial time series allowed for a wider variety of datasets to be generated than with the simulated spike train data. Here there were datasets with no causal relationships embedded (generated to test whether algorithms correctly find no causality when none is embedded), along with randomly generated sets of 20 and 40 relationships with either consistent or randomly generated lags, and a dataset including many-to-one relationships. In comparison with bivariate Granger causality (a method commonly applied to such data), false discovery rates were again extremely low (around 2%, with bivariate Granger being around 72%) with few false negatives. In datasets with no embedded causality, only the approach here was able to correctly infer no causes. On actual market data over long time periods, no causal relationships were inferred, suggesting that over the long term the market may be efficient at the timescale of daily returns. Over a period of one year of trading, though, relationships were inferred. This may have implications for portfolio construction, as a seemingly diversified set of stocks may carry more risk than thought when many are causally related.

In this book, I have described a general approach that can be applied to many areas, from politics (where a candidate's favorability ratings can be influenced by their choice of words in speeches and actions such as votes), to finance (where the price movement of a stock is a result of both hidden market factors and the movements of other individual stocks and sectors) to computational biology (where we want to find the genes responsible for particular traits). One of the most important emerging applications is in the analysis of electronic health records (EHRs), which contain valuable information on patients over long periods of time. These can potentially be used to find drug side effects and disease etiologies, yet they have been underexplored due to the dearth of methods for dealing with complex temporal data. The work here advances the state of the art for analyzing data in these types of challenging applications that can potentially have a large impact on practice.

8.1. Broader Connections

While this book has focused on empirical comparison against other computational methods and theoretical comparison against probabilistic theories (at the type level) and counterfactual ones (at the token level), there are implications for other frameworks. The goal here has been primarily methodological, but the resulting approach can be connected to metaphysical methods that conceive of causality in terms of processes or mechanisms. In particular, adding spatial information may enable connections to process theories of causality, and the underlying DTMCs (whether inferred or constructed) can potentially be understood mechanistically.

Process theories, such as those of Salmon (1994) and Dowe (2000), argue that causality involves the transmission of a property or information (such as momentum) and thus also requires locality in space-time. To illustrate this, say a stone is thrown from point A to point B. Then, if it is marked with chalk before it leaves point A, it will arrive at B with the same mark. On the other hand, we cannot mark or alter the stone's shadow in the same manner such that the change will persist until the second point. The idea is not necessarily transmitting chalk marks, but rather that causal processes can propagate a signal in a way that noncausal processes cannot. In the language of Dowe's conserved quantity theory, the stone can possess a quantity such as momentum, but its shadow cannot possess or transmit any such quantities. The concern in this book has been with the temporal relationship between potentially complex causes and events, without regard to the physical connection between these factors. While the conditions of process theories are stricter than those imposed here, it may be possible to bridge the gap between process and probabilistic methods by incorporating spatial information. Until now, process theories have been primarily investigated in philosophy, partly because calculation of probabilities is far easier than evaluation of the processes between cause and effect (at least outside of physics). However, since probabilistic theories can fall prey to counterexamples of causality without probability raising and probability raising without causality, while process theories may fail to handle cases such as omissions, incorporating ideas from process theories can make these more robust while also leading to methods for inferring causal processes. Spatiotemporal datasets such as those from fMRI (functional Magnetic Resonance Imaging) make this line of work of practical import. A primary challenge for probabilistic theories is weeding out which factors are not able to be causes even though they may seem to raise probabilities, a task that is further complicated when variables are missing. Process-based knowledge could be used to aid the hypothesis generation step, limiting which factors are considered as potential causes. Thus, even if we knew only of a stone's shadow, we would still not consider it to be a cause of an event such as a window breaking as it does not have the ability to transfer information as the stone does. Linking process theories to probabilistic ones may also broaden these beyond cases in physics, and may lead to an epistemological process theory of causality.

Mechanistic theories could also be related to the underlying structures of systems. One way of understanding probabilistic Kripke structures (DTMCs) causally (without needing to disentangle significant and insignificant causes) is by relating them to mechanistic explanation. There is dissent about what constitutes a mechanism and the purpose of mechanisms, but the rough idea is that there is some set of interactions or activities connecting the cause to the effect that function in invariant or predictable ways. The mechanisms are how the cause produces the effect (Glennan, 1996, 2002; Machamer et al., 2000). There is no single definition of what the parts of a mechanism are or how finely grained an explanation must be to be mechanistic. Whether there are "mechanisms all the way down" or if at some point they bottom out, is not a concern if we recognize that different levels of detail are desirable in different situations. For example, when describing the central dogma of molecular biology (Crick, 1970) the explanations will vary based on the audience. When describing this to someone with limited scientific background, we might simply leave it at "DNA is transcribed into RNA, which is then translated into proteins." If instead the audience were a group of biology students, we would go into more detail about each of those processes. Translation would be expanded into initiation, elongation and termination. Each of these in turn can be expanded into their components. Here the mechanism is something that gives evidence of the causal relationship by describing how it is possible.

The language of mechanisms, with their parts and connecting processes is analogous to that of states and transitions, though there is not necessarily a one-to-one correspondence. If we have or can infer the underlying structure of a system, we can understand it mechanistically by determining the processes connecting the states (e.g., how one might move from one to the other, not just the probability of this occurring). We should be able to fill in these transitions that occur with nonzero probability with some explanatory verbs. In the previous biological example, we can connect DNA to RNA by the activity of transcription. Whether or not this type of explanation is possible in general depends on the granularity of variables in the system, so we cannot automatically say that such a structure constitutes a mechanistic explanation. However, in some cases, this can be a useful way to understand them. The combination of mechanistic and probabilistic evidence for relationships is also in keeping with scientific practice in the biomedical sciences, as well as recent philosophical work that has suggested that while causality itself cannot be put into wholly probabilistic or mechanistic terms, these can provide complementary evidence for causal claims (Russo and Williamson, 2011a,b). Incorporating mechanisms into modeling would further the use of these in automated causal inference.

8.2. Looking Forward

This book is the first step in a new direction of causal inference and explanation focused on time series data and practical applications. The methodologies I have developed are only the beginning of what is needed, but open up a number of lines of work. We must first develop strategies for combining diverse data sources, including those at multiple scales (from populations to individuals to cells) and levels of granularity (to determine how short term processes influence longer term ones). There are many remaining problems in inference and explanation including finding and dealing with latent variables, inference in non-stationary time series, intelligently exploring the search space of hypotheses, and incorporating background knowledge. Here I outline a few of the most pressing areas.

A key problem is knowing whether the relationships we observe are genuine or if they are due to a chance distribution of the variables. Simpson's paradox occurs when we find a correlation between variables in a set of subpopulations, but this correlation is reversed when the populations are combined. We might find that a medication does not improve prognosis in a combined population of men and women, but that it is beneficial when we consider populations of just men or just women. This is a difficult problem to both detect and solve. However, it may be possible to address this using token-level knowledge, using instances where we know (or know with high probability) the true cause to refine our theory. If on many occasions the token and type-level causal relationships are in conflict, we may be observing this paradox.

In this book, it was assumed that both the data and relationships were stationary (the relationships did not themselves evolve over time), but this is not always true. In finance, the relationships between companies (due to mergers and acquisitions, for one) change, as do the legal rules governing their behavior. In medicine, a diabetic patient may oscillate between two states – one where their glucose is under control and one where it is not. However, only a subset of all relationships change in these cases (the entire system does not shift to a new regime). It will be important to determine the times when the underlying causal regime changes not just to know when our rules stop being true, but also for inference. If we assume the relationships in a long time series are stationary, but there are instead distinct periods with differing structures, we will likely fail to find the true relationships. In related work (Kleinberg, 2011) extending the method developed here to continuous-valued data, I found that relationships in the stock market did in fact change over time, and some could be found to begin and become increasingly strong until the end of the study period (measured by the magnitude of impact on a stock's expected price changes). When assuming that relationships do not change, we may fail to make these short term inferences.

Finally, there are important future directions in the area of token causality. These address practical problems such as determining who is to blame for an accident, why a patient developed a set of symptoms, or whether a change in policy affected a company's stock prices. Thus far, we have greatly simplified such tasks by assuming that for each possible fact, we either correctly know it to be true or false, or we do not know its truth value. However, individuals may have varying states of knowledge about the world and their information could be in conflict or incorrect. In some cases, there may also be deception, such as when a politician's statements are not reflective of their underlying beliefs. This area has similarities to argumentation and legal reasoning (where we perhaps need to understand the support for token-level hypotheses at the level of individuals), and applications in disease diagnosis. A patient's medical record may have incorrectly recorded tests and conflicting diagnoses, and we want to find both the best explanation for their symptoms and the best course of treatment. More broadly, automating the process of evaluating potential token causes has been largely ignored in the computational literature, yet it is a significant practical problem. Approaches that can do this from data without human intervention can have a large impact in medicine by analyzing the large quantity of streaming data from intensive care units (alerting doctors to events requiring intervention).

Much of causality remains an open problem, and as the field advances it becomes clearer how much is still to be done. The beauty of work in this area is that it permeates every other facet of research, so that discoveries can have a tangible impact not only on computational methods, but on biomedicine, finance, and politics among other areas.

Appendix A

A Little Bit of Statistics

We are frequently faced with the problem of determining whether a result is significant. People in a region may seem to have a high rate of cancer, but is it out of the ordinary? Are children much more likely to develop autism after being vaccinated? Which genes are differentially expressed in tumor and normal cells? In most cases, we end up with a numerical result, and must determine a threshold at which to call it significant. As we will see shortly, this becomes more complicated when we test many hypotheses at once, as it is then likelier that we will observe something that seems significant by chance. This chapter reviews the basic concepts in and approaches to evaluating statistical tests. We begin with the simplest case of a single result before discussing the modifications needed when doing many tests at once.

A.1. Preliminaries

Say we want to determine whether or not a coin is fair, so we flip it 10 times. Our assumption is that the coin is fair, meaning that the probability of heads (H) (or tails (T)) on any given flip is $1/2$. However, the sequence we observe is 9 heads and 1 tail. We then want to determine how likely it is that this would occur given our initial hypothesis (called the *null hypothesis*) that the coin is fair. The basic concept is that we attempt to determine whether the results conform to the null hypothesis, usually denoted H_0, that there is no difference, or whether the observations do deviate significantly, and might be more plausibly explained by an alternative hypothesis, usually denoted H_1.

One way of determining the significance of a result is by using its p-value. The p-value is the probability of seeing a result *at least as extreme* as the observation if the null hypothesis were true. That means that for the coin flipping case the p-value is:

$$P(9H1T) + P(10H) + P(10T) + P(9T1H). \qquad (A.1)$$

We could see all heads, all tails, or 9 tails and 1 head (which is as extreme as 9 heads and 1 tail). In this case, we are allowing that the coin could be biased for heads or for tails, so we examine the probabilities of many more or fewer heads. This is referred to as a two-tailed test. We could instead have examined the alternative hypothesis of the coin being biased just for heads or just for tails, conducting a one-tailed test. Then, when testing whether a coin is biased toward heads there would only be one more extreme result than $9H1T$ – all heads.

Going back to the previous case, where the coin may be biased for heads or tails, let us calculate the probabilities needed to determine the p-value. First,

$$P(10H) = P(10T) = (1/2)^{10} \approx 0.001. \tag{A.2}$$

The probability of a run of all heads or all tails is simply the probability of either of those outcomes 10 times in a row, meaning $(1/2)^{10}$. Next, when we calculate the probability of exactly one head, $P(9T1H)$, we do not care which position it is in, so the head might be on the first flip or on the eighth, but these results are identical from our perspective. Thus, there are 10 ways this can be satisfied (each of the 10 flips). Then:

$$P(9H1T) = P(9T1H) = (1/2)^{10} \times 10 \approx 0.01. \tag{A.3}$$

Finally, we can use these values and equation (A.1) to determine the p-value of the result, which is:

$$(1/2)^{10} \times 10 + (1/2)^{10} + (1/2)^{10} + (1/2)^{10} \times 10 \approx 0.021. \tag{A.4}$$

This convention goes back to Fisher (1925), who suggested 0.05 but also felt that this was not a hard and fast rule.

We must still determine at what level to call the coin unfair (rejecting the null hypothesis). Commonly, a threshold of 0.05 is used and the null hypothesis rejected if the probability of observing such an extreme result under it is less than 0.05. This threshold is referred to as α, and we reject the null hypothesis for tests where $P < \alpha$. Using $\alpha = 0.05$, we should then call the coin in question unfair, since $0.021 < 0.05$. Note however that 0.05 is simply a convention, and depending on the application, higher or lower values may be preferable.

A.2. Multiple Hypothesis Testing

In the previous section, we looked at the case of flipping one coin 10 times, but what if we flip 100 coins 10 times each? When testing a single hypothesis, we made the decision about whether to accept or reject the null hypothesis based on the probability of seeing such an extreme result under the null hypothesis. However, when we are testing multiple hypotheses at once, the likelihood that we will get such results – even under the null hypothesis – increases and we must account for this.

Say x is the event of getting 9 heads and 1 tail. Then, call y the set of events consisting of results at least as extreme as x (i.e., 9 tails and 1 head, all tails, or all heads). In the previous section, we calculated $P(y) \approx 0.021$. Now, to determine the probability of y being true at least once in N tries, we can calculate $1 - P(\neg y)^N$. Subtracting the probability of y not being true N times in a row from one gives the probability that we are interested in. Then,

$$P(\neg y) = 1 - P(y)$$

$$\approx 1 - 0.021$$

$$\approx 0.979$$

and the probability with $N = 100$ tries is:

$$1 - P(\neg y)^{100} \approx 0.88. \tag{A.5}$$

In the previous case (when doing only one test), we rejected the null hypothesis for p-values less than α. The significance level, α, corresponded to the probability of making an error in rejecting the null hypothesis. I now refer to the significance level for a single test as α_c, the per-comparison significance. When testing many hypotheses, the significance level for all tests will be denoted by α_e, the experiment-wide significance level. Intuitively, these will not be equal when doing a large number of tests, but let us look at an example to clarify this important point. Say we are doing $N = 100$ tests, and $\alpha_c = 0.05$. That means that the probability of a false positive (a seemingly significant result when the null hypothesis is true) is:

$$1 - (0.95)^{100} = 0.994. \tag{A.6}$$

Each comparison in this case is independent from each other comparison, and for each one the probability of an error is bounded by 0.05. That means we can use 1 minus the probability of an error on *any* of the 100 comparisons. As we can see, the probability is quite high.

Let us now generalize this. For N independent tests, with per-comparison significance-level α_e, the experiment-wide significance level α_e is given by:

$$\alpha_e = 1 - (1 - \alpha_c)^N. \tag{A.7}$$

However, if the tests are not independent, we can bound the experiment-wide significance as follows:

$$\alpha_e \leq N \times \alpha_c. \tag{A.8}$$

Table A.1. *Types of errors*

	Accept null	Reject null	Total
True null H	TN	FP	m_0
False null H	FN	TP	m_1
Total	$m - R$	R	m

Since (A.8) is greater than (A.7), we can bound the experiment-wide significance (in both the dependent and independent cases) by $N \times \alpha_c$. This means that when testing 100 fair coins, we may incorrectly deem 5 unfair when using $\alpha_c = 0.05$. Thus, it is necessary to account for the fact that we are performing many tests simultaneously, increasing the chances of seeing unlikely or anomalous behavior (Benjamini and Yekutieli, 2001; Efron, 2004; Storey and Tibshirani, 2003).

A.2.1. Basic definitions

Before discussing how to account for multiple tests, let us examine the types of errors that may be made. In the previous section, we considered the case of falsely calling a fair coin unfair, but we also could have failed to detect that a coin was unfair. Table A.1 shows the possible results for a set of m hypotheses being tested. We could correctly accept the null hypothesis in the case when it is true or correctly reject a false null (i.e., calling a coin unfair when that is the case). These are true negatives and true positives (TN and TP in the table). If instead we reject the null hypothesis when it is true, this is known as a false positive, or *Type I error* (α). As discussed before, the *per-comparison error rate* is the probability of making such an error during each significance test. We can also fail to reject the null hypothesis when we should, making a *Type II error* (β). Whereas Type I errors mean we have made a false discovery (false positive), Type II errors mean we have missed an opportunity for discovery (false negative). While it is desirable to reduce both types of error, it may sometimes only be possible to trade one kind off against the other. The best trade-offs are judged in terms of the relative costs of these errors in a particular domain of application.

The previous definitions related to individual comparisons, but we also want to determine the error rates over all the hypotheses being tested. The *familywise error rate* (FWER) is the probability of rejecting one or more true null hypotheses (i.e., the probability of having at least one Type I error), during all tests. That is, $P(FP \geq 1)$. For the FWER to approach a desired bound of α, we need each of the N tests to be conducted with an even stricter bound, such as $\frac{\alpha}{N}$, as required by the Bonferroni correction (Benjamini and Yekutieli, 2001). However, the FWER has low power, meaning that we have a good chance of making a Type II error (Benjamini and Hochberg, 1995). Another measure, called the *false discovery rate* (FDR), estimates the proportion of Type I errors among all rejected hypotheses (that is, the number of false discoveries divided by the total number of discoveries). Using the notation from the preceding table, this is FP/R. This measure results in more power than the FWER while still bounding the error rate. The main idea is that if we are rejecting only a few null hypotheses then each false discovery we make in that case is more significant than rejecting a large number of null hypotheses and making the same number of false discoveries. In the first case, the false discoveries are a larger percentage of the overall number of discoveries than they are in the later case. One final measure is the *false negative rate* (FNR), the proportion of falsely accepted null hypotheses out of all nulls, $FN/(m - R)$. In most cases, there is a tradeoff between controlling the FDR and FNR, so we must determine which type of error is most serious for the application at hand. For the applications in mind here, false discoveries are generally more concerning than false negatives, as we are using these relationships to make research and policy decisions and would rather have more confidence in the results, at the expense of missing a few potential discoveries.

A.2.2. Correcting for multiple tests

Before discussing methods for FDR control, let us look at the difference between this and control of the FWER. As noted in the previous section, the Bonferroni correction provides a method for controlling the FWER, but can result in many false negatives. The basic idea of the approach is that for α_e to be 0.05, each test needs to be conducted at a lower rate. Recall that the following is an upper bound for α_e:

$$\alpha_e = \alpha_c \times N. \tag{A.9}$$

To achieve a particular value of α_e, we can rearrange this to find α_c:

$$\alpha_c = \frac{\alpha_e}{N}. \tag{A.10}$$

That means that if we are doing 100 tests and want $\alpha_e = 0.05$, then each test must be conducted with $\alpha_c = 0.0005$. However, since this is controlling the probability of making even one false discovery, this test can result in many false negatives. Remember also that if the tests are independent, this greatly overestimates the needed α_c.

Instead of focusing on the probability of even one false discovery, we can focus on the rate of false discoveries. When doing 10 tests, 2 false positives might be significant, while if we were doing 1,000 tests, that would be much less serious. One procedure for controlling the FDR was introduced by Benjamini and Hochberg (1995). When testing m hypotheses, order the p-values $P_{(1)} \leq P_{(2)} \cdots \leq P_{(m)}$. Then with k selected as the largest i such that:

$$P_{(i)} \leq \frac{i}{m}\alpha, \tag{A.11}$$

reject all $H_{(i)}, i = 1, 2, \ldots, k$. In the case when all hypotheses are true this in fact controls the FWER, and otherwise controls the proportion of erroneous rejections of the null hypothesis. For independent (and positively dependent) test statistics, this procedure controls the FDR at rate α.

One downside of the Benjamini-Hochberg method for false discovery control is that in many cases we expect a large number of positive results. When detecting differential gene expression, we may have microarray data for thousands of genes and expect to find relationships between many pairs in this set. In practice, $0.05 \times m$ is too large, so a much lower value of α tends to be used. However, there are still many positives and potentially many false discoveries. One method introduced by Storey (2003) uses what is called the q-value to assess the significance associated with each hypothesis. The procedure is, as before, to order the p-values, and after determining the largest P where the null will be rejected, reject it for all p' where $p' \leq p$. To do this, we calculate the q-value, which is the expected proportion of false discoveries made if that hypothesis is called significant (the null rejected). Thus, we calculate q for each feature, and then reject the null where $q \leq \alpha$. The primary idea is that each test is being assessed individually, determining how rejection of that null affects the overall FDR.

While the q-value assesses the tests individually, the false discovery rate is for the entire tail (region of results with $p' \leq p$, where we rejected p). However, a hypothesis closer to the edge (near the largest p' where the null is rejected) will seem less likely than it should to be a false positive. For some test with $q = 0.05$, that particular q has a higher than 5% chance of being false, since the tests with smaller q-values are likelier to be true positives.

Another approach is to consider acceptance/rejection of the null for each test individually, based on its particular false discovery rate. This approach uses what is known as the *local false discovery rate* (fdr), and was introduced by Efron and Tibshirani (2002). This is similar to the q-value, but here the decision to accept or reject the null is made for each value individually based on how significantly it differs from the null. Here we assume that N is large, but the tests need not be independent.

Instead of p-values, this approach uses z-values, which are the number of standard deviations by which a result deviates from the mean. One property of these statistics is that, due to the large number of hypotheses tested, they should be normally distributed. With N hypotheses $H_1, H_2, \ldots, H_N$, we have the corresponding z-values $z_1, z_2, \ldots, z_N$. We begin by assuming the N cases fall into two classes: one where the effects are either spurious or not large enough to be interesting (and thus where we accept the null hypotheses), and another where the effects are large enough to be interesting (and where we will accept the non-null hypotheses as true). We also assume the proportion of non-null cases is small relative to N, say, around 10%. Then, p_0 and $p_1 = 1 - p_0$ are the prior probabilities of a case (here, a causal hypothesis) being in the "uninteresting" or "interesting" classes respectively. The densities of each class, $f_0(z)$ and $f_1(z)$, describe the distribution of these probabilities. When using a theoretical null, $f_0(z)$ is the standard $N(0, 1)$ density. Note that we need not know $f_1(z)$, though we must estimate p_0 (usually $p_0 \geq 0.9$, but this is simply a convention). We define the mixture density:

$$f(z) = p_0 f_0(z) + p_1 f_1(z), \tag{A.12}$$

then the posterior probability of a case being uninteresting given z is

$$P(null|z) = p_0 f_0(z)/f(z), \tag{A.13}$$

and the local false discovery rate, is:

$$fdr(z) \equiv f_0(z)/f(z). \tag{A.14}$$

Note that, in this formulation, the p_0 factor is ignored, yielding an upper bound on $fdr(z)$. Assuming that p_0 is large (close to 1), this simplification does not lead to massive overestimation of $fdr(z)$. One may also choose to estimate p_0 and thus include it in the FDR calculation, making $fdr(z) = P(null|z)$. The procedure is then:

1. Estimate $f(z)$ from the observed z-values;
2. Define the null density $f_0(z)$ either from the data or using the theoretical null;
3. Calculate $fdr(z)$ using equation (A.14);
4. Label H_i where $fdr(z_i)$ is less than a threshold (say, 0.10) as interesting.

Appendix B

Proofs

B.1. Probability Raising

Claim. *The following conditions for probabilistic causality are equivalent in non-deterministic cases:*

$$P(E|C) > P(E) \tag{B.1}$$

$$P(E|C) > P(E|\neg C) \tag{B.2}$$

Proof. Assume that $1 > P(C) > 0$ (and thus $1 > P(\neg C) > 0$). By definition:

$$P(E) = P(E|C) \times P(C) + P(E|\neg C) \times P(\neg C) \tag{B.3}$$

$$= P(E|C) \times P(C) + P(E|\neg C) \times (1 - P(C)) \tag{B.4}$$

$$= P(E|C) + (P(E|\neg C) - P(E|C)) \times (1 - P(C)) \tag{B.5}$$

Then, if $P(E|\neg C) > P(E|C)$, it must be that $P(E|C) < P(E)$ to maintain the equality, and if $P(E|C) > P(E|\neg C)$, then by the same reason $P(E|C) > P(E)$. Thus, if (B.2) is satisfied, (B.1) is satisfied. Conversely, if $P(E|C) > P(E)$, then we must have $P(E|C) > P(E|\neg C)$. Thus, if (B.1) is satisfied (B.2) is satisfied and finally we conclude that (B.1) $\leftrightarrow$ (B.2). $\square$

B.2. Equivalence to Probabilistic Theory of Causality

In this section, we show that the conditions proposed for prima facie causality are equivalent to Suppes's conditions. Recall that Suppes's notation A_t and $B_{t'}$, where $t' < t$, only implies that B occurs earlier than A, not that t and t' are specific times. We are implicitly summing over all t, considering any scenario where B is before A.

Suppes's conditions for prima facie causality (denoted SC):

1. $P(E_t|C_{t'}) > P(E_t)$,
2. $t' < t$, and
3. $P(C_{t'}) > 0$.

Our conditions for prima facie causality (denoted LC):

1. $c \overset{\geq 1, \leq \infty}{\underset{\geq p}{\leadsto}} e$,
2. $F_{>0}^{\leq \infty} c$, and
3. $F_{<p}^{\leq \infty} e$.

Restating theorem 4.2.1:

Theorem B.2.1. *Assume there is a structure $K = \langle S, s^i, L, \mathcal{T} \rangle$ representing the underlying system governing the occurrences of the events. Then the conditions for causality given in definition 4.2.1 (LC) are satisfied iff the conditions for causality given by Suppes in definition 2.3.2 are satisfied. (SC)*

We begin by showing $LC \to SC$ and then show $SC \to LC$.

Proposition B.2.1. $LC \to SC$

Proof. Assume that $c = C$, $e = E$ and that there is a structure, $K = \langle S, s^i, L, \mathcal{T} \rangle$, representing the underlying system governing the occurrences of these events. Also assume that states in K that satisfy c and e are labeled as such. If $t' < t$ in SC, we assume that in K there will be at least one transition between an event at t' and one at t. That is, the timescale of K is as fine as that of Suppes and vice versa. Further, we assume that the probabilities of Suppes's formulation and those in K come from the same source and thus if represented correctly, $P(E)$ in SC is equal to $P(e)$ in LC.

Condition 1 $P(E_t|C_{t'}) > P(E_t)$
By definition of $F_{<p}^{\leq \infty} e$, $P(E_t)$ – the probability of E occurring at any time, denoted t – is less than p. Recall that the probability of a path is the product of the transition probabilities along the path, and the probability of a set of paths is the sum of their individual path probabilities. For a structure to satisfy this formula, the set of paths from the start state that reach a state where e holds must be less than p, and the probability of reaching a state where e holds in this system is less than p. Thus,

$$P(E_t) < p.$$

Now we must show $P(E_t|C_{t'}) \geq p$, meaning that the probability of E_t is greater given that C has occurred at some time t' prior to E. We now show that this conditional probability is greater than or equal to p if:

$$c \overset{\geq 1, \leq \infty}{\underset{\geq p}{\leadsto}} e \tag{B.6}$$

is satisfied.

The probability p_1 of a transition from state s_1 to state s_2 that labels the edge between them,

$$s_1 \overset{p_1}{\to} s_2,$$

is the conditional probability:

$$P(s_{2,t+1}|s_{1,t}), \tag{B.7}$$

the probability of reaching s_2 one time unit after s_1. Then, for a path:

$$s_1 \overset{p_1}{\to} s_2 \overset{p_2}{\to} s_3,$$

we can calculate the probability, given s_1, of reaching s_3 (via s_2) within two time units:

$$P(s_{3,t+2}, s_{2,t+1}|s_{1,t}) = P(s_{3,t+2}|s_{2,t+1}, s_{1,t}) \times P(s_{2,t+1}|s_{1,t}), \tag{B.8}$$

and since s_3 and s_1 are independent conditioned on s_2 this becomes:

$$P(s_{3,t+2}, s_{2,t+1}|s_{1,t}) = P(s_{3,t+2}|s_{2,t+1}) \times P(s_{2,t+1}|s_{1,t}). \tag{B.9}$$

Note that the probabilities on the righthand side are simply the transition probabilities from s_1 to s_2, and s_2 to s_3 (since there is one time unit between the states, they can only be reached via a single transition). Thus, the conditional probability is precisely the path probability:

$$P(s_{3,t+2}, s_{2,t+1}|s_{1,t}) = p_2 \times p_1. \tag{B.10}$$

Then, if we have a set of paths from s_1 to s_3, the conditional probability $P(s_3|s_1)$ is the sum of these path probabilities. For example, we may have the following paths:

$$s_1 \overset{p_1}{\to} s_2 \overset{p_2}{\to} s_3$$

$$s_1 \overset{p_3}{\to} s_4 \overset{p_4}{\to} s_3$$

in which case:

$$P(s_{3,t+2}|s_{1,t}) = P(s_{3,t+2}, s_{2,t+1}|s_{1,t}) + P(s_{3,t+2}, s_{4,t+1}|s_{1,t}), \tag{B.11}$$

and from equation (B.10) this becomes:

$$P(s_{3,t+2}|s_{1,t}) = p_2 \times p_1 + p_4 \times p_3, \tag{B.12}$$

the sum of the individual path probabilities. Let us now say that s_1 is labeled with c and s_3 is labeled with e, these are the only c and e states in the system, and there are no other paths between the states taking less than or equal to 2 time units. Then, this probability we have computed is in fact the probability of:

$$c \overset{\geq 1, \leq 2}{\rightsquigarrow} e, \tag{B.13}$$

since the probability of reaching s_3 during a window of time simply means looking at the set of paths reaching s_3 during that window. Similarly, to find the probability of:

$$c \overset{\geq 1, \leq \infty}{\rightsquigarrow} e, \tag{B.14}$$

we must consider the set of paths from states labeled with c to those labeled with e that take at least 1 time unit. Since there can be cycles in our graph, calculating the probability associated with a leads-to formula with an infinite upper time bound requires a slightly different method. This is described in detail (and proven correct) in section B.3.

When this is calculated to be at least p, then:

$$P(E_t|C_{t'}) \geq p, \tag{B.15}$$

and since

$$P(E_t) < p, \tag{B.16}$$

we have:

$$P(E_t|C_{t'}) > P(E_t). \tag{B.17}$$

Thus condition (1) is satisfied.

Condition 2 $t' < t$

LC condition (1), states:

$$c \overset{\geq 1, \leq \infty}{\underset{\geq p}{\rightsquigarrow}} e. \tag{B.18}$$

That means that there is at least one transition (with a transition taking a nonzero amount of time) between c and e so c must be earlier than e and thus the second condition of SC (temporal priority) is satisfied.

Condition 3 $P(C_{t'}) > 0$

By definition of $F_{>0}^{\leq\infty}c$, condition (3) of SC is satisfied. If a structure K satisfies this formula it means that, from its starting state, c will be reached with nonzero probability and thus $P(C) > 0$.

Thus, if the three logical formulas (LC) are satisfied, so are Suppes's conditions (SC) for prima facie causality and thus $LC \rightarrow SC$. $\square$

Proposition B.2.2. $SC \rightarrow LC$

Proof. We begin with the same assumptions as for the $LC \rightarrow SC$ case. We also assume that the system of SC is first-order Markovian.

Conditions 1 and 3 $c \overset{\geq 1, \leq\infty}{\underset{\geq p}{\rightsquigarrow}} e$ and $F_{<p}^{\leq\infty}e$

Let us denote the probabilities of Suppes's conditions by:

$$P(E_t|C_{t'}) = p', \text{ and} \tag{B.19}$$

$$P(E_t) = p'', \tag{B.20}$$

and recall that $p' > p''$. From condition (2) of SC, we also know that $C_{t'}$ is earlier than E_t, i.e. $t' < t$. Then, the conditional probability in equation (B.19) represents the probability of E at any time after C has occurred. Again, we have assumed the same time granularity in both sets of conditions, and thus if C is earlier than E in SC, there is at least one transition between a state where c holds and one where e holds. That is, applying the same reasoning as we did earlier, C can cause E any number of time units after C occurs. Thus, we can show that the probability $P(E_{t'}|C_t)$ is the probability of the set of paths from states where C holds to states where E holds. That is, it is the μ_m measure. In the previous section, we showed that the path probability yields the conditional probability, now we must show that the conditional probability yields the path probability and thus the μ_m-measure for the leads-to formula. We have two cases to consider. First, if there is one time unit between t and t', i.e., $t = t' + 1$, then:

$$P(E_t|C_{t'}) = p', \tag{B.21}$$

where for all states s where C holds, there is a transition to some state s' where E holds such that $\mathcal{T}(s, s') \geq p'$.

In the second case, if $t' > t + 1$, then in the path from C to E there will be at least one other state s'' between the C and E states (called s and s'

as before). Say there are two time units between C and E. We can then rewrite the probability as:

$$P(E_t|C_{t'}) = \sum_{s'' \in S} P(E_t, s''|C_{t'}) \tag{B.22}$$

$$= \sum_{s'' \in S} P(E_t|C_{t'}, s'') \times P(s''|C_{t'}), \tag{B.23}$$

where S is the set of all states between C and E at t''. Since we have assumed the system to be first-order Markovian, we know that time t and t' are independent given t''. Thus,

$$P(E_t|C_{t'}) = \sum_{s'' \in S} P(E_t|s'') \times P(s''|C_{t'}). \tag{B.24}$$

We have now reduced the problem to the first case, and each of the conditional probabilities represent transitions from one time unit to the next, and may be replaced as such:

$$P(E_t|C_{t'}) = \sum_{s'' \in S} T(s, s'') \times T(s'', s'). \tag{B.25}$$

Thus, this is the sum of the probabilities of the set of paths from s for which E is true in two time units. This is easily extended to any arbitrary t.

This corresponds to the probability of:

$$c \overset{\geq 1, \leq \infty}{\leadsto} e. \tag{B.26}$$

Then, since there are p' and p'' such that

$$c \overset{\geq 1, \leq \infty}{\leadsto} e \tag{B.27}$$

holds with probability p' and $F^{\leq \infty} e$ with probability p'', we can set $p = p'$ and satisfy both conditions (1) and (3) of LC.

Condition 2 $F_{>0}^{\leq \infty} c$

If $P(C_{t'}) > 0$ it means that if we represent the system as a probabilistic Kripke structure, it will be possible to reach a state where C is true with nonzero probability and thus K satisfies $F_{>0}^{\leq \infty} c$.

Thus, if all conditions in SC are satisfied, so are those in LC and $SC \rightarrow LC$. $\qquad\square$

We have proven $LC \rightarrow SC$ and $SC \rightarrow LC$ and can conclude $SC \leftrightarrow LC$.

B.3. Leads-to with Both Lower and Upper Time Bounds

Recall that in definition 4.2.1, there is a window of time in which c leads to e. In the formulation in this book, I add a minimum time after c is true before which e is true. Here it is shown that it is possible to add such a lower bound. By definition:

$$f \overset{\geq t_1, \leq t_2}{\underset{\geq p}{\leadsto}} g \equiv AG[f \rightarrow F^{\geq t_1, \leq t_2}_{\geq p} g], \tag{B.28}$$

where $t_1 \leq t_2$. Thus, we are actually only adding a minimum time to the consequent of the conditional. If we can label states where $F^{\geq t_1, \leq t_2}_{\geq p} g$ is true, then we can proceed as in the algorithms of Hansson and Jonsson (1994). This is defined as:

$$F^{\geq t_1, \leq t_2}_{\geq p} g \equiv true\ U^{\geq t_1, \leq t_2}_{\geq p} g. \tag{B.29}$$

Thus, we now focus on formulas of the form:

$$h U^{\geq t_1, \leq t_2}_{\geq p} g, \tag{B.30}$$

where for a F formula, $h = true$.

Claim. *The formula $g_1 U^{\tau_1, \tau_2}_{\geq p} g_2$, where $0 \leq \tau_1 \leq \tau_2 \leq \infty$ and $\tau_1 \neq \infty$ can be checked in a structure $K = \langle S, s^i, L, \mathcal{T} \rangle$, if it can be checked when $\tau_2 < \infty$ (Theorem B.3.1) and when $\tau_2 = \infty$ (Theorem B.3.2).*

Corollary. *If a state can be correctly labeled with $g_1 U^{\tau_1, \tau_2}_{\geq p} g_2$, it can also be correctly labeled with $f \leadsto^{\geq t_1, \leq t_2}_{\geq p} g$.*

Since,

$$f \overset{\geq t_1, \leq t_2}{\underset{\geq p}{\leadsto}} g \equiv AG[f \rightarrow F^{\geq t_1, \leq t_2}_{\geq p} g], \tag{B.31}$$

and

$$F^{\geq t_1, \leq t_2}_{\geq p} g \equiv true\ U^{\geq t_1, \leq t_2}_{\geq p} g, \tag{B.32}$$

then let $g_1 = true$, $g_2 = g$ and $\tau_1 = t_1$, $\tau_2 = t_2$. All other components of the leads-to formula can be checked and each subformula is independent of the others. If we replace $F^{\geq t_1, \leq t_2}_{\geq p} g$ by x in the preceding formula, the resulting leads-to formula can be checked. Since as is shown x can be checked, the entire formula can be checked.

We begin with the case where the upper bound, t_2, is non-infinite and then show how this extends to the case where it is infinite.

Case 1: $t_2 \neq \infty$

Theorem B.3.1. *For structure $K = \langle S, s^i, L, T \rangle$, we begin with all states that satisfy g or h labeled as such. Then, for $0 \leq t_1 \leq t_2$, with $t_2 < \infty$ the μ_m-measure for the set of paths σ from s where $\sigma \models_K hU^{\geq t_1, \leq t_2}g$ is given by $P(t_1, t_2, s)$.*

$$
P(t_1, t_2, s) = \begin{cases}
1 & \text{if } t_1 \leq 0, t_2 \geq 0 \text{ and} \\
& \quad g \in L(s); \\
0 & \text{else if } t_2 < 0 \text{ or} \\
& \quad h \notin L(s); \\
\sum_{s' \in S} T(s, s') \times P(t_1 - 1, t_2 - 1, s') & \text{otherwise.}
\end{cases}
$$

(B.33)

Then, following this recurrence, states s will be labeled with $hU_{\geq p}^{\geq t_1, \leq t_2}g$ if $P(t_1, t_2, s) \geq p$. Now, we prove that the recurrence correctly yields the μ_m-measure.

Proof. For the set of states s and integer times t_1 and t_2 take $\Pi(t_1, t_2, s)$ to be the set of finite sequences of states $s \rightarrow \cdots \rightarrow s_i \rightarrow \cdots \rightarrow s_j$, beginning in s, such that there is some j for which $t_1 \leq j \leq t_2$, where $s_j \models_K g$ and for all i with $0 \leq i < j$, $s \models_K h$ and $s \nvDash_K g$.

Let $\mu_m^{t_1, t_2}(s)$ be the μ_m-measure of the set of paths $\sigma \in \Pi(t_1, t_2, s)$ from s where $\sigma \models_K hU^{\geq t_1, \leq t_2}g$. Then, by definition, $\mu_m^{t_1, t_2}(s)$ is:

$$
\mu_m^{t_1, t_2}(s) = \sum_{s \rightarrow s_1 \cdots \rightarrow s_j \in \Pi(t_1, t_2, s)} T(s, s_1) \times \cdots \times T(s_{j-1}, s_j).
$$

(B.34)

We have the following cases to consider:

Case 1: $s \models_K g$, with $t_2 \geq 0$ and $t_1 \leq 0$
Then any path σ from s satisfies $\sigma \models_K hU^{\geq t_1, \leq t_2}g$. Thus, $\mu_m^{t_1, t_2}(s) = 1$.

Case 2: $s \nvDash_K h$, and $s \nvDash_k g$
Then for any path σ from s, $\sigma \nvDash_K hU^{\geq t_1, \leq t_2}g$. Since s does not satisfy g or h, one cannot satisfy the formula by extending the path, as h must hold until g holds. Thus, $\mu_m^{t_1, t_2}(s) = 0$.

Case 3: $s \nvDash g$
Here there are two sub cases.

(a) $t_2 = 0$
Here, $\sigma \nvDash_K hU^{\geq t_1, \leq 0}g$ iff $s \models_K g$. Thus, $\mu_m^{t_1, 0} = 0$.

(b) $t_2 > 0$

In this case, there must be at least two states on the path. We can rewrite such paths $\sigma \in \Pi(t_1, t_2, s)$ in terms of a transition from s to σ' where σ' is σ after its first state. That is,

$$\sigma \in \Pi(t_1, t_2, s) \text{ iff } \sigma' \in \Pi(t_1 - 1, t_2 - 1, \sigma[1]),$$

where:

$$\sigma = \langle \sigma[0], \sigma[1], \sigma[2], \ldots \rangle.$$

Then,

$$\sigma' = \langle \sigma[1], \sigma[2], \ldots \rangle.$$

Thus,

$$\mu_m^{t_1, t_2}(s) = \sum_{s \to \cdots \to s_j \in \Pi(t_1, t_2, s)} \mathcal{T}(s, s_1) \times \cdots \times \mathcal{T}(s_{j-1}, s_j)$$

$$= \sum_{s_1} \mathcal{T}(s, s_1) \times \sum_{s_1 \to \cdots \to s_j \in \Pi(t_1-1, t_2-1, s_1)} \mathcal{T}(s_1, s_2) \times \cdots$$

$$\times \mathcal{T}(s_{j-1}, s_j)$$

$$= \sum_{s_1} \mathcal{T}(s, s_1) \times \mu_m^{t_1-1, t_2-1}(s_1)$$

The equation for $\mu_m^{t_1, t_2}(s)$ satisfies exactly the recurrence of equation (B.33). We conclude that due to the uniqueness of the solution to this equation, $\mu_m^{t_1, t_2}(s) = P(t_1, t_2, s)$. $\quad\square$

Case 2: $t_2 = \infty$

When t_2 is infinite we cannot use the recurrence of equation (B.33), as this will lead to an infinite number of computations. Since we are looking for paths of minimum length t_1, we also cannot immediately proceed as Hansson and Jonsson (1994) do. We will instead identify three sets: P, Q, and R. Q is the set of states from which there is no path to g (in any amount of time) or where neither h nor g holds. P is the set of states, including those labeled with g, from which there exists at least one path to g that is shorter than t_1. Finally, R is the set of states that always reach g (i.e., $F_{\geq 1}g$). Note that it is possible for a state to be in both R and P, as it may have only paths resulting in reaching a state where g holds, but perhaps at least some of these may do so in fewer than t_1 time units.

We begin by decomposing K into strongly connected components (SCCs), resulting in a directed acyclic graph (DAG). We add one condition,

Algorithm B.1 form-Q

$S_s = \{s : s \in S \text{ and } g \in L(s)\}$
$S_i = \{s : s \in S \text{ and } h \in L(s), g \notin L(s)\}$
unseen $= S_i \bigcup S_s$
fringe $= S_s$
mark $= \emptyset$
$P = \emptyset$
for $i = 0$ to $|S_i|$ **do**
  if $i < t$ **then**
    mark $=$ mark $\cup \{s : (s \in$ fringe and s is an SCC$)\vee$
                    $(s \in$ fringe $\wedge \exists s' \in$ mark $: (\mathcal{T}(s, s') > 0))\}$
    $P = P \cup$ fringe
  else
    mark $=$ mark $\cup$ fringe
  end if
  unseen $=$ unseen $-$ fringe
  fringe $= \{s : (s \in$ unseen $\wedge \exists s' \in$ fringe $: \mathcal{T}(s, s') > 0)\}$
end for
$Q = S - ($ mark $\cup P)$

---

which is that all states in an SCC must either be labeled with h or $\neg h$. Note that when testing a leads-to formula, $h = true$, and since all states are labeled with this, the condition is automatically met. First, we define a non-trivial SCC as one with at least one state and one edge (that is, there is one state with a self loop or there are multiple states in the SCC). We replace non-trivial SCCs with new states that are labeled with all of the labels of the states comprising the SCC. For an SCC, C, $f \in L(C)$ if there is a state $s \in C : f \in L(s)$. As we are checking whether a formula, g, will eventually hold, it is enough to know that we can reach an SCC where it holds.

Now we can partition the states into the three sets described earlier. We begin by identifying the failure states Q and inconclusive states P. Akin to the algorithm of Hansson and Jonsson, we form Q and P as shown in algorithm B.1. When there are SCCs in the sets, this means that all states in the SCC are removed when an SCC is removed from a set. Similarly, if Q contains any SCCs, we consider it to contain the set of states comprising the SCC. Then, Q is equivalent to the set Q identified by the algorithm of Hansson and Jonsson (1994).

Now that we have the set of states from which no success is possible, we find those (R) for which the probability of reaching a state where g holds

---

Algorithm B.2 form-R

form-Q
$S_s = \{s : s \in S \text{ and } g \in L(s)\}$
$S_i = \{s : s \in S \text{ and } h \in L(s), g \notin L(s)\}$
$S_f = \{s : s \in S \text{ and } h \notin L(s), g \notin L(s)\}$
unseen $= S_i$
fringe $= Q \cup S_f$
mark $= \emptyset$
for $i = 0$ to $|S - S_s|$ **do**
    mark $=$ mark $\cup$ fringe
    unseen $=$ unseen $-$ fringe
    fringe $= \{s : (s \in \text{ unseen } \wedge \exists s' \in \text{ fringe } : T(s, s') > 0)\}$
end for
$R = S -$ mark

(i.e., a success) is 1. Here we do not concern ourselves with the amount of time as we already have P and thus know which states will not always reach g in at least t_1 time units. Now we find whether it is also possible to transition to states from which we will never reach g or whether these P states guarantee reaching g. As we are not checking the length of the paths, we do not need to worry about termination and can proceed as Hansson and Jonsson do, without decomposing the graph into SCCs.

Theorem B.3.2. *For structure $K = \langle S, s^i, L, T \rangle$ states satisfying g or h have been labeled as such. For $0 \leq t < \infty$, the μ_m-measure of the set of paths σ from s where $\sigma \models_K hU^{\geq t, \leq \infty}g$ is given by $P(t, \infty, s)$.*

$$P(t, \infty, s) = \text{if } s \in R \text{ and } s \notin P \text{ then } 1$$

$$\text{else if } s \in R \text{ and } s \in P \text{ and } t \leq 0 \text{ then } 1$$

$$\text{else if } s \in Q \text{ then } 0$$

$$\text{else if } t > 0 \text{ then}$$

$$\sum_{s' \in S} T(s, s') \times P(t - 1, \infty, s') \tag{B.35}$$

$$\text{else}$$

$$\sum_{s' \in S} T(s, s') \times P(\infty, s')$$

$$P(\infty, s) = \text{if } s \in R \text{ then } 1$$
$$\text{else if } s \in Q \text{ then } 0$$
$$\text{else } \sum_{s' \in S} T(s, s') \times P(\infty, s') \qquad \text{(B.36)}$$

Proof. We have three cases to consider.

Case 1: $s \in Q$

By the definition of Q (it is not possible to reach a state where g holds), $\mu_m^{t,\infty}(s) = 0$.

Case 2: $s \in R$

(a) if $s \notin P$

By the definition of R and by s only being in R, this means that not only will a state where g holds be reached with probability 1, but that there are no paths from s where this will happen in less than t time units. Thus, $\mu_m^{t,\infty}(s) = 1$.

(b) if $s \in P$ and $t \leq 0$

Now that $t \leq 0$, we are only concerned with whether we will reach a g state – in any amount of time – i.e., at any state beginning at s. Thus, since $s \in R$, g is inevitable and $\mu_m^{t,\infty}(s) = 1$.

(c) if $s \in P$ and $t > 0$.

See case 3.

Case 3: Here we have the cases where we have not yet achieved success or failure and thus we consider transitions to the next states on the paths σ from s. The recurrences are similar to that of equation (B.33), with the difference being that once $t \leq 0$, if we have still not reached a success/failure state, we no longer need to keep track of t and thus use exactly the recurrence of Hansson and Jonsson in equation (B.36). If $t > 0$, then we proceed as we did for the finite case, rewriting the paths in terms of their sequences after the first state. We know that paths in this category must consist of at least two states and, as before, where σ' is σ after its first state:

$$\sigma \in \Pi(t, \infty, s) \text{ iff } \sigma' \in \Pi(t - 1, \infty, \sigma[1]). \qquad \text{(B.37)}$$

The uniqueness of the solution for $P(\infty, s)$ was shown by Hansson and Jonsson (1994). For the cases where $P(t, \infty, s)$ is used, once we know that $P(\infty, s)$ is unique, this recurrence also has a unique solution and since the μ_m-measure satisfies the same equation, we conclude that $P(t, \infty, s) = \mu_m^{t,\infty}(s)$. $\qquad \square$

When handling the case of an infinite upper bound on the path length Hansson and Jonsson (1994) assure that their algorithm for computing the probabilities recursively will terminate by first partitioning the set of states, S, into those that guarantee success (g holds), failure (neither h nor g hold, or it is not possible to reach a state where g holds) or are inconclusive (h holds, and there is a path to a state where g holds). In determining these sets, they begin with success states and expand the "frontier" being explored by one transition during each iteration, only extending successful paths by previously unseen states. We could not do this, as we sometimes want to revisit states. This is necessary as we stipulate a lower bound on the leads-to formula, so we may extend a too-short path by visiting a cycle. However, if we do not keep track of unseen states, we again have the problem of an infinite number of computations.

Instead, we recognized that if we revisit a state, it must be due to a cycle in the graph. Further, if we know that we have visited a cycle on a path between some state s and some other state labeled with g, then we know that we can find a path of at least length t_1 between these states for any t_1, where $t_1 \geq 0$ and $t_1 \neq \infty$.

Glossary

actual cause In this book the term is synonymous with genuine cause, and applies to both type and token-level cases.

Bayesian network A directed acyclic graphical model that represents probabilistic dependencies between variables.

causal background context Relative to a particular effect, this is the set of all factors relevant to its occurrence. When looking at a particular cause of the effect, this may be reduced to the set of all relevant factors that are independent of the cause.

causal chain A sequence of relationships, $x_1 \rightarrow x_2 \rightarrow \ldots \rightarrow x_n$, where each x_i occurs before and causes the next x_{i+1}.

causal relationship There is a causal relationship between x and y if either x causes y or y causes x.

causal structure The underlying DTMC (a probabilistic Kripke structure) that is assumed to be generating the behavior of the systems being observed.

causal sufficiency A set of variables is causally sufficient if it includes all of the common causes of pairs on that set.

causally connected Two events are causally connected if one is a cause of the other, or if they have a common cause.

causally relevant x is causally relevant to y if it is a positive cause or negative cause of y. A factor with mixed relevance may also be called causally relevant depending on the theory.

common cause principle (Reichenbach) If two events are probabilistically dependent, then if there is a third event such that conditional on this event, the first two are no longer dependent, this third event screens off the first two, and is a common cause of both.

context unanimity The notion that a causal relationship must hold in all background contexts. For x to be a positive cause of y, there cannot be any backgrounds in which it is a negative or neutral cause.

counterfactual causal dependence With distinct events c and e, e causally depends on c if were c to occur, e would occur as well and if c were not to occur, e would not occur either.

deterministic cause Synonymous with sufficient cause.

direct cause This is the most immediate cause of the effect. Direct causes are relative to the scale at which we are viewing a system. See indirect cause.

dynamic Bayesian network A graphical model that describes the dependencies between variables across time. A common implementation is one Bayesian network describing the initial state of the system, with a set of Bayesian networks (one for each time slice) and connections between them describing the dependencies across time.

genuine cause This refers to the true cause of an effect and is independent of theory. Synonymous with actual cause in this book.

Granger cause One time series, C, is a Granger cause of another time series, E, if the probability of E, given lagged values of all available information including C, is statistically different from the probability of E when the information does not include the lagged values of C.

indirect cause A cause that acts through some intermediate effects. There are other events and factors between an indirect cause and its effect. See direct cause.

insignificant cause An insignificant cause is one that makes little difference to the effect. Note that some causes may seem insignificant based on particular datasets, even though they are genuine.

INUS condition An insufficient but non-redundant part of an unnecessary but sufficient condition.

necessary cause c is necessary for e if e cannot occur without c.

negative cause A cause that inhibits, or prevents, the effect. In the case of probabilistic causality, a negative cause decreases the probability of the effect.

omission (causation by) The absence of a factor bringing about the effect. For example, forgetting to water a plant can cause it to die.

overdetermination Overdetermined cases are those where multiple causes of an effect actually occur in such a way that either could have been the cause of the effect. See redundant causation and preemption.

positive cause A cause that brings about the effect. In the case of probabilistic causality, a positive cause increases the probability of the effect.

preemption This is a special case of redundant causation. Here the potential causes are not symmetric. One cause actually occurs earlier, bringing about the effect and preempting the other from causing it.

prima facie cause A seeming, or possible, cause. In probabilistic theories, this is simply one that occurs earlier than and raises the probability of the effect.

redundant causation This generally refers to token-level cases where multiple causes of an effect are present, and either alone would cause the effect. The term is sometimes used synonymously with overdetermination. There are two primary cases of redundant causation: preemption, where one cause is actually responsible for the effect, and overdetermination, where it is not possible to determine which cause was actually responsible.

significant cause A significant cause is one that makes a large difference to the effect. These are comprised of just so and genuine causes.

Simpson's paradox A correlation (positive or negative) between two variables is found in a general population but one can find subpopulations such that in every subpopulation the relationship is reversed.

spurious cause A cause that may seem genuine – by appearing to raise the probability of the effect – but that does not actually cause it.

sufficient cause For an effect e and cause c, c is sufficient for e if c alone is enough to bring about e. Also called deterministic causes. Note that this is not synonymous with causal sufficiency.

temporal priority That a cause must be earlier than its effect. Note that this does not always mean strictly earlier, as some theories allow cause and effect to be simultaneous.

token cause The cause of a particular, actually occurring, event.

token level Token-level claims relate to specific events, such as an individual's diagnosis at a particular time and place.

transitivity (of causation) The notion that if A causes B and B causes C, that A causes C.

type level Type-level claims refer to general properties between factors or events, such as that between smoking and lung cancer.

Bibliography

Agbabiaka, T. B., Savovic, J., and Ernst, E. (2008). Methods for Causality Assessment of Adverse Drug Reactions: A Systematic Review. *Drug Safety*, 31(1):21–37.

Alicke, M. D. (1992). Culpable Causation. *Journal of Personality and Social Psychology*, 63(3):368–378.

Anscombe, G. E. M. (1971). *Causality and Determination: An Inaugural Lecture*. Cambridge University Press, London. Reprinted in Sosa and Tooley, 1993.

Benjamini, Y. and Hochberg, Y. (1995). Controlling the False Discovery Rate: A Practical and Powerful Approach to Multiple Testing. *Journal of the Royal Statistical Society. Series B (Methodological)*, 57(1):289–300.

Benjamini, Y. and Yekutieli, D. (2001). The Control of the False Discovery Rate in Multiple Testing under Dependency. *Annals of Statistics*, 29(4):1165–1188.

Bickel, P. J., Hammel, E. A., and O'Connell, J. W. (1975). Sex Bias in Graduate Admissions: Data from Berkeley. *Science*, 187(4175):398–404.

Blinowska, K. J., Kuś, R., and Kamiński, M. (2004). Granger causality and information flow in multivariate processes. *Physics Review E*, 70(5):050902.

Brandt, P. (2009). MSBVAR R package version 0.4.

Bressler, S. L. and Seth, A. K. (2011). Wiener-Granger Causality: A well established methodology. *Neuroimage*, 58(2):323–329.

Broadbent, A. (2012). Causes of causes. *Philosophical Studies*, 158(3):457–476.

Brown, E. N., Kass, R. E., and Mitra, P. P. (2004). Multiple neural spike train data analysis: state-of-the-art and future challenges. *Nature Neuroscience*, 7(5):456–461.

Cartwright, N. (1979). Causal Laws and Effective Strategies. *Noûs*, 13(4):419–437.

——— (1989). *Nature's Capacities and Their Measurement*. Clarendon Press, Oxford.

——— (2001). What Is Wrong with Bayes Nets? *The Monist*, 84(2):242–264.

——— (2002). Against Modularity, the Causal Markov Condition, and Any Link Between the Two: Comments on Hausman and Woodward. *British Journal for the Philosophy of Science*, 53(3):411–453.

——— (2007a). Causal Powers: What Are They? Why Do We Need Them? What Can Be Done with Them and What Cannot? Technical report, Centre for Philosophy of Natural and Social Science, London School of Economics and Political Science, London.

———— (2007b). *Hunting Causes and Using Them: Approaches in Philosophy and Economics.* Cambridge University Press, Cambridge.

Chan, K., Poernomo, I., Schmidt, H., and Jayaputera, J. (2005). A Model-Oriented Framework for Runtime Monitoring of Nonfunctional Properties. In *Quality of Software Architectures and Software Quality,* volume 3712 of *Lecture Notes in Computer Science,* pp. 38–52. Springer, New York.

Chowdhury, A. R. (1987). Are causal relationships sensitive to causality tests? *Applied Economics,* 19(4):459–465.

Ciesinski, F. and Größer, M. (2004). On Probabilistic Computation Tree Logic. In *Validation of Stochastic Systems,* volume 2925 of *Lecture Notes in Computer Science,* pp. 333–355. Springer, New York.

Clarke, E. M., Emerson, E. A., and Sistla, A. P. (1986). Automatic Verification of Finite-State Concurrent Systems Using Temporal Logic Specifications. *ACM Transactions on Programming Languages and Systems,* 8(2):244–263.

Clarke, E. M., Grumberg, O., and Peled, D. A. (1999). *Model Checking.* The MIT Press, Cambridge, MA.

Cooper, G. F. (1999). An Overview of the Representation and Discovery of Causal Relationships Using Bayesian Networks. In C. Glymour and G. F. Cooper (eds.), *Computation, Causation, and Discovery,* pp. 3–62. AAAI Press/The MIT Press, Cambridge, MA.

Crick, F. (1970). Central Dogma of Molecular Biology. *Nature,* 227(5258):561–563.

Davidson, D. (1998). The Individuation of Events. In C. Macdonald and S. Laurence (eds.), *Contemporary Readings in the Foundations of Metaphysics,* pp. 295–309. Wiley-Blackwell, Oxford.

Davis, R. (1989). Expert Systems: How Far Can They Go? *AI Magazine,* 10(1):61–67.

Dekkers, O. M., Elm, E., Algra, A., Romijn, J. A., and Vandenbroucke, J. P. (2010). How to assess the external validity of therapeutic trials: a conceptual approach. *International Journal of Epidemiology,* 39(1):89–94.

Ding, M., Chen, Y., and Bressler, S. L. (2006). Granger Causality: Basic Theory and Application to Neuroscience. In B. Schelter, M. Winterhalder, and J. Timmer (eds.), *Handbook of Time Series Analysis: Recent Theoretical Developments and Applications,* pp. 437–460. Wiley-VCH Verlag GmbH & Co. KGaA, Weinheim.

Dondelinger, F., Lebre, S., and Husmeier, D. (2010). Heterogeneous Continuous Dynamic Bayesian Networks with Flexible Structure and Inter-Time Segment Information Sharing. In *Proceedings of the 27th International Conference on Machine Learning.*

Dowe, P. (2000). *Physical Causation.* Cambridge University Press, Cambridge.

Dupré, J. (1984). Probabilistic Causality Emancipated. *Midwest Studies in Philosophy,* 9(1):169–175.

———— (1990). Probabilistic Causality: A Rejoinder to Ellery Eells. *Philosophy of Science,* 57(4):690–698.

Edgington, D. (1995). On Conditionals. *Mind,* 104(414):235–329.

Eells, E. (1987a). Probabilistic Causality: Reply to John Dupré. *Philosophy of Science*, 54(1):105–114.

––––––– (1987b). Cartwright and Otte on Simpson's Paradox. *Philosophy of Science*, 54(2):233–243.

––––––– (1991). *Probabilistic Causality*. Cambridge University Press, Cambridge.

Eells, E. and Sober, E. (1983). Probabilistic Causality and the Question of Transitivity. *Philosophy of Science*, 50(1):35–57.

Efron, B. (2004). Large-Scale Simultaneous Hypothesis Testing: The Choice of a Null Hypothesis. *Journal of the American Statistical Association*, 99(465):96–104.

––––––– (2007). Size, Power, and False Discovery Rates. *The Annals of Statistics*, 35(4):1351–1377.

––––––– (2010). *Large-Scale Inference: Empirical Bayes Methods for Estimation, Testing, and Prediction*. Institute of Mathematical Statistics Monographs. Cambridge University Press, Cambridge.

Efron, B. and Tibshirani, R. (2002). Empirical Bayes Methods and False Discovery Rates for Microarrays. *Genetic Epidemiology*, 23(1):70–86.

Eichler, M. (2009). Causal inference from multivariate time series: What can be learned from Granger causality. In C. Glymour, W. Wang, and D. Westerstahl (eds.), *Logic, Methodology and Philosophy of Science: Proceedings of the 13th International Congress*, pp. 481–496. College Publications, London.

Entner, D. and Hoyer, P. O. (2010). On Causal Discovery from Time Series Data using FCI. In *Proceedings of the 5th European Workshop on Probabilistic Graphical Models*.

Fagin, R., Halpern, J. Y., Moses, Y., and Vardi, M. Y. (1995). *Reasoning About Knowledge*. The MIT Press, Cambridge, MA.

Fama, E. F. and French, K. R. (1992). The Cross-Section of Expected Stock Returns. *The Journal of Finance*, 47(2):427–465.

––––––– (1993). Common risk factors in the returns on stocks and bonds. *Journal of Financial Economics*, 33(1):3–56.

Fienberg, S. E. (1980). *The Analysis of Cross-Classified Categorical Data*. The MIT Press, Cambridge, MA, 2nd edition. Reprint, Springer-Verlag, 2007.

Fisher, R. A. (1925). *Statistical Methods for Research Workers*. Oliver and Boyd, Edinburgh.

Fitelson, B. and Hitchcock, C. R. (2011). Probabilistic Measures of Causal Strength. In P. M. Illari, F. Russo, and J. Williamson (eds.), *Causality in the Sciences*, pp. 600–627. Oxford University Press, Oxford.

Freedman, D. and Humphreys, P. (1999). Are There Algorithms That Discover Causal Structure? *Synthese*, 121(1–2):29–54.

French, K. R. and Fama, E. F. (2011). Fama French – Data Library. URL http://mba. tuck.dartmouth.edu/pages/faculty/ken.french/data_library.html.

Friedman, N., Murphy, K., and Russell, S. (1998). Learning the Structure of Dynamic Probabilistic Networks. In *Proceedings of the 14th Conference on Uncertainty in Artificial Intelligence*.

Gillies, D. (2000). *Philosophical Theories of Probability*. Routledge, London.

Glennan, S. (1996). Mechanisms and the Nature of Causation. *Erkenntnis*, 44(1):49–71.

—— (2002). Rethinking Mechanistic Explanation. *Philosophy of Science*, 69(3): S342–S353.

Glymour, C., Spirtes, P., and Richardson, T. (1999). On the Possibility of Inferring Causation from Association without Background Knowledge. In C. Glymour and G. F. Cooper (eds.), *Computation, Causation, and Discovery*, pp. 305–322. AAAI Press / The MIT Press, Cambridge, MA.

Glymour, C., Scheines, R., Spirtes, P., and Ramsey, J. (2004). TETRAD IV software.

Godfrey-Smith, P. (2010). Causal Pluralism. In H. Beebee, C. R. Hitchcock, and P. Menzies (eds.), *Oxford Handbook of Causation*, pp. 326–337. Oxford University Press, Oxford.

Good, I. J. (1961a). A Causal Calculus (I). *British Journal for the Philosophy of Science*, 11(44):305–318.

—— (1961b). A Causal Calculus (II). *British Journal for the Philosophy of Science*, 12(45):43–51.

Gopnik, A. (2004). Finding Our Inner Scientist. *Daedalus*, 133(1):21–28.

Gopnik, A. and Schulz, L. (eds.) (2007). *Causal Learning: Psychology, Philosophy, and Computation*. Oxford University Press, Oxford.

Granger, C. W. J. (1969). Investigating Causal Relations by Econometric Models and Cross-Spectral Methods. *Econometrica*, 37(3):424–438.

—— (1980). Testing for Causality: A Personal Viewpoint. *Journal of Economic Dynamics and Control*, 2:329–352.

—— (2007). Causality in Economics. In P. K. Machamer and G. Wolters (eds.), *Thinking about Causes: From Greek Philosophy to Modern Physics*, pp. 284–296. University of Pittsburgh Press, Pittsburgh.

Grzegorczyk, M. and Husmeier, D. (2009). Non-stationary continuous dynamic Bayesian networks. In *Proceedings of the 23rd Annual Conference on Neural Information Processing Systems*.

Halpern, J. Y. and Hitchcock, C. R. (2010). Actual Causation and the Art of Modeling. In R. Dechter, H. Geffner, and J. Y. Halpern (eds.), *Heuristics, Probability and Causality: A Tribute to Judea Pearl*, pp. 383–406. College Publications, London.

Halpern, J. Y. and Pearl, J. (2005). Causes and Explanations: A Structural-Model Approach. Part I: Causes. *British Journal for the Philosophy of Science*, 56(4):843–887.

Halpern, J. Y. and Shoham, Y. (1991). A Propositional Modal Logic of Time Intervals. *Journal of the ACM*, 38(4):935–962.

Hansson, H. and Jonsson, B. (1994). A Logic for Reasoning about Time and Reliability. *Formal Aspects of Computing*, 6(5):512–535.

Hartemink, A. J. (2008). Banjo: Bayesian Network Inference with Java Objects. URL http://www.cs.duke.edu/~amink/software/banjo/.

Hausman, D. M. (1998). *Causal Asymmetries*. Cambridge University Press, Cambridge.

—— (2005). Causal Relata: Tokens, Types, or Variables? *Erkenntnis*, 63(1):33–54.

Hausman, D. M. and Woodward, J. (1999). Independence, Invariance and the Causal Markov Condition. *British Journal for the Philosophy of Science*, 50(4):521–583.

——— (2004). Modularity and the Causal Markov Condition: A Restatement. *British Journal for the Philosophy of Science*, 55(1):147–161.

Hesse, W., Möller, E., Arnold, M., and Schack, B. (2003). The use of time-variant EEG Granger causality for inspecting directed interdependencies of neural assemblies. *Journal of Neuroscience Methods*, 124(1):27–44.

Hill, A. B. (1965). The Environment and Disease: Association or Causation? *Proceedings of the Royal Society of Medicine*, 58(5):295–300.

Hintikka, J. (1962). *Knowledge and Belief: An Introduction to the Logic of the Two Notions*. Cornell University Press, Ithaca.

Hitchcock, C. R. (1995). The Mishap at Reichenbach Fall: Singular vs. General Causation. *Philosophical Studies*, 78(3):257–291.

——— (2003). Of Humean Bondage. *British Journal for the Philosophy of Science*, 54(1):1–25.

——— (2007). How to be a Causal Pluralist. In P. K. Machamer and G. Wolters (eds.), *Thinking about Causes: From Greek Philosophy to Modern Physics*, pp. 200–221. University of Pittsburgh Press, Pittsburgh.

Hlavackova-Schindler, K., Palus, M., Vejmelka, M., and Bhattacharya, J. (2007). Causality detection based on information-theoretic approaches in time series analysis. *Physics Reports*, 441(1):1–46.

Hoover, K. D. (2001). *Causality in Macroeconomics*. Cambridge University Press, Cambridge.

Hopkins, M. and Pearl, J. (2007). Causality and Counterfactuals in the Situation Calculus. *Journal of Logic and Computation*, 17(5):939–953.

Hripcsak, G., Elhadad, N., Chen, Y. H., Zhou, L., and Morrison, F. P. (2009). Using Empiric Semantic Correlation to Interpret Temporal Assertions in Clinical Texts. *Journal of the American Medical Informatics Association*, 16(2):220–227.

Hume, D. (1739). *A Treatise of Human Nature*. London. Reprint, Prometheus Books, 1992. Citations refer to the Prometheus edition.

——— (1748). *An Enquiry Concerning Human Understanding*. London. Reprint, Dover Publications, 2004.

Humphreys, P. and Freedman, D. (1996). The Grand Leap. *British Journal for the Philosophy of Science*, 47(1):113–123.

Hyttinen, A., Eberhardt, F., and Hoyer, P. O. (2010). Causal Discovery for Linear Cyclic Models with Latent Variables. In *Proceedings of the 5th European Workshop on Probabilistic Graphical Models*.

Jacobs, R. L., Leamer, E. E., and Ward, M. P. (1979). Difficulties with Testing for Causation. *Economic Inquiry*, 17(3):401–413.

Jaynes, E. T. (2003). *Probability Theory: The Logic of Science*. Cambridge University Press, Cambridge.

Jennings, D. L., Amabile, T. M., and Ross, L. (1982). Informal covariation assessment: Data-based versus theory-based judgments. In D. Kahneman, P. Slovic, and

A. Tversky (eds.), *Judgment Under Uncertainty: Heuristics and Biases*, pp. 211–230. Cambridge University Press, Cambridge.

Jin, J. and Cai, T. T. (2007). Estimating the Null and the Proportion of Nonnull Effects in Large-scale Multiple Comparisons. *Journal of the American Statistical Association*, 102(478):495–506.

Joffe, M. (2011). The gap between evidence discovery and actual causal relationships. *Preventive Medicine*, 53(4–5):246–249.

Johnson, M. L., Crown, W., Martin, B. C., Dormuth, C. R., and Siebert, U. (2009). Good research practices for comparative effectiveness research: analytic methods to improve causal inference from nonrandomized studies of treatment effects using secondary data sources: the ISPOR Good Research Practices for Retrospective Database Analysis Task Force Report–Part III. *Value in Health*, 12(8):1062–1073.

Kamiński, M., Ding, M., Truccolo, W. A., and Bressler, S. L. (2001). Evaluating causal relations in neural systems: Granger causality, directed transfer function and statistical assessment of significance. *Biological Cybernetics*, 85(2):145–157.

Kim, J. (1976). Events as Property Exemplifications. In M. Brand and D. Walton (eds.), *Action Theory*, pp. 159–177. Reidel, Dordrecht. Reprinted in Laurence and Macdonald, 1998.

Kim, M., Kannan, S., Lee, I., Sokolsky, O., and Viswanathan, M. (2001). Java-MaC: A Run-time Assurance Tool for Java Programs. *Electronic Notes in Theoretical Computer Science*, 55(2):218–235.

Kleinberg, S. (2011). A Logic for Causal Inference in Time Series with Discrete and Continuous Variables. In *Proceedings of the 22nd International Joint Conference on Artificial Intelligence*.

Kleinberg, S. and Hripcsak, G. (2011). A review of causal inference for biomedical informatics. *Journal of Biomedical Informatics*, 44(6):1102–1112.

Kleinberg, S. and Mishra, B. (2009). The Temporal Logic of Causal Structures. In *Proceedings of the 25th Conference on Uncertainty in Artificial Intelligence*.

——— (2010). The Temporal Logic of Token Causes. In *Proceedings of the 12th International Conference on the Principles of Knowledge Representation and Reasoning*.

Kleinberg, S., Kolm, P., and Mishra, B. (2010). Investigating Causal Relationships in Stock Returns with Temporal Logic Based Methods. *arXiv e-prints/1006.1791*.

Knobe, J. (2009). Folk judgments of causation. *Studies In History and Philosophy of Science*, 40(2):238–242.

Koch, R. (1932). Die Aetiologie der Tuberkulose. *Journal of Molecular Medicine*, 11(12):490–492.

Koller, D. and Friedman, N. (2009). *Probabilistic Graphical Models: Principles and Techniques*. The MIT Press, Cambridge, MA.

Kolmogorov, A. N. (1956). *Foundations of the Theory of Probability*. Chelsea Publishing Co., New York.

Korb, K. B. and Nicholson, A. E. (2010). *Bayesian Artificial Intelligence*. CRC press, Boca Raton, 2nd edition.

Kripke, S. (1963). Semantical Considerations on Modal Logic. *Acta Philosophica Fennica*, 16(1963):83–94.

Lagnado, D. (2011). Thinking about Evidence. In P. Dawid, W. Twining, and M. Vasilaki (eds.), *Evidence, Inference and Enquiry*, pp. 183–224. Oxford University Press/British Academy, Oxford.

Laurence, S. and Macdonald, C. (eds.) (1998). *Contemporary Readings in the Foundations of Metaphysics*. Wiley-Blackwell, Oxford.

Lauritzen, S. L. and Wermuth, N. (1989). Graphical Models for Associations Between Variables, some of which are Qualitative and some Quantitative. *The Annals of Statistics*, 17(1):31–57.

Leibovici, L. (2001). Effects of remote, retroactive intercessory prayer on outcomes in patients with bloodstream infection: randomised controlled trial. *BMJ*, 323(7327):1450–1451.

Leucker, M. and Schallhart, C. (2009). A Brief Account of Runtime Verification. *Journal of Logic and Algebraic Programming*, 78(5):293–303.

Lewis, D. (1973). Causation. *The Journal of Philosophy*, 70(17):556–567. Reprinted in Lewis, 1986a.

———— (1986a). *Philosophical Papers*, volume 2. Oxford University Press, Oxford.

———— (1986b). Postscripts to "Causation". In *Philosophical Papers*, volume 2, pp. 172–213. Oxford University Press, Oxford.

———— (2000). Causation as Influence. *The Journal of Philosophy*, 97(4):182–197.

Lunze, J. and Schiller, F. (1999). An Example of Fault Diagnosis by Means of Probabilistic Logic Reasoning. *Control Engineering Practice*, 7(2):271–278.

Machamer, P., Darden, L., and Craver, C. F. (2000). Thinking about Mechanisms. *Philosophy of Science*, 67(1):1–25.

Mackie, J. L. (1965). Causes and Conditions. *American Philosophical Quarterly*, 2(4):245–264.

———— (1974). *The Cement of the Universe*. Clarendon Press, Oxford.

McDermott, M. (1995). Redundant Causation. *British Journal for the Philosophy of Science*, 46(4):523–544.

McIntosh, N. (2002). Intensive care monitoring: past, present and future. *Clinical Medicine*, 2(4):349–355.

Mill, J. S. (1843). *A System of Logic*. London. Reprint, Lincoln-Rembrandt Pub., 1986.

Moor, J. H. (ed.) (2003). *The Turing Test: The Elusive Standard of Artificial Intelligence*. Kluwer Academic Publishers, Dordrecht.

Morris, A. and Gardner, R. (1992). Computer applications. In J. Hall, G. Schmidt, and L. Wood (eds.), *Principles of Critical Care*, pp. 500–514. McGraw-Hill, New York.

Murphy, K. (2002). *Dynamic Bayesian Networks: Representation, Inference and Learning*. Ph.D. thesis, University of California, Berkley.

Naranjo, C. A., Busto, U., Sellers, E. M., Sandor, P., Ruiz, I., Roberts, E. A., Janecek, E., Domecq, C., and Greenblatt, D. J. (1981). A method for estimating the probability of adverse drug reactions. *Clinical Pharmacology and Therapeutics*, 30(2):239–245.

Neapolitan, R. (2004). *Learning Bayesian Networks*. Pearson Prentice Hall, Upper Saddle River, NJ.

Otte, R. (1981). A Critique of Suppes' Theory of Probabilistic Causality. *Synthese*, 48(2):167–189.

——— (1985). Probabilistic Causality and Simpson's Paradox. *Philosophy of Science*, 52(1):110–125.

Papineau, D. (1992). Can We Reduce Causal Direction to Probabilities? In *PSA: Proceedings of the Biennial Meeting of the Philosophy of Science Association*, volume 2, pp. 238–252.

——— (2001). Metaphysics over Methodology – Or, Why Infidelity Provides No Grounds To Divorce Causes from Probabilities. In M. C. Galavotti, P. Suppes, and D. Costantini (eds.), *Stochastic Causality*, pp. 15–38. CSLI, Stanford, CA.

Parascandola, M. and Weed, D. L. (2001). Causation in epidemiology. *Journal of Epidemiology and Community Health*, 55(12):905–912.

Pearl, J. (2000). *Causality: Models, Reasoning, and Inference*. Cambridge University Press, Cambridge.

Pnueli, A. (1977). The Temporal Logic of Programs. In *Proceedings of the 18th Annual Symposium on Foundations of Computer Science*.

Prior, A. N. (1967). *Past, Present, and Future*. Clarendon Press, Oxford.

Psillos, S. (2010). Causal Pluralism. In R. Vanderbeeken and B. D'Hooghe (eds.), *Worldviews, Science and Us: Studies of Analytical Metaphysics*, pp. 131–151. World Scientific Publishers, Singapore.

Reichenbach, H. (1956). *The Direction of Time*. University of California Press, Berkeley. Reprint, Dover Publications, 2000.

Reiss, J. (2007). Time Series, Nonsense Correlations and the Principle of the Common Cause. In F. Russo and J. Williamson (eds.), *Causality and Probability in the Sciences*, pp. 179–196. College Publications, London.

Reiter, R. (1980). A Logic for Default Reasoning. *Artificial Intelligence*, 13(1–2):81–132.

Richardson, T. (1996). A Discovery Algorithm for Directed Cyclic Graphs. In *Proceedings of the 12th Conference on Uncertainty in Artificial Intelligence*.

Rizzi, D. A. (1994). Causal Reasoning and the Diagnostic Process. *Theoretical Medicine and Bioethics*, 15(3):315–333.

Robins, J. M. and Wasserman, L. (1999). On the Impossibility of Inferring Causation from Association without Background Knowledge. In C. Glymour and G. Cooper (eds.), *Computation, Causation, and Discovery*, pp. 305–321. AAAI Press / The MIT Press, Cambridge, MA.

Robinson, J. W. and Hartemink, A. J. (2010). Learning Non-Stationary Dynamic Bayesian Networks. *Journal of Machine Learning Research*, 11(Dec):3647–3680.

Rosen, D. A. (1978). In Defense of a Probabilistic Theory of Causality. *Philosophy of Science*, 45(4):604–613.

Rothman, K. J. (1976). Causes. *American Journal of Epidemiology*, 104(6):587–592. Reprinted in 141(2), 1995.

Rothwell, P. M. (2006). Factors That Can Affect the External Validity of Randomised Controlled Trials. *PLoS Clinical Trials*, 1(1):e9.

Russo, F. (2006). The Rationale of Variation in Methodological and Evidential Pluralism. *Philosophica*, 77(1):97–124.

——— (2009). *Causality and Causal Modelling in the Social Sciences: Measuring Variations*. Springer, New York.

Russo, F. and Williamson, J. (2007). Interpreting Causality in the Health Sciences. *International Studies in the Philosophy of Science*, 21(2):157–170.

——— (2011a). Epistemic Causality and Evidence-Based Medicine. *History and Philosophy of the Life Sciences*, 33(4):563–581.

——— (2011b). Generic versus single-case causality: the case of autopsy. *European Journal for Philosophy of Science*, 1(1):47–69.

Salmon, W. C. (1980a). Causality: Production and Propagation. In *PSA: Proceedings of the Biennial Meeting of the Philosophy of Science Association*, volume 2, pp. 49–69.

——— (1980b). Probabilistic Causality. *Pacific Philosophical Quarterly*, 61:50–74.

——— (1994). Causality without Counterfactuals. *Philosophy of Science*, 61(2):297–312.

Schmidt, M. and Murphy, K. (2009). Modeling Discrete Interventional Data using Directed Cyclic Graphical Models. In *Proceedings of the 25th Conference on Uncertainty in Artificial Intelligence*.

Schulz, K. F., Chalmers, I., Hayes, R. J., and Altman, D. G. (1995). Empirical Evidence of Bias: Dimensions of Methodological Quality Associated with Estimates of Treatment Effects in Controlled Trials. *JAMA*, 273(5):408–412.

Seth, A. K. (2010). A MATLAB toolbox for Granger causal connectivity analysis. *Journal of Neuroscience Methods*, 186(2):262–273.

Shoham, Y. (1988). *Reasoning About Change: Time and Causation from the Standpoint of Artificial Intelligence*. The MIT Press, Cambridge, MA.

Simpson, E. H. (1951). The Interpretation of Interaction in Contingency Tables. *Journal of the Royal Statistical Society. Series B (Methodological)*, 13(2):238–241.

Skyrms, B. (1980). *Causal Necessity*. Yale University Press, New Haven.

——— (1984). EPR: Lessons for Metaphysics. *Midwest Studies in Philosophy*, 9(1):245–255.

Sloman, S. A. (2005). *Causal Models: How People Think about the World and its Alternatives*. Oxford University Press, Oxford.

Sloman, S. A., Fernbach, P. M., and Ewing, S. (2009). Causal Models: The Representational Infrastructure for Moral Judgment. In D. M. Bartels, C. W. Bauman, L. J. Skitka, and D. L. Medin (eds.), *Moral Judgment and Decision Making: The Psychology of Learning and Motivation*, vol. 50, pp. 1–26. Elsevier, San Diego, CA.

Sober, E. (2001). Venetian Sea Levels, British Bread Prices, and the Principle of the Common Cause. *British Journal for the Philosophy of Science*, 52(2):331–346.

Sober, E. and Papineau, D. (1986). Causal Factors, Causal Inference, Causal Explanation. *Proceedings of the Aristotelian Society, Supplementary Volumes*, 60:97–136.

Sosa, E. and Tooley, M. (eds.) (1993). *Causation*. Oxford University Press, Oxford.

Spirtes, P. (1995). Directed Cyclic Graphical Representations of Feedback Models. In *Proceedings of the 11th Conference on Uncertainty in Artificial Intelligence*.

Spirtes, P., Glymour, C., and Scheines, R. (2000). *Causation, Prediction, and Search*. The MIT Press, Cambridge, MA, 2nd edition. First published 1993.

Stalnaker, R. (1968). A Theory of Conditionals. In N. Rescher (ed.), *Studies in Logical Theory*, American Philosophy Quarterly Monograph Series, pp. 98–112. Blackwell, Oxford.

Storey, J. D. (2003). The positive false discovery rate: A Bayesian interpretation and the q-value. *Annals of Statistics*, 31(6):2013–2035.

Storey, J. D. and Tibshirani, R. (2003). Statistical significance for genomewide studies. *Proceedings of the National Academy of Sciences*, 100(16):9440–9445.

Strimmer, K. (2008). fdrtool: a versatile R package for estimating local and tail area-based false discovery rates. *Bioinformatics*, 24(12):1461–1462.

Suppes, P. (1970). *A Probabilistic Theory of Causality*. North-Holland, Amsterdam.

Susser, M. (1973). *Causal Thinking in the Health Sciences: Concepts and Strategies of Epidemiology*. Oxford University Press, New York.

Thurman, W. N. and Fisher, M. E. (1988). Chickens, Eggs, and Causality, or Which Came First. *American Journal of Agricultural Economics*, 70(2):237–238.

Wiener, N. (1956). The theory of prediction. In E. Beckenbach (ed.), *Modern Mathematics for the Engineer*, pp. 165–190. McGraw-Hill, New York.

Wikipedia (2008). Ronald Opus – Wikipedia, The Free Encyclopedia. URL http://en.wikipedia.org/w/index.php?title=Ronald_Opus&oldid=247157374.

Williamson, J. (2006). Causal Pluralism versus Epistemic Causality. *Philosophica*, 77(1):69–96.

Woodward, J. (2005). *Making Things Happen: A Theory of Causal Explanation*. Oxford University Press, New York.

Yoon, Y., Guimaraes, T., and O'Neal, Q. (1995). Exploring The Factors Associated With Expert Systems Success. *MIS quarterly*, 19(1):83–106.

Zou, C. and Feng, J. (2009). Granger causality vs. dynamic Bayesian network inference: a comparative study. *BMC Bioinformatics*, 10:122.

Index

Printed in the United States
By Bookmasters